2013

The Origins of Active Social Policy

The Origins of Active Social Policy

Labour Market and Childcare Policies
in a Comparative Perspective

Giuliano Bonoli

OXFORD
UNIVERSITY PRESS

OXFORD
UNIVERSITY PRESS

Great Clarendon Street, Oxford, OX2 6DP,
United Kingdom

Oxford University Press is a department of the University of Oxford.
It furthers the University's objective of excellence in research, scholarship,
and education by publishing worldwide. Oxford is a registered trade mark of
Oxford University Press in the UK and in certain other countries

First Edition published in 2013

Impression: 1

British Library Cataloguing in Publication Data

Data available

ISBN 978–0–19–966976–9

Printed in Great Britain by
MPG Books Group, Bodmin and King's Lynn

To Luca, Margit, and Susi

Acknowledgements

My interest in the reorientation of post-war welfare states goes back to the late 1990s. At the time, most researchers were interested in retrenchment. However, it was clear to me that the notion of retrenchment was unable to capture the broad range of transformations European welfare states were going through. My initial take on the multifaceted nature of welfare state transformation was based on the notion of 'new social risks'. I assumed that retrenchment concerned mostly traditional social policies. At the same time, policies providing coverage against new social risks (such as long-term unemployment, lone parenthood, working poverty) were being expanded. This assumption was only partly confirmed by the empirical analysis of actual policy trajectories, and towards the late 2000s it became clear to me that what determined whether policy was expanding or contracting was not the degree of exposure to social risk of its clientele. What really mattered was the expected impact of policy on employment. Since the late 1990s, most of the time, expansion in social policy has concerned policies that have a positive impact on labour supply. These include most notably active labour market policies and subsidized childcare.

The objective of this book is to account for the reorientation of European welfare states: from providers of economic security to employment promoting institutions. It is a profound transformation that is having a major impact on the lives of many Europeans, hence the importance of understanding why this reorientation came to be.

In my search for the determinants of the emergence of 'active welfare states', I was fortunate enough to be able to count on the help and support of many colleagues. At IDHEAP, during the various phases of this book project, I was able to count on the direct or indirect support of colleagues, students, and particularly Aurélien Abrassart, Michel Berclaz, Fabio Bertozzi, Cyrielle Champion, Frank Reber, Regula Schlanser, and Nicolas Turtschi.

Much of the thinking behind this book was done while I was involved in the network of excellence RECWOWE, financed by the EU under FP VI. In particular, this book benefitted from discussions which took place in a parallel book project entitled 'The Politics of the New Welfare State' (Oxford University Press, 2012), which I co-edited with David Natali. Project participants deserve a big thank you as do the coordinators of the network, Denis Bouget and Bruno Palier.

This book is based, too, on secondary literature, so that I had to rely on good quality studies produced by others in order to identify policy trajectories. Some of the most helpful studies were actually PhDs in the making or just finished, but not yet published. I am thankful to their authors, Daniel Clegg, Monique Kremer, Nathalie Morel, and Ingela Naumann, who were kind enough to make them available to me. This book would not have been possible without their studies.

Above all, however, this book benefitted from discussions with a large number of colleagues, on many occasions: Christian Albrekt Larsen, Jochen Clasen, Daniel Clegg, Eric Crettaz, Johan Bo Davidsson, Bernhard Ebbinghaus, Patrick Emmenegger, Maurizio Ferrera, Timo Fleckenstein, Ana Guillen, Silja Häusermann, Anton Hemerijck, Takeshi Hieda, Karl Hinrichs, Jane Jenson, Matteo Jessoula, Kimberly Morgan, David Natali, Ingela Naumann, Moira Nelson, Bruno Palier, Joakim Palme, Martin Seeleib-Kaiser, John Stephens, Patrik Vesan, and Tim Vlandas. My sincerest thanks to all of them and my apologies to those I may have forgotten.

I finalized the manuscript while on research leave in Berlin, where the Hertie School of Governance provided me with excellent facilities and an intellectually stimulating environment. I also had a much appreciated opportunity to discuss my project with colleagues there. My thanks go to Anke Hassel, Stein Kuhnle, and particularly Christof Schiller, who helped me make sense of the German case.

I would also like to thank the Swiss National Science Foundation, who sponsored the research which has made this book possible (project: Adapting Western Welfare States to New Structures of Social Risk, Grant 100012–115937).

Finally, at Oxford University Press I am very grateful to Dominic Byatt and Sarah Parker for encouragement and support. But the very last thank you goes to Ramsey Wise, who read the whole manuscript and helped a lot improving the quality of the English language.

Berlin, May 2012

Contents

List of Figures

List of Tables

1

Introduction

The twenty-first century has witnessed the rebirth of consensus in social policy-making. After three decades of political struggles over the crisis, the dismantling, or the defence of the welfare state, most academics, international agencies, and, increasingly, national political actors throughout Organisation of Economic Co-operation and Development (OECD) countries have come to support the idea of an 'active welfare state'. The terminological issue may not have been settled yet since the terms used to qualify the new policy paradigm are varied and include 'social investment', 'flexicurity', or the 'Third Way'. The vision behind all these labels is nonetheless clear. Social policies should give a high priority to employment. They must deal with social problems chiefly by promoting labour market participation of disadvantaged people. Active social policies include labour market policies that aim at facilitating labour market entry and re-entry—policies that make it easier for parents to reconcile work and family life, and policies that invest in the human capital of disadvantaged people. Active social policy promises to simultaneously improve the living conditions of disadvantaged people, and to provide returns for society as a whole, through lower welfare spending and a more efficient labour market.

The adoption of an active approach to social policy can be considered as a true paradigm shift in social policy-making. The post-war welfare state was, above all, about protecting incomes. The social programmes that were set up during that period, and that today are responsible for the bulk of social expenditure, had one key objective: to protect the incomes of the family father, or the male breadwinner, should he be unable to work as a result of unemployment, sickness, invalidity, or old age. The post-war welfare state did little to help people gain access to employment. The welfare state of the early twenty-first century, while it continues to perform this important function, is pursuing another major objective as well: the promotion of labour market participation for all. This shift is reflected in the language used to describe welfare settlements. The images associated with the post-war welfare state were those of protection and security: the Swedish 'People's home' or the

British notion of income security 'from the cradle to the grave'. The new paradigm, instead, insists on 'opportunity', 'promotion', or 'advancement'. Today's blueprints for the reform of the welfare states have titles like *Extending Opportunities* (OECD 2005) or *From Safety Net to Springboards* (World Bank 2001).

The shift towards active social policy has been clearly led by academics, leading national politicians, and international agencies. Politically influential scholars like Anthony Giddens, Gøsta Esping-Andersen, Maurizio Ferrera, and Anton Hemerjick along with politicians like Tony Blair, Gerhard Schröder, and Frans Vanderbroucke have vastly contributed to spreading these new policy ideas among policy-makers, especially within European institutions. Moreover, the European Union, through the European Employment Strategy, is perhaps one of the most enthusiastic proponents of the new paradigm; however, other international organizations are not far behind. Support for this approach can be identified in the bulk of OECD publications on social policy since the mid-1990s. Active social policy has clearly replaced dismantling and deregulation as the international consensus in social policy.

Many have pointed out that active social policy is not a new idea. The notion that social policy should play an active and not only a protective role has influenced policy developments in some Nordic countries since the early post-war years. Sweden's emphasis on active labour market policies and heavy investments in childcare services go back to the 1950s and 1970s, respectively. To some authors the active dimension is one of the defining features of the social democratic welfare state (Esping-Andersen 1990; Huber and Stephens 2001; Huo et al 2008). As we will see below (Chapter 4), this view is controversial. In addition, a careful study of policy trajectories in the Nordic countries shows that while the emphasis on promoting employment was strong in the early post-war years and again at the beginning of the twenty-first century, in-between we find a period during which policy in countries like Sweden and Denmark developed in a more passive direction.

Today, however, the idea of an active social policy is rapidly gaining ground at the national level in Scandinavia and beyond, with countries as diverse as the UK, Germany, and the Netherlands having started investing in new labour market programmes aimed at activating various categories of non-working people. These countries have also declared childcare services, a key element of an active social policy, as a major policy priority.

This book addresses how countries are reorienting the welfare states they have inherited from the post-war years. Its focus is on Western Europe because it is in this part of the world that the notion of a protective welfare state went further. By the end of the post-war years, Western European countries had developed comprehensive systems of income and job protection. Since the late 1990s, however, a key objective of social policy has been to promote labour market participation. This book tries to explain how this happened.

The puzzles

The emergence and spread of active social policies poses a number of research problems, or puzzles. First, this development is taking place in a context of serious budgetary pressures, which makes expansion of social policy unlikely. Lower rates of growth, population ageing, and welfare state maturation have resulted in an economic climate characterized by, as Pierson aptly put it, 'permanent austerity'. In such a situation, social policy-making is expected to be about reducing or at least containing rising expenditures. Theories of retrenchment have also emphasized the political risks involved in cutting social programmes, and have claimed that governments will engage in this exercise reluctantly (Pierson 1994, 2001; Weaver 1986). They would expect governments with some 'spare cash' to use it to moderate retrenchment rather than to expand in new areas of social policy (Bonoli 2012). True, sometimes expansion was part of policy packages that contained also substantial retrenchment measures. However, there are many instances of expansion measures unrelated to the retrenchment measures that were going on at the same time, in other parts of the welfare state. Clearly, what we are seeing is higher spending in some parts of the welfare state: this is the case in the field of labour market services, childcare, and in the area of policies that help parents reconcile work and family life. How can we account for this development? Existing welfare state theories are better at explaining retrenchment or the absence of it than expansion in these new policy fields.

The second puzzle one encounters when studying active social policy is the reduced relevance of differences among welfare regimes. Until the mid-1990s the consensus among social policy specialists was that different welfare regimes had developed radically different responses to similar socio-economic problems. In short, facing an employment and a budgetary crisis in the late 1970s and early 1980s, English-speaking countries turned to neo-liberal solutions such as welfare retrenchment, labour market deregulation, and a general liberalization of their economies. In contrast, continental European countries responded to the same shock by using the welfare state in order to reduce labour supply; early retirement and easily accessible invalidity benefit were the tools. The Nordic countries took another route, based on investment in public services and active labour market policies. As a result observers concluded that different welfare regimes tend to develop very different types of responses to broadly similar social and economic problems (Esping-Andersen 1996; Pierson 2001).

What is striking today is that the reorientation of welfare states towards active social policies spans across welfare regimes. To be sure, differences between, say, Sweden, the UK, and Germany remain substantial. But the direction of policy change is remarkably similar across these three countries: more active social policies. Even a country like Sweden, which many have singled out as the pro-employment welfare state *par excellence*, has further strengthened the active dimension of its welfare state in the late 1990s and early 2000s. The vast majority of OECD countries likewise are implementing the active social policy paradigm, certainly with different emphases and in different ways, but they clearly are moving in the same direction. This observation contradicts what we thought we knew about the influence of past policies and welfare arrangements, more in general, on the current process of social policy adaptation. It demands an explanation.

The third puzzle refers to differences. The move towards active social policy is fairly generalized, but some countries, located essentially in Southern Europe, are clearly lagging behind. In these countries, childcare services and active labour market policies have not featured prominently among the areas of welfare state expansion over the past few years. True, these countries have generally seen an increase in labour force participation rates, but this is a result of some relaxation in labour law, mostly through the introduction of new types of labour contracts that do not enjoy all the protections available to core workers. The result of this development has been an increase in labour force participation rates as well as a growing cleavage between those who continue to enjoy good social and employment protection, often referred to as insiders, and those on the new types of contracts, or the outsiders (Rueda 2007; Palier and Thelen 2010).

Why is Southern Europe seemingly taking a different route in relation to welfare state adaptation? It is true that some social developments that are likely to have created the demand for active social policies are occurring more slowly in Southern Europe in comparison to the Nordic countries. This is the case, for example, of the process of women's emancipation, which started earlier in protestant Northern Europe and reached other parts of the European continent with a delay of 20 to 30 years. This process may be a precondition for the development of childcare services, and its relative delay may explain the lack of such services in some parts of Europe. According to this view, the current divergence should be only a temporary phenomenon. Given sufficient time, Southern European countries will develop active welfare states like those that exist in the North.

This possibility cannot be ruled out in the long term; however, there is currently little sign of Southern Europe embracing an active approach to social policy, despite relatively strong pressures pushing it in this direction. These pressures take various shapes: international agencies (EU (European Union) and the OECD) are encouraging their member states to develop active labour market and work–life balance policies; persistent high unemployment constitutes an ever-present economic and political problem for governments seeking re-election; and Southern European women now express the same aspiration to participate in labour markets as their counterparts elsewhere in Europe. The employment rate of younger cohorts of Italian and Spanish women, for instance, is catching up rapidly (Esping-Andersen 2009: 7). Why is the move towards active social policy uneven across otherwise similar OECD advanced economies? Why are Southern European countries not embracing the promising policy model which is being promoted by the OECD and the EU alike?

The objective of this book is to provide answers to these three puzzles. They can also be seen as anomalies or gaps between the predictions that theory makes and what observers see in actuality. Anomalies sometimes lead to new theories (Kuhn 1962). This is not the case with this book, which instead seeks to reconcile existing scholarship on welfare state transformation with what we have witnessed in terms of actual policy-making over the past two decades or so. Theories are revisited and adapted, but the basic principles on which our understanding of social policy-making is based remain intact.

On methodology

Students of comparative public policy know how difficult it is to provide convincing answers to the type of questions raised above. The key obstacle we face in this endeavour is the well-known many variables, small-N problem. Basically, the number of cases we can rely upon for this type of analysis is limited to advanced industrial countries that have been democratic for a sufficient number of years (a few decades) so as to allow the type of political mechanisms that we are interested in to take root. This leaves us with a sample of twenty-two to twenty-three countries in the best-case scenario. On the other hand, the number of variables likely to impact a complex phenomenon like the reorientation of modern social policy is huge. Good candidates are found in economic and social structures, political institutions, party systems, institutional legacies, and policy ideas, to mention a few.

Faced with this methodological problem, I rely on a number of strategies that will allow me to obtain results as robust as possible. First, contrary to the standard hypothetico-deductive approach of Popperian inspiration, I follow Fritz W. Scharpf's approach by taking seriously the issue of how hypotheses are generated (Scharpf 1997: 28). The standard approach does not care much about the process of formulating hypotheses. What matters is the test and the scientific quality of it. This prescription makes perfect sense in fields where relatively safe tests are available, such as, say, epidemiology, where hypotheses can be tested on samples with tens of thousands of observations. Things are different in the field of comparative public policy. The small number of cases reduces dramatically the power of hypothesis testing. In such circumstances, it is essential that more attention be paid on the quality and the plausibility of hypotheses.

Of course, this is a second best solution. Defining the quality of a hypothesis through other means than by its ability to withstand empirical tests is problematic. Yet a hypothesis can be just 'thrown up' by assuming relationships between variables, they can be elaborated on the basis of the theoretical understanding of the mechanisms behind policy-making processes or generated, inductively, on the basis of the observation of a few cases. Some quantitative papers in comparative public policy do the former. Hypotheses are typically presented in a few lines of text. Better studies spend time and text to illustrate why a given effect is plausible, what type of mechanism is behind it, and the basis upon which the understanding of policy-making is founded. This book belongs to the latter category. Hypotheses capable of answering the three puzzles presented above are put forward in Chapter 4. They are based on existing theories that attempt to provide ways of understanding social policy-making in advanced democracies.

The empirical material comes from two different sources. First, I present case studies of social policy-making in two key fields of active social policy: active labour market policy and childcare. Case studies are available for seven Western European countries: Sweden, Denmark, the Netherlands, Germany, France, Italy, and the UK. They have been selected so as to represent different types of political economies, welfare state regimes, political institutions, and cultural traditions. They also represent the various parts of Western Europe. Former communist countries are not included in this study. The theoretical framework I use emphasizes the role of politics and institutions over time. In this respect, it can be applied to countries that have developed extensive protection-oriented welfare states in a democratic context, that have faced similar socio-economic challenges over the past three decades, and that now find themselves in a context of permanent austerity. A study of active social policy in Eastern Europe would be extremely valuable, but would require other analytical tools.

Second, using expenditure data, the same two policy fields are investigated through statistical analysis. Using a pooled time series setup, it is possible to simultaneously study the effects across time and space, thereby, increasing the number of relevant observations. Though controversial, this method can provide additional information that complements the finding obtained in the qualitative studies, of course if used appropriately. It is explained in more details in Chapter 7. The combination of qualitative and quantitative research methods in a single study is increasingly common practice in comparative social policy (see, e.g., Huber and Stephens 2001; Huo 2009; Häusermann 2010). It is an approach that promises more robust and convincing results, which explains why it is followed in this study.

The argument in brief

The three puzzles presented above need complex answers. These are developed throughout the book and presented in Chapter 8. Unsurprisingly, a number of factors are found to have played a role in the development of active social policies. First, I argue, active social policies emerge in post-industrial societies, characterized by an employment problem for the low skilled and by high rates of female labour force participation. 'Activation' would have made little sense in the context of male full employment that prevailed in the OECD world during the 1950s and 1960s. Active social policy can thus be seen as a response to the new types of problems brought about by post-industrialization. Socio-structural change alone, however, does not explain the pattern of conversion to active social policy that we have observed in Western Europe over the past two decades. The timing of the turn towards an active welfare state differs across countries in a way that is not always related to the timing of post-industrial trends. For example, France is an early post-industrializer, but one must wait until the late 2000s to see the beginning of an activation turn in that country. In Southern Europe, typical post-industrial trends such as low-skill unemployment and increased female labour market participation have progressed quickly over the past decade. However, this has had little impact on the orientation of social policies, which have remained essentially passive. The socio-structural transformations going under the rubric of post-industrialization are best viewed as a necessary but not sufficient condition for the development of active social policies.

A social learning explanation is only partly helpful here. True, as it is often the case with public policies, the most adequate responses to a changed socioeconomic environment are not necessarily adopted quickly and simultaneously across countries. Policy-makers tend to go through more or less successful processes of trial and error and to rely on experiences made by their peers in other countries. All this may produce the particular pattern of the shift to active social policy that has been observed in Western Europe. But there are problems with this explanation too. For example, the activation turn begins well before a clear picture of the actual potential of these policies is available. These policies seem to be seen as attractive by policy-makers long before any positive effect is visible or demonstrated. In addition, Southern European countries, though increasingly affected by post-industrial employment and social problems, seem to fail to learn. That is why, in the account of the reorientation of European social policy, I put much emphasis on political competition.

Politics has been known to influence social policy since the early days of welfare state analysis. However, different periods have witnessed different effects. The reorientation towards active social policy can be seen as driven in the political arena by the notion of 'affordable credit claiming', inspired by the work of R. Kent Weaver on credit claiming and blame avoidance (1986). Weaver argued that much of current policy-making is about taking unpopular decisions and discussing the strategies developed by governments in order to minimize the political and particularly electoral consequences of these tough choices, what he called blame avoidance. He spent much less time discussing the notion of 'credit claiming', an activity in which government engage less often, at least in the current climate of widespread austerity.

True, economic and budgetary constraints do make credit claiming more difficult. However, it is reasonable to expect that when an opportunity for credit claiming is in sight, policy-makers will be inclined to take advantage of it. The idea of an active social policy provided precisely such an opportunity, at a reasonable cost for cash-strapped public finances. Interventions like active labour market policies and childcare can be popular. Helping disadvantaged people by improving their chances of finding a job or helping parents to reconcile work and family life are both policies that can find the support of the middle classes, who may benefit indirectly as tax payers (via active labour market policy) or, those with young children, directly.

These policies also tend to be considerably less costly than more traditional components of the welfare state. Big spenders on childcare and active labour market policy assign to these functions between 1 and 2 per cent of GDP. In contrast, spending on old age pensions averages around 7 per cent in OECD countries. I argue that this imbalance in the fiscal implications of different social policies constitutes an incentive for politicians to turn to active social policies for credit claiming purposes. Constructing a party programme on raising pensions could be popular, but clearly unaffordable in the current context and probably not very credible. Promising the status quo or cuts that are smaller than those proposed by the competitors is unlikely to inspire many new voters. In this context it is easy to see that active social policy is attractive because it provides opportunities for affordable credit claiming.

Active social policy turned out to be attractive independently of existing welfare state institutions, hence the convergence of countries across Europe on the notion of an active welfare state. Instead, the success of active social policy in the political arena is strongly related to policy-makers willingness and ability to use these tools as credit claiming devices. This has been often the case with the social democratic governments that were in power in the 1990s.

Most countries reoriented their welfare states in this direction during the 1990s/early 2000s. Often, the reorientation was presided upon by social democratic parties that were back in power after a more or less prolonged period in opposition. Key moments in the implementation of the new policy perspective were the Danish 1994 labour market policy reform, adopted just after the election of Poul Nyrup Rasmussen as prime minister. Wim Kok, the head of the Dutch government who played an instrumental role in promoting an 'activation turn', was elected in the same year. Tony Blair and the Third Way were to follow in the UK in 1997, and in Germany in 1998 Gerhard Schröder, who was also a loud proponent of an active social policy, both in both words and actions.

These newly elected social democratic governments faced two common problems. First, they had to demonstrate that they were capable of running the economy in difficult economic times. Second, they also had to distinguish themselves from their conservative predecessors. Traditional social democratic policies of Keynesian inspiration were off the menu, given the limits to increased state spending imposed by globalization, population ageing, European constraints, and in short, the context of permanent austerity (Pierson 1998). Active social policy provided them with a solution that could be related to some of the traditional values of social democracy, equality, and the defence of the weakest in society (Huo 2009) while at the same time be fully compatible with the constraints imposed by the context of permanent austerity.

The most favourable conditions for the development of active social policy were found in countries where the social democrats were in power in the late 1970s and where during the 1980s right-wing governments turned to retrenchment. When back in power, the social democrats found in active social policy a solution that allowed them to demonstrate that they were capable of running the economy in the context of globalization, while at the same time relating to left-wing values. This sequence is found in two of the most enthusiastic adopters of active social policies: the UK and Denmark. The Netherlands and Germany have followed a similar trajectory. In contrast, one does not find this sequence in the countries where active social policy has progressed more slowly, such as in France and Southern Europe.

Southern Europe may have missed the opportunity to develop an active welfare estate. There were attempts to adopt an active social policy, sometimes made by social democratic governments (like the 1996–8 Prodi government in Italy). However, there was very little success. Budgetary constraints were stronger in Southern Europe, which made it difficult to develop any sort of new policy. At the same time, Southern European countries have clearly emphasized the selective deregulation of their labour market as a way to increase employment rates. Labour markets have been deregulated at the margin, introducing new labour contracts with low levels of employment and social protection. These changes are now responsible for the bulk of job creation in Southern Europe, leading to a strong dualization of the labour market, which is increasingly characterized by a cleavage between insiders (who still enjoy the projections of the post-war welfare state) and the outsiders (Palier 2010; Palier and Thelen 2010; Emmenegger et al. 2012).

Reality is complex, as are the origins of active social policy. That is why in the final chapter, I identify a range of other factors that have contributed to the development of active social policies. These include institutional antecedents, which sometimes played a surprising role, the type of political competition—whether centripetal or centrifugal, the role of women's political influence in the development of comprehensive systems of subsidized childcare, and the timing of post industrialization relative to other developments such as population ageing and welfare state maturation. These other factors are helpful in understanding cross-national variation in the spread of active social policies. However, the main drivers behind the activation turn are to be found in the changed socio-economic circumstances and in political competition.

The book's structure

The book begins by discussing different attempts to characterize the 'new welfare state'—or the welfare settlement that is emerging at the beginning of the twenty-first century—and by putting forward a definition of active social policy. It then moves on to map the development of active social policy across OECD countries. The conclusion of this empirical part is that active social policies have expanded across the OECD, except in Southern Europe. Chapter 4 begins the search for an explanation for this development or lack thereof. On the basis of political science welfare state theories, it presents a number of hypotheses. It also discusses some attempts that have already been made to explain the emergence of active social policies. Next, Chapters 5 and 6 provide narrative accounts of policy-making in the two areas covered by this study: active labour market policies and childcare. This evidence is complemented in Chapter 7 with analysis expenditure data for these two fields of policy. Finally, Chapter 8 provides an assessment of the hypotheses presented in Chapter 4 in light of the available empirical evidence. It concludes by pointing out the implications for welfare state theory and whether very recent policy developments prompted by the 2008 financial crisis have some bearing on the argument put forward in the book.

2

Defining Active Social Policy

Social policy in Organisation of Economic Co-operation and Development (OECD) countries took an unexpected turn in the late 1990s–early 2000s. While in the previous two decades the key direction of welfare restructuring was retrenchment and cost containment, more recent reforms, at least up to the 2008 financial crisis, have favoured a new, more active role for social policy. For advanced welfare states, this shift has meant the adoption of a new function. In addition to the traditional income protection function, social programmes are increasingly expected to promote labour market participation through a great variety of means. Of course, the income protection function of welfare states still plays a very important (and controversial) role, which is increasingly obscured by the very strong emphasis on employment promotion and investment in human capital. This shift has been recognized by many, and I have had the chance to discuss it more thoroughly in work carried out jointly with David Natali (Bonoli and Natali 2012). This chapter provides first an overview of the interpretations that have been given to the shift in social policy. It then puts forward a definition of active social policy and discusses its key components.

Perspectives on the new welfare state

The reorientation of welfare states away from income maintenance and towards the promotion of labour market participation has been recognized by several authors (see Bonoli and Natali 2012 for a discussion). Earlier attempts to capture this movement made reference to the notion of recalibration, understood as shifting emphasis away from the protection of traditional welfare state clienteles, such as older people, towards new social groups such as women and younger people (Ferrera and Rhodes 2000; Ferrera et al 2000; Pierson 2001). Others understood this movement in terms of rationalization of Western welfare state, especially those of continental Europe, where the passive income protection function had gone too far (Levy 1999).

Since then, many have made reference to a fundamental shift in welfare state development, taking place between the late 1990s and the early 2000s. Studies of the Third Way contributed to identifying the emergence of a new approach: Emphasizing the role of the welfare state in promoting equality of opportunity as opposed to income protection (Powell 1999; White 2001). The notion of flexicurity, a contraction of the terms 'flexibility' and 'security', has also been used to describe a combination of labour market and social policy oriented towards the promotion of market employment.

Other authors who have focused on the changing nature of the problems social policy is designed to address identify a shift in the direction of social policy that can be more or less sensitive to the emergence of new social risks (Taylor-Gooby 2004; Bonoli 2005; Armingeon and Bonoli 2006). In his more recent work, Taylor-Gooby refers to a 'new welfare settlement' for Europe. This concept is based on the view that 'the role of government is to promote national competitiveness in an increasingly international market, and away from a passive providing state to one which seeks to enhance self-activity, responsibility and mobilisation into paid work among citizens' (2008: 4). Anton Hemerijck also identifies a 'social investment turn' around the mid-1990s across OECD countries, resulting from a growing dissatisfaction with the previously near-hegemonic, neo-liberal paradigm and prompted also by the economic success obtained by the Nordic countries. It constitutes a third phase of welfare state development, after expansion in the post-war years and retrenchment in the 1980s (Hemerijck 2011). Similarly, Jane Jenson identifies in the 'social investment perspective' a novel approach to social policy that rests between the Keynesian welfare state and the neo-liberal paradigm (Jenson 2011).

Some of the authors briefly mentioned above have discussed definitional as well as content issues at great length. The labels used as well as the precise focus of these analyses are somewhat different, but they all make reference to what one could call the adoption of a more active role in social policy, oriented towards promoting labour market participation for all, directly and through investment in human capital. Next I review some of the most influential attempts at capturing this type of change in social policy.

The Third Way

Many of the themes that are included in the discussion of active social policies are strongly reminiscent of the debate on the Third Way, which kept Social Democrats busy at the end of the 1990s. By the end of the 2000, the term Third Way was nearly forgotten. However, many of the policy ideas that were put forward under this label are now clearly mainstreamed and implemented by governments of different political orientation.

The Third Way debate can be traced back to the writings of Anthony Giddens from the mid-1990s onwards (Giddens 1994, 1998). These ideas proved extremely influential in shaping the agenda of the British Labour Party, before and especially after the 1997 election victory and accession of Tony Blair to the position of Prime Minister. The ideas and the discourse were then popularized throughout Europe, resulting in some high profile publications, such as a paper jointly authored by Tony Blair and the then German Chancellor, Gerhard Schröder (Blair and Schröder 1999).

These events resulted in the development of a literature, academic as well as political, which attempted to define the 'new' orientation of social democracy in terms of Third Way. At times, confusion arose within these debates as different authors focus on different levels of analysis: rhetoric, values, or actual policies. It was nonetheless possible to identify a number of key Third Way themes: an emphasis on equality of opportunity (as opposed to equality of outcomes), a shift away from the state and towards civil society (the voluntary sector) but also towards the private sector as providers of public goods, a re-balancing of rights and responsibilities in social policies. In addition, all accounts of the Third Way included also a strong focus on the reorientation of the welfare state towards active social policy, along the lines put forward here (see, e.g., Giddens 1998; Powell 1999; White 2001).

It is most likely the case that the policy ideas that were subsumed under the label 'Third Way' went far beyond a simple updating of Social Democratic party policies. First, this has been made clear in empirical studies trying to identify Third Way ideas in the real world of politics and policy, which found that the Left did not have a monopoly over them. Looking at party manifestoes, Volkens (2004) found that Third Way ideas had indeed gained ground in Western European politics over the past few decades. But this trend was in no way limited to Social Democratic parties. It was equally discernible among their centre-right competitors (Volkens 2004). Country-level studies showed that key Third Way ideas have been championed by Social Democrats and Liberals alike. This was the case in Belgium, the Netherlands (Hoop 2004), and Spain, where the corresponding concept of *Via Media* was developed by the Center-Right *Partido Popular* (Moreno 2000).

But a more fundamental critique of the notion of a new Third Way came from the North, more specifically from Sweden. Swedish Social Democrats had been practising with Third Way ideas since the early post-war years. Unlike the British Labour Party, Swedish Social Democrats did not feel they had to promote a new image of economic competence since they had been successfully running economic policy for several decades. According to Charlotte

Svensson, a political adviser to former Social Democratic leader and Prime Minister Goran Persson:

> Many of the Third Way notions constitute fundamental parts of the Swedish social-democratic programs and the concrete policy practice by the social-democratic government [...]. The notion of 'from welfare to work' does not seem new to a Swede. Modern Swedish labour market policy was conceived more than 30 years ago.... Active labour market policies have the task of preventing social exclusion and act as a good incentive to look for work or to pursue education. (Svensson 2001: 224)

In reality, as will be shown below (Chapter 4), Swedish labour market policy in the 1970s temporarily shifted away from the promotion of market employment and acquired a more passive, Continental, flavour. But one must acknowledge that most of the time, at least formally, Swedish policy has put strong emphasis on helping people back to the labour market.

The Third Way project aimed at modernizing social democracy. The welfare state was only one element of it, though admittedly a crucial one. The understanding of the role of welfare in the Third Way project, however, is clearly in line with the idea of an active social policy. According to Jingjing Huo, this idea appealed to Social Democrats because it allowed them to maintain the emphasis on their traditional values of solidarity and egalitarianism. What they managed was a simple shift of priorities between passive and active measures (Huo 2009: 2).

Flexicurity

The notion of 'flexicurity' has become extremely popular in labour market policy debates at the international and especially EU level, but also at the national level in several countries. Popularity notwithstanding, there is no clear, generally accepted definition or precise meaning. Lack of precision may be an advantage for concepts in politics as it facilitates 'ambiguous agreements' (see Palier 2005), but it is a problem in research. This problem has been exacerbated by the fact that the meaning of the term flexicurity has evolved over time to include a vast variety of aspects broadly related to social policies and labour markets. A quick look at the relevant literature shows that there is a great variety of ways to understand the term (see Viebrock and Clasen 2009).

Initially, the notion of flexicurity was used to describe the combination of a relatively liberal labour market with the provision of income security through a generous welfare state. This arrangement describes the Danish approach to labour market regulation, based on flexible employment contracts, high replacement rates for unemployment insurance, and a developed system of active labour market policies designed to move back into employment those who lose their jobs (Madsen 2002). Low job protection facilitates entry into the labour market. It also facilitates exit, but a generous unemployment compensation system offsets most of the financial consequences of unemployment. Finally, activation ensures that high replacement rates do not impact negatively on re-employment.

During the 1990s, Denmark succeeded in reducing its unemployment rate dramatically (see Chapter 5). According to many observers, this was a result of its particular mix of social and labour market policy. The Danish approach was soon recognized as a possible model for southern and continental European countries, where economic security to wage earners had traditionally been provided not so much by the welfare state, but much more through employ-ment protection legislation (Bonoli 2003). This feature of Southern European labour markets was considered to be at least in part responsible for their rather bad employment performance (Esping-Andersen 2000; Nickell 2003).

As a result, the idea of flexicurity gained momentum, especially at the EU level, with the publication of a communication on flexicurity by the Commis-sion (European Commission 2007). Here, and in the work of flexicurity experts, the concept was defined in much broader terms to include, for instance, aspects related to work–family reconciliation, referred to as 'combin-ation security' (Wilthagen and Tros 2004). The European Commission further included in its vision of flexicurity a very broad range of objectives and policy fields, such as lifelong learning, active labour market policies, gender equality, and social dialogue (European Commission 2007: 6, 10). Understood in such broad terms, flexicurity reflects well the notion of active social policy explored in this chapter. First, flexicurity emphasizes helping disadvantaged people by facilitating labour market entry. Second, flexicurity embodies the win-win quality that is also typical of active social policies: the strategy promises flexibility for employers and security for employees.

New social risks

An alternative approach to capturing the reorientation of Western welfare state focused on shifts in what is considered as social risks. The notion of new social risks is being used with increasing frequency in the literature on the welfare state (see, e.g., Esping-Andersen 1999; Hemerijck 2002; Taylor-Gooby 2004; Bonoli 2005, 2007). However, a precise definition of what is considered under this label is generally missing. Elsewhere, I have used the label 'new social risks' to denote 'situations in which individuals experience welfare losses and which have arisen as a result of the socio-economic transformations that have taken place over the last three to four decades, and that are generally subsumed under the heading of post-industrialisation' (Bonoli 2007: 498). These include a number of contingencies such as:

- *Reconciling work and family life*—The domestic and childcare work that used to be performed on an unpaid basis by housewives now needs to be externalized. It can be either obtained from the state or bought on the market. The difficulties faced by families in this respect (but most significantly by women) are a major source of frustration and can result in important losses of welfare (i.e., if a parent reduces working hours because of the unavailability of adequate childcare facilities).

- *Single parenthood*—Change in family structures and behaviour have resulted in increased rates of single parenthood across OECD countries, which presents a distinctive set of social policy problems (access to an adequate income, childcare, and the relationship between parenthood and work). Moreover, it is obvious that difficulties in reconciling work and family life are of course more serious for single parents than they are for two-parent households.

- *Having a frail relative*—Like in the case of children, care for frail elderly or disabled people during the post-war years was mostly provided by non-employed women on an unpaid, informal basis. Again, with the femininization of labour market participation, this task needs to be externalized too. The inability to do so (because of lack of services) may also result in important welfare losses.

- *Possessing low or obsolete skills*—Low-skill individuals have probably always been disadvantaged. However, during the post-war years, low-skill workers were predominantly employed in manufacturing industry. They were able to benefit from productivity increases possible thanks to technological advances, so that their wages rose together with those of the rest of the population. Today, low-skill individuals are mostly employed in the low-value-added service sector or unemployed. Low-value-added services such as retail sale, cleaning, and catering are known for providing very little scope for productivity increases (Pierson 1998). In countries where wage determination is essentially based on market mechanisms, this means that low-skill individuals are seriously exposed to the risk of being paid a poverty wage (US, UK). The situation is different in countries where wage determination is controlled by governments (through generous minimum wage legislation) or by the social partners (through encompassing collective agreements). Under these conditions, the wages of low-skill workers are protected, but given the limited job creation availability in these sectors, many low-skill individuals are in fact unemployed (Iversen and Wren 1998). Overall, the fact of possessing low or obsolete skills today entails a major risk of welfare loss, considerably higher than in the post-war years.

- *Insufficient social security coverage*—The shift to a post-industrial employment structure has resulted in the presence of career profiles in modern labour markets that are very different from that of the standard male workers of the post-war years. These profiles are characterized by full-time, continuous employment from an early age and with a steadily rising salary. Yet the social security schemes (most notably pensions) that we have inherited from the post-war years are still clearly based on these traditional assumptions regarding labour market participation. Pension coverage, in most Western European countries, is optimal for workers who spend their entire working life in full-time employment. Part-time work usually results in reduced pension entitlements, as do career interruptions due to childbearing.

These situations are caused by different factors but have a number of things in common. First, they are all 'new' in the sense that they are typical of the post-industrial societies in which we live today. During the *trente glorieuses*—the period of male full employment and sustained economic growth that characterized the post-war years—these risks were extremely marginal, if they existed at all. In addition, new social risks share another feature: They tend to concentrate amongst the same groups of people, usually younger people, families with small children, or working women. While it is difficult to set clear borders around the section of the population that bears most new social risks, it is clear that the categories mentioned here are largely overlapping, making it possible to identify in post-industrial society a fairly large minority of the population that struggles daily against the consequences of new social risks.

The new social risks approach emphasizes the shift that has occurred in what is considered to constitute a social problem or a social risk. In common with the perspective adopted in this book, it implies that the social context of social policy has undergone some profound changes since the post-war years and reflects now a qualitatively different type of society and economy. The main difference lies in the fact that the notion of new social risks refers to social structures, whereas 'active social policy' focuses on the interventions that are adopted in response to the emergence of the new risks. This book being about policy, the latter terminology has been preferred.

Social investment

Recent thinking on welfare state transformation has focused also on the notion of 'social investment', which makes reference to policies that aim to help disadvantaged people by improving their life chances, particularly their chances to enter and succeed in education and in the labour market. From an abstract point of view, they can be distinguished both from the more traditional social policy approach based on income or job protection and from the neo-liberal one based on deregulation and re-commodification (Jenson 2009).

Social investment emphasizes investment in human capital as a strategy to deal with social problems and to reduce inequalities. As a result, education and training are the key instruments of a social investment strategy. Investment in human capital is promoted throughout the life course. Much emphasis is placed on investing in children so as to maximize their chances of succeeding in education and in the labour market (Esping-Andersen 2002, 2009; Jenson 2002, 2009; Jenson and Saint Martin 2006). Other age groups are also targeted by investments in human capital, including older people who are often strongly disadvantaged in rapidly changing labour markets. Social investment refers also to measures that remove obstacles to employment or to career advancement. These include the provision of subsidized childcare to parents of young children so that they can enter or remain in the labour market, but also active labour market policies that assist jobless people in their efforts to look for employment.

The use of the term 'investment' suggests that these policies can generate 'returns' for the 'investor' (i.e., society). Of course, the ability to impact positively on societal well being is not a specificity of the social investment approach. Social policies, in general, do produce positive returns for society in terms of improved social cohesion, which benefits all, or in terms of sustained demand for goods and services, thus promoting economic growth. These positive effects of social policies are well known, but are extremely difficult to measure. Benefits in terms of social cohesion may be particularly difficult to quantify, as the value that people attach to it may vary across individuals. The social investment perspective understands returns in stricter, quantifiable terms. Investing in education, childcare, or active labour market policy increases the productivity and earning capacity of individuals, who as a result are less likely to require benefits and more likely to be paying taxes. Esping-Andersen insists on this quality of some of the new policies, arguing that spending on them should not count as consumption but as investment. Spending on childcare, for instance, can produce net returns to the exchequer through increased labour market participation by the mother (Esping-Andersen 2009: 96).

The notion of social investment is often used in a prescriptive, normative way. Esping-Andersen (2002) calls for a new 'social investment' welfare state. Its key features are the focus on investing in human capital in general. It emphasizes the need for policy-makers to take a life-course perspective and hence a strong focus on child well being and development. Vandenbroucke et al. (2011) call for a social investment pact for Europe, which even in the current tough budgetary context should prioritize investment in policies that support children, lifelong learning, work and family reconciliation, and so forth. Hemerijck calls for 'affordable social investment' or policies that can be developed despite the dire state of public finances (Hemerijck 2012a).

Like the other labels discussed in this chapter, the notion of 'social investment' tries to capture a new way to help disadvantaged people by improving their life chances, especially through investment in human capital. There are differences though between the notions of 'social investment' and 'active social policy'. Social investment, as used by the authors mentioned above, emphasizes human capital development and a notion of equality of opportunity that entails also some equality in outcomes. In contrast, little attention is paid to work incentives. These aspects of the social investment perspective are strongly present in the academic discussions but have been much less influential in policy developments. The reorientation examined in this book, instead, stresses much more stronger work incentives.

At the same time, social investment, like all the notions discussed above, sees a role for social policy that is clearly different from the passive, compensatory function fulfilled by post-war income replacement schemes. With different emphases, these assessments of current developments in social policy agree that something has changed in the way welfare states provide economic security. Facilitating access to employment is a key function of a modern welfare state.

Active social policies

My definition of 'active social policy' relies to a large extent on the analysis presented above. Conceptually, I concur with the widespread view that, in a one-dimensional ideological space, the new paradigm is located somewhere between Keynesian or traditional social democracy and neo-liberalism. However, a wide variety of policy options fulfil the condition of being neither of Keynesian origin nor of neo-liberal inspiration. In this respect, it is helpful to think of social policies as a continuum, going from income and job protection—the traditional Keynesian, social democratic solution to social problem—to active policy and to re-commodification, the standard neo-liberal response. This view is represented in Figure 2.1.

Active social policies prioritize human capital investment and the removal of obstacles to labour market participation. They may focus on the promotion of capabilities or on removing incentive traps. In fact, we can think of active social policies that are more oriented towards protection, such as job creation schemes, and other ones that are closer to the notion of re-commodification, such as tax credits or welfare to work programmes. Of course, the borders

Employment protection Early retirement Cash benefits	Job creation schemes Social insertion programmes Parental leave Anti-child poverty programmes	Full vocational training Education Early childhood education	Job search programmes Tax credits Childcare	Retrenchment Workfare Deregulation
PROTECTION	ACTIVE SOCIAL POLICY			(RE-) COMMODIFICATION

Figure 2.1. Social policy options arranged according to three principles: protection, active social policy, and commodification

between the three social policy paradigms are not watertight. The objective of Figure 2.1 is to clarify the concept of active social policy rather than to provide a tool for classifying policies.

By defining the new welfare state by its ideological location between traditional social democracy (protection) and neo-liberalism (re-commodification), this approach reflects previous ones (e.g., Giddens 1998; Jenson 2009). However, by differentiating types of active social policies, it permits distinctions between different variants in the implementation of the new paradigm. This more fine-grained understanding of policies belonging to the rubric of 'active social policy' is essential in order to make sense of countries' trajectories. As we will see in Chapter 5, policy often shifts within the space defined as 'active social policy'.

Active social policies have some important qualities that are likely to affect the politics they generate. First, active social policies can be credibly presented as win-win solutions to social problems. They provide help to disadvantaged people, and at the same time, they promise to produce returns for society in the shape of lower social expenditure and higher tax receipts. Both sides of the welfare relationship, the beneficiary and the contributor, are winners in this exchange. This win-win quality distinguishes active policies from the traditional redistributive social policies of the post-war welfare state. Redistributive policies are, by definition, zero-sum-games: what some people gain, others must pay. This putative win-win quality of active social policies makes them particularly suitable for credit claiming since there are no obvious losers involved. In addition, credit claiming must not be limited to the receivers of the policy (i.e., non-working individuals who may be helped into employment by the new policies), but also by those who see themselves as contributors (i.e., from the middle classes upwards). This means that the 'pool' of voters targeted through a credit-claiming exercise can be particularly large.

Second, active social policies have a positive impact on labour supply. This is true for both labour market and family policies. In this regard, they differ completely from the traditional protective social policies, which tend to remove people from the labour market. As a result, the type of class-based cleavages that are behind the development of the traditional post-war welfare states is unlikely. In contrast, active social policy can be equally attractive for representatives of capital and labour. Of course, this does not mean that disagreement between political actors of the Left and the Right is absent in this field, quite the contrary. However, it is clear that active social policy is more likely to be the result of cross-class coalitions than was the case with the traditional protective policies. In fact, some of these policies were imposed by powerful left-wing governments against reluctant employers (see, e.g., Korpi 1983). This was particularly the case with employment protection legislation (Emmenegger 2009).

Finally, since the ideological space occupied by active social policy is rather broad, we can allow for different 'varieties of active social policy'. In fact, a parallel with Keynesianism comes useful here. After 1945 the majority of industrial countries developed countercyclical demand management in their economic policies. But they did so in different ways that reflected their respective political economy traditions and balance of political power. In the 1960s, for example, we could find that Keynes' recipes were followed more closely in countries like Britain and France than Germany or the USA (Shonfield 1964; Hall 1989). Similarly, we can expect the notion of an active social policy to provide some broad indications concerning the direction of social interventions. Its application is likely to vary across countries, again depending on their own political economy traditions, balance of political power, and budgetary constraints. Although virtually all the countries studied in this book developed policies over the past 20 years or so under the rubric of active labour market policy and childcare, they did so to very different extents and with different emphases. This topic will be presented more fully in Chapters 5 and 6.

The tools of active social policy

The re-orientation of Western welfare states towards active social policy takes place through different channels. Sometimes new policies are introduced; sometimes old ones are transformed and take up new objectives, a process that can be seen as one of 'institutional conversion' (Streeck and Thelen 2005).

Next, I discuss some of the most important policy fields in which the active paradigm can be implemented.

Active labour market policies

Active labour market policy constitutes the cornerstone of the active welfare state. Rather than simply providing a cash benefit to those who are unable to work, active labour market policy aims to remove obstacles to employment, upskill workers, or provide access to work experience. Active labour market policy differs also from the neo-liberal approach to worklessness, based on strengthening incentives only through measures such as time limits on benefit recipiency, lower benefit rates, and sanctions.

The label 'active labour market policy' (ALMP) is used to describe an extremely diverse range of policies, going from vocational retraining to welfare-to-work or workfare schemes for social assistance beneficiaries. The result is that discussions of ALMPs are often confusing. For this reason, I propose a more fine-grained approach here, distinguishing between different types of ALMPs. These different types are used in the analyses presented in this book, wherever possible.

ALMPs have different origins. In Sweden, ALMPs were developed as early as the 1950s, with the objective of improving the match between demand and supply of labour in the context of a rapidly evolving economy, essentially by financing extensive vocational training programmes (Swenson 2002). At the opposite extreme, the term 'active' has been used to describe the approach developed in various English-speaking countries, which combines placement services with stronger work incentives, time limits on recipiency, benefit reductions, and the use of sanctions. This has also been referred to as the so-called 'workfare' approach (King 1995; Peck 2001).

In fact, as many have pointed out, ALMP is a particularly ambiguous category of social policy (Clasen 2000; Barbier 2001, 2004; Clegg 2005). In particular, ALMPs cannot be subsumed under a traditional one-dimensional view of social policy, making reference to expansion and retrenchment. As Jochen Clasen put it:

> it is sometimes difficult to classify a particular policy as an example of either welfare retrenchment or welfare expansion. For instance, the potential expenditure involved in activation programmes is higher than in maintaining passive cash support. [...However,] from the perspective of individual claimants, obligatory activation might be seen exclusively as welfare restriction. (Clasen 2000: 90)

In order to deal with this problem, various authors have tried to develop a more differentiated view of this policy area, based on the identification of different types of ALMPs. These classifications tend to draw a line between the 'good' activation policies, which are about improving human capital, and the 'bad' ones, which use essentially negative incentives to move people from social assistance into employment. Examples of such classifications are found in Torfing, who distinguishes between 'offensive' and 'defensive' workfare (1999). Offensive workfare, which is the term used to describe the Danish variant of activation, relies on improving skills and empowering jobless people rather than on sanctions and benefit reduction, which is the 'defensive' variant found in the USA. Taylor-Gooby makes the same point using instead the terms of 'positive' and 'negative' activation (2004).

In a similar vein, Barbier distinguishes between 'liberal activation' (characterized by stronger work incentives, benefit conditionality, and the use of sanctions) and 'universalistic activation', which is found in the Nordic countries and relies on extensive investment in human capital essentially through training (Barbier 2004; Barbier and Ludwig-Mayerhofer 2004). Barbier also hypothesizes the existence of a third type, found within Continental Europe. This third type of activation emphasizes 'insertion sociale', a notion that refers more to full participation in society and less to the fact of actually having a job. Its tools are job creation programmes in the public or non-profit sector (Barbier 2001; Enjolras et al. 2001).

Dichotomies between human investment and incentive-based approaches to activation are a useful starting point in making sense of an ambiguous concept. However, they probably constitute an oversimplification of the real world and run the risk of carrying value judgements. A different type of distinction is found in Clegg, who identifies two policy mechanisms that can be subsumed under activation: circulation and integration. The idea behind circulation is to improve the chances of an unemployed person to enter in contract with a potential employer (i.e., through placement services). Instead, integration refers to instruments that more directly bring the jobless into employment, like benefit conditionality or sheltered employment (Clegg 2005: 56). Clegg's approach is promising, insofar as it focuses on the mechanisms behind the active approach and avoids the risk of making value judgments by simply drawing a distinction between 'good' and 'bad' active policy.

Here, I also want to depart from the dichotomic, value-laden distinction that has dominated debates on ALMPs and suggest a more complex view of what can be subsumed under the heading active labour market policy. This discussion will also contribute to clarify the meaning of the various terms used in the debate on ALMPs, such as 'activation' or 'workfare'. These have flourished over the past few years and are not always used consistently.

My understanding of ALMPs makes reference to two dimensions (see Bonoli 2010). The first dimension concerns the extent to which the objective of policy is to put people back into unsubsidized market employment, provided

Table 2.1. Four types of active labour market policy

		Investment in human capital		
		None	Weak	Strong
Pro-market employment orientation	Weak	(Passive benefits)	**Occupation** • Job creation schemes in the public sector • Non-employment-related training programmes	(Basic education)
	Strong	**Incentive reinforcement** • Tax credits, in work benefits • Time limits on recipiency • Benefit reductions • Benefit conditionality	**Employment assistance** • Placement services • Job subsidies • Counselling • Job search programmes	**Upskilling** • Job-related vocational training

Source: adapted from Bonoli 2010.

by either private or public employers.[1] Many programmes have this objective, but some, especially in continental and Northern Europe during the 1980s and early 1990s, looked more like alternatives to market employment. These took the shape of temporary jobs created in the public or in the non-profit sector. They were often used to re-create an entitlement to unemployment insurance rather than to increase the chances of landing an unsubsidized job. As will be seen in the narrative accounts below, the extent to which ALMPs favour labour market re-entry varies across countries and across time. I call this dimension the 'pro-market employment orientation'.

The second dimension refers to the extent to which programmes are based on investing in jobless people's human capital. Investment can take the shape of vocational training or help in developing the sort of soft skills employers look for when selecting candidates. Intersecting these two dimensions allows us to identify different types of labour market policy and to map the variety that exists under the label 'active labour market policy' (Table 2.1).

Of course, there are several dimensions of variation in ALMPs that can be used to develop alternative typologies. The two selected here are particularly important in defining the impact that ALMPs can have on the broader political economy. An ALMP that aims to provide an alternative to market employment can be seen as part of the strategy known as 'labour reduction route' adopted in continental European countries in the 1980s. In contrast, one that

---

[1] By 'unsubsidized market employment' I mean jobs that are created as a result of a demand for labour by private or public employers, and not in order to absorb excess labour supply.

aims to reinstate people back into employment will have a positive impact on labour supply. However, the pro-market employment orientation tells us little about the type of jobs that are being promoted. This is why it is important to consider also the content of policy in terms of investment in human capital.

Of the six possible combinations between the two dimensions selected, four describe different orientations in ALMP. These can be labelled as incentive reinforcement, employment assistance, occupation, and human capital investment. The other two, passive benefits and basic education, are not generally considered as part of ALMPs.

The first type of ALMPs, 'incentive reinforcement', refers to measures that intend to strengthen work incentives for benefit recipients. This objective can be achieved in various ways (i.e., by curtailing passive benefits, in terms of both benefit rates and duration). Benefits can also be made conditional upon participation in work schemes or other labour market programmes. Finally, incentives can be strengthened by providing in-work cash benefits to low-paid workers, such as tax credits (Myles and Pierson 1997). Elements of incentive reinforcement exist everywhere, but they are particularly strong in English-speaking countries.

The second type, which I term 'employment assistance', consists of interventions aimed at removing obstacles to labour market participation. These include placement services or job search programmes that increase the likelihood of a jobless person establishing contact with a potential employer. Counselling and job subsidies may be particularly useful to beneficiaries who have been out of the labour market for a long time or have never had a job and are often shunned by employers. For parents, an obstacle to employment may be the lack of childcare, and help in finding (and paying for) a suitable daycare service may also be included under the employment assistance variant. These interventions may provide modest improvements in the human capital of beneficiaries, mostly in the shape of improved soft skills. Above all, however, they allow beneficiaries to put their human capital to good use. This approach is common in English-speaking countries (combined with incentive reinforcement), since the mid- to late 1990s as well as in Nordic and continental European countries.

A third type of active labour market policy can be labelled 'occupation'. Its objective is not primarily to promote labour market re-entry, but to keep jobless people busy and to prevent the depletion of human capital associated with an unemployment spell. This type of ALMP consists of job creation and work experience programmes in the public or non-profit sector as well as training, in some cases, such as shorter courses, which do not fundamentally change the type of job a person can do. Continental European countries in the 1980s and early 1990s have been among the main users of this type of ALMP.

Finally, ALMPs can rely on 'upskilling' or providing vocational training to jobless people. The idea here is to offer a second chance to people who were not able to profit from the training system or whose skills have become obsolete. The provision of vocational training to jobless people is most developed in the Nordic countries.

Work–life balance policies

The promotion of labour market participation has not been confined to labour market policy. Family policies have also been reoriented so as to pursue this goal, essentially through policies that facilitate labour market participation for parents. The provision of subsidized childcare is the main pillar of this reorientation, which is why this book focuses essentially on this service. However, one could include also under this rubric policies that allow parent-workers time off to care for their young children, more flexibility in working hours, or other sorts of help in reconciling work and family life. These policies, even though some of them are about allowing temporary interruptions in employment, are clearly meant to maximize labour force participation. Relevant policy measures here include maternity and parental leave, flexible working time policies, and, above all, subsidized childcare.

The provision of subsidized childcare may be used to pursue different aims. As seen above, it can facilitate maternal employment, but it can also impact child well being. Childcare and early education programmes have been shown to be beneficial to child development, especially insofar as their later school performance is concerned. The beneficial effect concerns above all children from disadvantaged families (Kamerman et al. 2003; Esping-Andersen 2009). In this book, I focus on the 'active social policy' aspect of childcare services, in other words, its role in facilitating access to employment for parents of young children. This means that, although very important, the educational function of childcare is not considered in this study.

Parental leave as well as other policies that allow parents to take time off to care for their children may at first seem of a rather passive nature. After all, they allow workers to temporarily withdraw from the labour force. In fact, the overall impact of parental leave depends very much on how it is structured. Long periods of parental leave with low-income replacement benefits tend to negatively impact female labour supply. This was the case of the German parental leave introduced in the 1980s, which provided a low means-tested benefit for up to 36 months. The similar French APE was found to have a discouraging effect on labour market re-entry, especially for low-skilled women (Fagnani 2000). It is easy to understand why. First, 36 moths out of the labour market is a rather long period, which can of course be even longer in case of siblings. Second, a low cash benefit means that the household may become accustomed to relying essentially on one breadwinner, most often the father. As a result, when the benefit runs out, the pressure to re-enter the labour market is rather low.

Things are different with shorter parental leaves that have a higher benefit, such as those found in the Nordic countries and in Germany after 2007. In such cases the career interruption is limited to about 1 year, making it easier to re-enter employment. Second, a high replacement rate, of say 70–80 per cent of previous earnings, means that once the benefit runs out, the household will face a rather abrupt fall in income, unless the partner who took parental leave goes back to the labour market. Under such conditions (around 12 months with a high replacement rate), parental leave can be considered as active social policy.

Social policies can play an active role in different areas and through different channels. Above I have briefly presented the most obvious places within a welfare state where an active approach can be introduced. An active approach could conceivably concern other areas of policy, such as old age pensions, which could encourage retired people to earn part of their living though labour market participation. In this book, I focus on the core components of active social policy, including active labour market policy, broadly understood to encompass interventions that emphasize stronger incentives and focus on human capital investment. They also include work–life balance and childcare policies, the latter being a key tool in facilitating access to employment for young women. My empirical analysis of active social policy, therefore, focuses on these two key policy areas.

3

Mapping Variation in Active Social Policies

In Chapter 2, I identified the main policy areas and instruments that can be seen as being part of the active social policy paradigm. In this chapter, my objective is to map cross-national variation in practices. It focuses on the two most important areas of active social policy: active labour market policy (ALMP) and work–life balance policies. These are the fields of government intervention where labour market participation is promoted. Strengthening these two policy fields is a necessary condition for the reorientation of social policy towards the active approach. As a result, a focus on them will demonstrate how far countries have gone in this direction.

More precisely, this chapter aims to provide answers to three questions. First, it paints a picture of the current degree of cross-national variation in relation to these two policy areas. Second, it aims to find out what the trends are in relation to the development of the ALMPs and work–life balance policies. Are we really seeing a clear expansion movement as assumed in the Introduction of this book?

The third question is more complicated. It refers to the empirical justification of the joint treatment of two different policy areas. In Chapter 2, I argued that interventions in these two fields fulfil at least one common function, the promotion of labour market participation for individuals not involved in paid work. From a theoretical point of view, it seems justified to consider the two areas together. But what about the empirical level? Do developments in these two policy areas tend to co-vary, so as to justify the joint treatment perspective adopted in this book? Or do they follow different trajectories most of the time? I will get back to these questions in the final section of the chapter after having presented a map of active social policy across time and space.

Active labour market policies

There are several difficulties in mapping ALMPs. First, as seen in Chapter 2, the label is used to denote a vast variety of measures that are very different with regard to at least two dimensions: the extent to which they aim at putting beneficiaries back into market employment and the degree of investment in human capital. Obviously, one could solve this problem by distinguishing between different types of ALMPs as suggested above. However, the difficulty then will be in finding suitable indicators to measure the extent of, for example, occupation-oriented ALMPs or incentive reinforcement policies. The Organisation of Economic Co-operation and Development (OECD) produces statistics on ALMP spending by type that distinguish among half a dozen different categories. This breakdown is helpful, although it does not follow the same distinction used in the typology developed in Chapter 2. OECD data on spending by type will nonetheless be used below as a second best alternative.

In addition to OECD spending data, researchers have recently begun collecting institutional data on ALMPs. Two such data sets are publicly available and aim to reflect the rules that are applied in relation, for example, to job search requirements or benefit conditionality (Hasselpflug 2005; OECD 2007a). This information is helpful, but also problematic. The data set includes information on unemployment benefit claimants, but the programmes compared do not necessarily cover the same type of jobless people across countries. For example, unemployment benefits in the USA cover only short-term unemployment, whereas in Denmark people can rely on it for up to 4 years. In addition, the data sets are based on formal rules, which tend to emphasize a quick return to the labour market everywhere. In practice, however, implementation in this field can be very different from formal rules.

An additional problem one encounters when assessing comparatively the degree of development of ALMP is the partly automatic relationship between the rate of unemployment and the level of spending on these policies. Increases in the number of unemployed people, for example because of a recessions, will *ceteris paribus* result in higher spending on ALMPs, at least to the extent that funds are available to finance additional participation to the various relevant programmes. This automatic link between unemployment and ALMP spending may distort the picture one gets when looking only at spending as a percentage of GDP. Some authors (e.g., Huo et al. 2008) simply divide spending on ALMP by the unemployment rate. This procedure also has its drawbacks. As unemployment drops, spending per percentage point of unemployment increases quite dramatically, even in the absence of additional policy efforts. This is because ALMPs, like all policies, suffer from a form of inertia that makes them slow in adapting to changed economic circumstances. For this reasons, this chapter considers both unemployment unweighted and weighted figures of spending on ALMPs.

More in general, this analysis should not be affected by the huge fluctuations in both unemployment and GDP that we have witnessed since 2008.

For this reason, I consider developments only up to pre-crisis 2007. More recent trends are examined in Chapter 8.

Spending on ALMPs: an overview

Over the past 20 years, most advanced welfare states have increased the proportion of GDP spent on ALMPs, regardless of the measurement (weighted or unweighted) used (Table 3.1). One country, Sweden, has followed the opposite direction with spending declining dramatically in both absolute and unemployment weighted terms. This development can be explained with reference to the fact that in the 1980s, ALMPs were more or less explicitly used in order to avoid open unemployment and to provide a costly alternative to market employment to otherwise jobless people (see Chapter 5 for a detailed account).

Table 3.1. Spending on active labour market policies in 1985 and 2007 according to two measures

	Spending on ALMPs as a percentage of GDP		Spending on ALMPs as a percentage of GDP per percentage point of unemployment	
	1985	2007	1985	2007
Denmark (1986–2007)	0.8	1.3	0.16	0.33
Finland	0.7	0.9	0.12	0.13
Norway	0.6	0.6	0.23	0.24
Sweden	2.1	1.1	0.71	0.18
Unweighted average of Nordic countries	*1.05*	*0.98*	*0.31*	*0.20*
Austria	0.3	0.7	0.07	0.16
Belgium	1.2	1.2	0.12	0.16
France	0.6	0.9	0.06	0.11
Germany	0.5	0.8	0.06	0.09
Netherlands	1.3	1.1	0.17	0.34
Switzerland	0.2	0.6	0.23	0.18
Unweighted average of Continental countries	*0.68*	*0.88*	*0.12*	*0.15*
Australia	0.4	0.3	0.04	0.07
Canada	0.6	0.3	0.06	0.05
New Zealand	0.9	0.3	0.21	0.08
Ireland	1.1	0.6	0.06	0.13
United Kingdom	0.7	0.3	0.06	0.06
United States	0.3	0.1	0.04	0.02
Unweighted average of English-speaking countries	*0.67*	*0.32*	*0.08*	*0.07*
Greece (1985–2005)	0.1	0.1	0.02	0.01
Italy (1990–2007)	0.2	0.4	0.03	0.06
Portugal (1986–2007)	0.2	0.5	0.02	0.06
Spain	0.3	0.8	0.02	0.10
Unweighted average of Southern European countries	*0.20*	*0.45*	*0.02*	*0.06*
Unweighted average of above countries	*0.66*	*0.65*	*0.12*	*0.11*
Unweighted average of above countries except Sweden	*0.58*	*0.70*	*0.09*	*0.12*

Source: OECD Stat.

With the exception of Sweden, the other countries in Table 3.1 have seen a fair increase in spending on ALMPs, at least according to one of the two measures used. In some instances the increase is substantial. In Denmark, spending as a proportion of GDP has more than doubled over the 20-year period of study. In the UK, spending has also doubled if one takes into account the drop in unemployment. Austria, Germany, and France have likewise seen impressive increases. Proportionally, the biggest rise has taken place in Southern Europe, but this is above all due to the very low level of spending in 1985.

Table 3.1 shows also some more or less persistent differences amongst countries and welfare regimes. The Nordic countries are the biggest spenders on ALMPs according to either measure. In the past (1985), however, this was almost entirely due to very high spending in Sweden. At that time, other Nordic countries were not so different from continental European ones with regard to ALMP spending. Things were different in 2005, when all four Nordic countries became top ALMP spenders, especially if one takes into account the unemployment rate (see Table 3.1).

Continental Europe has generally lower levels of spending, but also more internal variation, as it includes big spenders like the Netherlands and Belgium as well as countries with less developed systems like Switzerland. English-speaking countries are in general low spenders. This does not necessarily mean that ALMPs are underdeveloped here. Rather, this result can be interpreted with reference to the fact that the type of policies these countries mostly rely upon are the least costly. Rather than job creation programmes and training, the emphasis here is often on public employment services and incentives. Lastly, southern Europe displays the lowest levels of spending, especially when using unemployment weighted data.

Different types of ALMPs

The figures presented in Table 3.1 show that the effort countries are putting into ALMPs has increased over the past two decades. However, this result underestimates the extent to which a reorientation of labour market policy towards the active paradigm is actually taking place. In fact, not only do we see an increase in overall spending levels, but also the composition of ALMPs expenditure by type has changed.

Figure 3.1 shows the development of spending on four different categories of ALMPs across a 20-year period. The most striking result is the decline in spending on the category 'direct job creation', which reflects the type 'occupation' identified in Chapter 2. The least market employment-oriented policies have run out of fashion over the past 20 years. At the same time, spending on categories that reflect ALMPs of the 'employment assistance

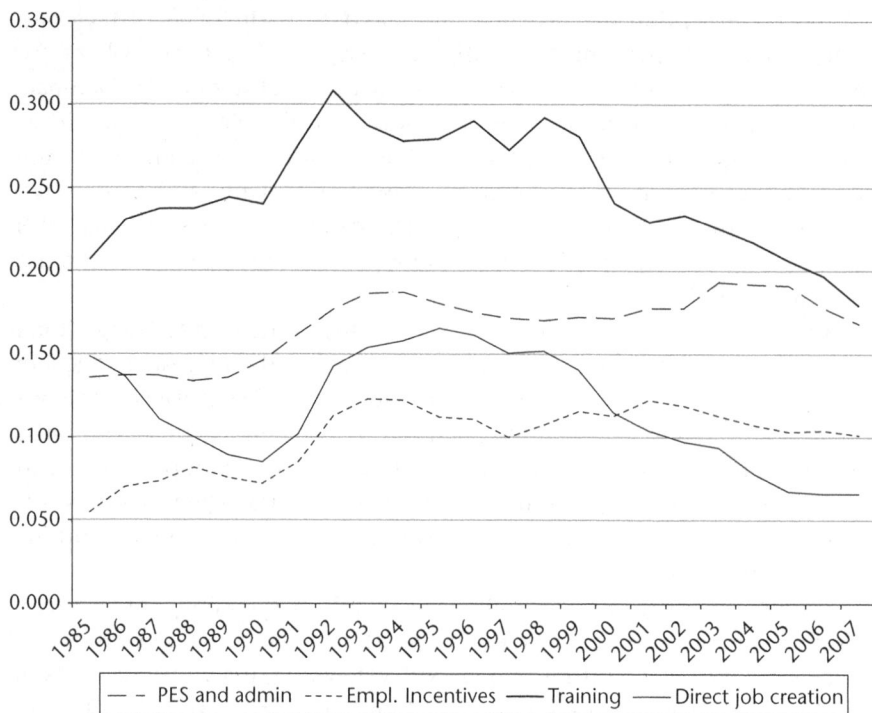

Figure 3.1. Spending on ALMP as a proportion of GDP by type, 1985–2007, unweighted average of 22 OECD countries
Source: OECD *Stat*.

type'—including public employment services (PES) and employment incentives for employers—has increased. Spending on training followed a more curious trajectory, with an increase in the early 1990s and a decline since the early 2000s. It should be noted that the general drop in ALMP spending that one can see in the period 2003–7 is due to the lower unemployment rates during these years. This decline disappears if the graph is made using unemployment weighted figures.

Figures on ALMPs from 1985 to 2007 strongly confirm the claim that labour market policy has taken an active turn. Most countries are not only spending significantly more on ALMPs, they are also putting a stronger emphasis on policies that promote entry into unsubsidized jobs and less on those that that tend to constitute alternatives to market employment. This trend in the composition of ALMP spending is visible in all main welfare regimes: liberal, conservative, and social democratic (graphs not reproduced). However, such trends are less prominent in Southern Europe since ALMPs were virtually non-existent in 1985; therefore, there is no decline of direct job creation. At the same time, one does see an expansion on the other components of ALMP.

Spending figures reflect only part of the active turn in labour market policy. In fact, not all relevant policy changes result in more spending. Important reforms concerning the strengthening of work incentives for jobseekers, such as job search requirements or benefit conditionality, do not necessarily impact spending, but they certainly do put pressure on beneficiaries to reintegrate the labour market. For this reason, they should be included in our assessment of the extent to which policy has taken an active turn.

As mentioned earlier, data problems severely limit our ability to summarize changes in this field. With all required caution, institutional data can nonetheless complement the spending figures presented above. Table 3.2 provides an indication of the intensity of work incentives to which unemployed people are subjected in different countries. It looks at the replacement rate, whether or not activation is systematic (i.e., whether all unemployed people are required to participate in a labour market programme), and the continuation of job search requirement during participation in a programme. These three indicators provide a picture of the intensity of work incentives, which is summarized in a synthetic index in column (4).

The data presented in Table 3.2 are consistent with the expectations put forward earlier. Focusing on regime averages, activation relies mostly on work incentives in the liberal, English-speaking countries. Incentives are fairly strong also in the Nordic countries; however, there is a decline as one moves southward across the European continent. An examination of individual countries reveals a more contrasted picture. Greece, for example, scores higher than Canada on work incentives; yet this is largely due to a very low replacement rate. Contrastingly, Norway scores very low. Given the data problems discussed above, it may be preferable to focus on regime averages than on individual countries, as measurement errors are more likely to even each other out.

The information contained in Table 3.2 may be complemented with data concerning the use of sanctions, as provided in Table 3.3. A high frequency of sanctions may be an indicator of stronger emphasis on work incentives. Here, too, data problems must prompt caution. In addition, information is missing for most continental and southern European countries. The available results, however, confirm the picture emerging from Table 3.2, in other words, that liberal welfare states rely mostly on work incentives, whereas continental and Southern European countries do the least. The Nordic world is somewhere in-between.

Unfortunately, the data used to examine the incentive reinforcing character of ALMPs are available only at one point in time (late 1990s to mid-2000s). As a result, we cannot say much about tendencies over time. There is nonetheless evidence elsewhere that a trend towards more pressure to enter in the labour market is occurring. Comparing his 2005 study with a smaller scale, earlier one, Hasselpflug concludes that between 1997 and 2004, access to benefits

Table 3.2. Indicators of the intensity of work incentives, mid-2000s

	(1)	(2)	(3)	(4)
	Short-term unemployment benefit replacement rate	Systematic activation (every beneficiary receives an offer after a given time)	Continuing job search requirement and verification during participation in ALMPs	Synthetic index of work incentive intensity
Denmark	63.0	1	1	6.09
Finland	54.0	0	1	4.08
Norway	64.0	0	0	1.78
Sweden	62.0	1	2	7.65
Unweighted average of Nordic countries	*60.8*	*0.5*	*1.0*	*4.9*
Austria	55.0	0	0	3.36
Belgium	58.0	0	1	3.75
France	67.0	0	0	1.9
Germany	60.0	0.5	1	4.96
Luxembourg	86.0	0	0	0.00
Netherlands	65.0	1	2	7.41
Switzerland	70.0	0	2	4.26
Unweighted average of Continental countries	*65.2*	*0.3*	*0.7*	*3.7*
Australia	33.0	1	2	10
Canada	63.0	0	0	1.86
New Zealand	38.0	0	1	5.37
Ireland	31.0	0	0	4.46
United Kingdom	41.0	1	0	6.39
United States	62.0	0	1	3.43
Unweighted average of English-speaking countries	*44.7*	*0.3*	*0.7*	*5.3*
Greece	36.0	0	0	4.05
Italy	63.0	0	0	1.86
Portugal	82.0	0	0	0.32
Spain	62.0	0	0	1.95
Unweighted average of Southern Europe	*60.8*	*0.0*	*0.0*	*2.0*

Notes: (1) Net replacement rate of unemployment benefit at initial phase of unemployment, for single person without children, 100% of average wage in 2005 (source: OECD Benefits and Wages); (2) indicator developed on the basis of information provided in OECD (2007a), according to the following scores: 0 = no automatic activation; 0.5 = for some groups; 1 = for all; (3) indicator developed on the basis of information provided in OECD (2007a) and Hasselpflug (2005), according to the following scores: 0 = no requirement; 1 = job search requirement but no verification or various requirements; 2 = job search requirement and verification; (4) synthetic index based on indicators presented in columns 1–3. Unweighted average of z-scores of these indicators are standardized to vary between 0 and 10.

became more difficult in a majority of the countries covered (12 out of 16). Countries that introduced stricter access are found across welfare regimes, suggesting that the trend is a general one (Hasselpflug 2005). These findings are confirmed by a similar survey carried out by the OECD, which found that 'Countries seem to be increasing the number and variety of instruments used

Table 3.3. Sanction rate and spending on ALMPs, selected countries

	Sanction rate (number of sanctions/average number of beneficiaries) in the late 1990s
Denmark	2.12
Finland	10.19
Norway	7.32
Unweighted average of Nordic countries	*6.54*
Belgium	0.78
Germany	1.14
Unweighted average of Continental countries	*0.96*
Australia	3.3
United Kingdom	5.52
United States	35.4
Unweighted average of English-speaking countries	*14.74*
Switzerland	38.5

Note: Sanctions concerning only labour market behaviour (e.g., refusal of a job offer), not administrative sanctions.

Source: OECD 2000b: 136.

to "activate" jobseekers, focusing on density of contacts, verification of job search, the set-up of individual action plans and referrals to ALMPs after a period of unsuccessful job search' (OECD 2007a: 209).

A nearly general activation turn

The evidence presented here shows that the vast majority of OECD countries over the past 20 years have reoriented their unemployment policies in a more active direction. The objective of policy is increasingly promoting a quick return to market employment. Unlike in the past, the objective is not simply stated; it is also translated into actual policy measures, such as more investment in public (and private) employment services, temporary job subsidies, or more pressure on beneficiaries to re-enter the labour market.

This trend is a general one and seems to be happening across welfare regimes. The shift is perhaps clearest in continental Europe because it constitutes a clear reverse after the development of a policy in the early 1980s geared towards reducing labour supply (Esping-Andersen 1996). Contrary to widespread perceptions, the Nordic welfare states have not always been 'active welfare states'. In the mid-1980s, Denmark had an underdeveloped system of ALMPs, and Sweden used its own system to provide alternatives to market employment. Nonetheless, these two countries did undergo a major reorientation towards the active paradigm in the mid- to late 1990s, as will become clearer in Chapter 5. The shift is perhaps less visible in Southern Europe. Even though spending on ALMPs has increased over the past two decades, it remains very low in comparison to other parts of the OECD world. In addition, as it is apparent in Table 3.2, unemployment compensation systems put relatively little pressure on beneficiaries to re-enter the labour market.

Work–life balance policies

Work–life balance policies are another major area of welfare expansion. This label encompasses a wide range of policy tools, the most important of which are subsidized childcare services and time to care policies (i.e., parental and maternity leave). The conciliation of work and family life can be promoted also through other tools, like labour market regulations that encourage flexibility of working time. Some countries have introduced a right for parents to work part-time, meaning that a request to reduce working hours can only be rejected if the employer can prove that a given job can only be performed on a full-time basis. Some employers have been experimenting and developing new ways of increasing work-time flexibility so to better accommodate parents' needs (Cressey 2002). When it comes to reconciling work and family life, such employer level arrangements can be very important. However, given this book's focus on social policy, they are not dealt with here.

Welfare regimes and work–life balance policies

Traditional typologies and classification tools are of little use in relation to work–life balance policies. If we apply the standard three- or four-type regime classification to this field, we discover several outliers. For example, although considered conservative welfare states in many respects, France and Belgium have developed a work–life balance policy regime that is more reminiscent of the Nordic variant. Liberal Switzerland is more similar to conservative Germany than to English-speaking countries.

Difficulties in classifying work–life balance policies may be related to their multi-purpose character. Their main aim is certainly not decommodification, and in this respect, these interventions differ from the traditional policies of the post-war welfare state. One objective is to improve the living conditions of commodified workers by facilitating employment, not by reducing their dependence on labour market participation. Some authors refer to this objective as positive commodification (Knijn and Ostner 2002). But there are certainly other goals. These include promoting gender equality and increasing labour supply (by making it possible for mothers to enter the labour market). In response to the sharp and apparently stable decline in fertility rates, work–life balance policies in many countries are also adopted with a demographic objective.

Feminist analyses of social policies emphasize the concept of defamilialization. One objective of social policy in general and of work–life balance policies in particular is to 'defamilialize' the life course of women, or in other words, to help women reduce their economic dependence on their male partners (Lewis 1992; Sainsbury 1994). Work–life balance policies are obviously relevant to defamilialization, and for the reasons outlined in the feminist literature, are not well captured by Esping-Andersen's regime typology. In fact, subsequent attempts to classify welfare states according to the extent by which countries defamilialize women's life experiences or the degree to which they assume a male breadwinner role have produced rather different results.

Table 3.4 presents some influential attempts at providing alternative classifications of welfare states on the basis of how they deal with work–life balance aspects. It is clear that there is a great degree of variation in the results produced. This is partly due to the fact that different typologies focus on different dimensions. One can nonetheless identify a common pattern, at least in relation to a majority of countries.

Most typologies tend to identify four different variants. The first one, which includes only the Nordic countries, is described as promoting employment amongst women, defamilialization, and gender equality. Second, English-speaking liberal welfare states are also seen as supporting female employment, not so much through dedicated policies but as a result of market mechanisms. In these countries, gender equality is relatively strong, not resulting so much from social policy, but from anti-discrimination legislation (Orloff 2006). Third is a cluster of countries that facilitate the reconciliation of work and family life, but are not as gender egalitarian as the Nordic countries. These

Table 3.4. Three typologies of work–life balance policies and gender orientation of welfare states

Author(s)	Dimension(s)	Clusters of countries identified
Lewis (1992)	Strength of male breadwinner model	Strong male breadwinner (Ireland, UK); modified male breadwinner (France); weak male breadwinner (Sweden)
Siaroff (1994)	Female work desirability and family welfare orientation	Protestant social democratic (Sweden, Finland, Denmark, Norway); Protestant liberal (UK, Canada, USA, Australia); advanced Christian democratic (France, Belgium, Netherlands, Austria); late female mobilization (Switzerland, Japan, Spain, Italy, Greece, Portugal, Ireland)
Daly (2000)	Extent and continuity of female labour market participation	High extent, high continuity (Sweden, Denmark, Portugal, Finland, Norway, Austria, Canada, USA, France); high extent, low continuity (UK, Germany, Australia); low extent, high continuity (Belgium, Netherlands); low extent, low continuity (Greece, Italy, Luxembourg, Ireland, Spain)

include France and sometimes Belgium, the Netherlands, and Portugal. Finally, the fourth group of countries includes countries where policy assumes a traditional male breadwinner family model and where reconciliation of work and family life is particularly difficult, typically Germany, Italy, Spain, and Greece, but also Switzerland and Japan.

The case that variation in family-related policies is not well captured by traditional welfare state typologies is persuasive. However, in order to guarantee comparability with the other policy sector analysed in this study, active labour market policy, it is essential to stick to an understanding of regimes that is compatible with the more traditional one based on labour market policy. For this reason, the data discussed in this section are structured according to the same four regimes used in the previous one. However, in order to take into account systematic differences within regimes, some countries are extracted from the relevant cluster and analysed separately. This special treatment particularly concerns France and Belgium among the continental European countries and Ireland among the English-speaking ones.

Childcare

Childcare is the key element of any policy package aiming at facilitating the conciliation of work and family life. It is also a major area of welfare state development across OECD countries. On average, OECD countries spent 0.76 per cent of their GDP on various childcare services in 2007. Yet cross-national differences are striking: the amount of public spending on childcare and pre-school services varies between 0.16 (Canada) and 1.86 (Sweden) per cent of GDP (Table 3.5).

Country differences are also visible in relation to coverage rates, though these data stop in 2004.[1] These tend to be highest in the Nordic countries, especially for the age group 0–3 years. As already highlighted, continental Europe appears divided here, with countries like France, Belgium, and the Netherlands displaying figures rather similar to those found in Northern Europe. As will be shown in Chapter 6, this is a rather recent development for the Netherlands, less so for France.

Other continental European countries (Germany, Austria, and Switzerland) have considerably lower coverage rates, especially for the age group 0–3 years. A few countries, all located in 'neo-Latin' Europe (France, Italy, Spain, and Portugal), stand out as having a very high level of coverage of the age group

---

[1] The OECD provides more recent data, but for several countries, these are based on surveys rather than administrative data, with the result that in some cases, coverage rates are obviously implausible. For this reason, I prefer to rely on somewhat older but more reliable administrative data.

Table 3.5. Coverage of formal childcare arrangements (percentage of age group) and spending on family services (percentage of GDP) in selected OECD countries

	Aged 0–3 yrs	Aged 3–6 yrs	Spending on family services	
	(2004)	(2004)	1998	2007
Denmark	62	90	1.73	1.80
Finland	22	46	1.35	1.34
Norway	44	85	1.33	1.45
Sweden	39	87	1.58	1.86
Unweighted average of Nordic countries	*42*	*77*	*1.50*	*1.61*
Belgium	34	100	0.79	0.95
France	28	100	1.78	1.66
Unweighted average of Belgium and France	*31*	*100*	*1.29*	*1.31*
Austria	7	74	0.38	0.45
Germany	9	80	0.71	0.75
Netherlands	29	70	0.73	1.40
Switzerland		45	0.25	0.32
Unweighted average of continental countries	*15*	*67*	*0.61*	*0.87*
Australia	29	71	0.56	0.65
Canada	19		0.21	0.16
New Zealand	32	93	0.66	0.79
United Kingdom	26	80	1.09	1.11
United States	35	62	0.62	0.55
Unweighted average of English-speaking countries	*28*	*77*	*0.63*	*0.65*
Ireland	15	68	0.12	0.28
Greece	7	47	0.32	0.39
Italy	6	100	0.56	0.75
Portugal	23	78	0.31	0.44
Spain	20	99	0.55	0.70
Unweighted average of Southern European countries	*14*	*81*	*0.43*	*0.61*
Unweighted average of countries above	*26*	*78*	*0.78*	*0.91*

Note: Family services include childcare services and pre-school education as well as other minor programmes for families.
Source: OECD 2007b, OECD.Stat SOCX database, accessed 20/02/2012.

3–6 years. This is the result of a relatively early development of a comprehensive pre-school system that generally did not have the objective of allowing mothers to work. As will be shown in Chapter 6, France and Italy developed pre-school systems before the emergence of work–family reconciliation as a social or political issue, but rather mostly for pedagogical reasons. As a result, these tools are not necessarily suitable for parents wishing to engage in paid employment, for example, because of too short opening hours. These are nonetheless often adapted to the new function, help parents reconcile work and family life, with relatively little difficulty.

Looking at spending figures, the period between 1998[2] and 2007 has been characterized by an increase in the funds assigned to early education and

---

[2] OECD data collected before 1998 are not suitable for cross-national comparisons because spending on pre-school programmes was included in some countries only.

childcare in most countries. The exceptions are the Nordic countries as well as France and Belgium, where spending was stable. This can be explained with reference to the high level of services already developed in the late 1990s. Even though they cover a short time span, data regarding spending on family services show that this is an expanding area of social policy.

Spending on family services and coverage rates are related, but high spending does not seem to be a precondition for high levels of service development. Liberal welfare states, such as the USA, achieve relatively high levels of childcare coverage despite investing very little public money in this field (Figure 3.2).

This observation suggests that there are at least two routes to high childcare coverage. One, followed in the Nordic countries, relies on extensive public spending. The alternative approach, found in liberal welfare states, is based on the development of market services. But why does the market seem to function only in liberal welfare states? Morgan (2005) has put forward an explanation for this puzzle. Building on work by Esping-Andersen (1999), she argues that one finds the answer in wage regulation. In liberal welfare states, flexible

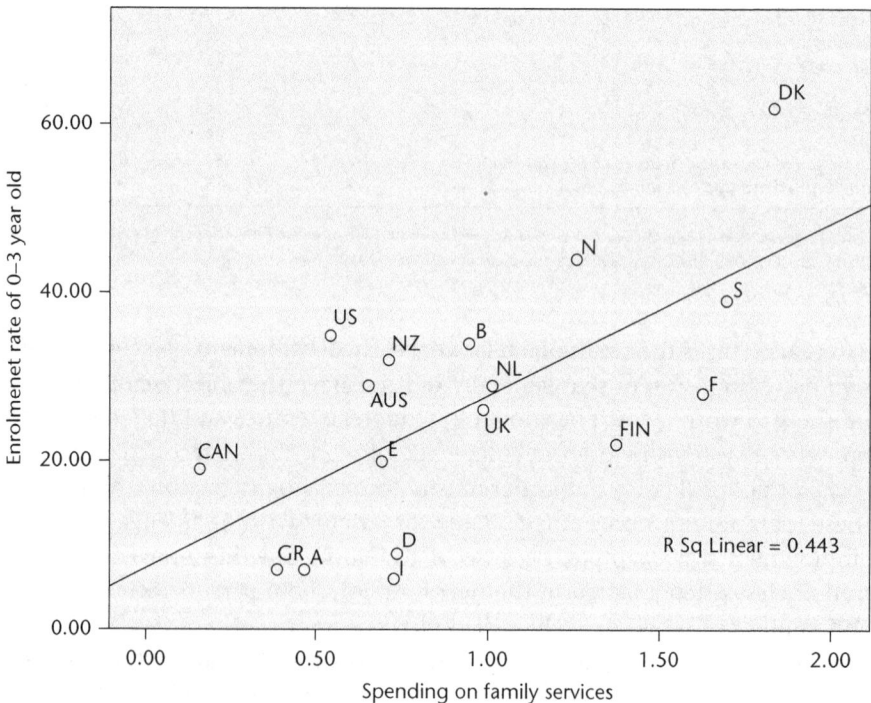

Figure 3.2. Coverage of childcare (age group 0–3 years) and spending on family services, mid-2000s

Source: see Table 3.5.

wage setting mechanisms have allowed markets to respond to increasing demand for childcare services. High levels of inequality make it also easier in these countries for middle-class parents to afford services produced by low-paid workers. This explains why the USA and other liberal welfare states have seen the development of above average levels of childcare coverage with very little public expenditure. In contrast, continental and Northern Europe demonstrate high minimum wages, lower income inequality, and strong union influence in wage setting, all of which in turn have prevented the market from responding to rising demand for services. Higher wage levels make such services, if unsubsidized, simply too costly for the middle classes. The only way to develop childcare in this context is through massive public spending, as again visible in Figure 3.2. This hypothesis is supported by Bonoli and Reber (2010), who found that when controlling for spending on family services, earnings inequality is positively correlated to coverage rates for the age group 0–3 years.

Care leave policies

Over the past decades, care leave policies (e.g., parental leave, maternity benefit) have developed to a significant extent in a majority of OECD countries (Morgan and Zippel 2003). In the field of parental leave, the European Union, by adopting a directive in 1998, has arguably played an important role, at least in some of the member states (Treib and Falkner 2004). Cross-national differences, however, remain substantial (see Table 3.6). With regard to parental leave, the Nordic countries provide generous compensation for the loss of earnings over a fairly long period of time, usually around a year. Continental European countries, in contrast, tend to provide less generous provisions, often in the shape of flat-rate benefits, but in some cases over a longer period of time (e.g., in France). Note that in 2008 Germany introduced a shorter but better paid leave (see Chapter 6). Lastly, English-speaking and Southern European countries have the least developed systems, with the exception of Italy, which with regard to this policy area is more closely related to continental countries.

Moving upwards at different speeds

Work–life balance policies have been a major area of welfare expansion over the past few years. This development is only partly reflected in the data presented above as coverage rates for childcare, for instance, are difficult to estimate accurately. However, spending data, which are more easily comparable across time, show a clear upward trend across regime types, with the high spending countries showing more stability. A similar point has been made by

Table 3.6. Parental leave periods by duration in weeks and full-time equivalent of the leave period if paid at 100% of last earnings, 2006–7

	Weeks of parental leave (paid or not)	FTE paid leave
Denmark	32	32
Finland	156	35.8
Norway	48	38.4
Sweden	72	52.8
Unweighted average of Nordic countries	*77*	*40*
Belgium	12	2.6
France	156	31.1
Unweighted average of Belgium and France	*84*	*17*
Austria	104	16.7
Germany	156	34.8
Netherlands	13	9.8
Switzerland	0	0
Unweighted average of continental European countries	*68*	*15*
Australia	52	0
Canada	35	19.3
New Zealand	na	na
United Kingdom	13	0
United States	na	na
Unweighted average of English-speaking countries	*33*	*6*
Ireland	14	0
Greece	14	0
Italy	26	7.8
Portugal	12	0
Spain	156	0
Unweighted average of Southern European countries	*52*	*2*

Source: OECD Family database, indicator PF7 (<http://www.oecd.org>).

Castles (2005), who looking at previous OECD expenditure data noted an increase in the relative size of social expenditure going towards social services. While the general trend is clearly upwards, differences across regimes persist. The Nordic countries still provide the most encompassing arrangements in this field. Many indicators suggest that some continental European countries, particularly France, Belgium, and, in recent years, the Netherlands and Germany, are closer to the Nordic model than to other Bismarckian continental European countries. Southern Europe, despite a modest increase in spending on family services, lags behind, according to most indicators (i.e., coverage rate of childcare services or length of paid parental leave). Pre-school coverage in Italy and Spain seems to be an exception in this respect, which can be explained by the existence of a long-standing tradition that has little to do with the policy objective of allowing parents to reconcile work and family life.

Active welfare states

The above discussion of active labour market and work–life balance policies has highlighted a number of trends in relation to the development of an active orientation in current social policy. While different policy areas reflect different logics, there seems to be some regularity in the extent to which countries, or clusters of countries, have reoriented their welfare states. Independent from the policy area on which this chapter focuses, the Nordic countries demonstrate the greatest trend towards a more active social policy. Continental European countries have also moved in this direction, albeit to a lesser extent. Clearly, this second group of countries has embarked on the modernization of its welfare state considerably later than Northern Europe. ALMPs and work–life balance policies are an area of rapid growth in most continental European countries, like France and Germany. Whether these countries will eventually catch up with their northern neighbours is an open question.

Liberal welfare state invest relatively little public money in ALMPs and childcare, but are able to obtain at least some of the result that in Northern Europe require large investments of public money. The pro-employment orientation of social security is very strong in liberal welfare states, but it is based more on strengthening work incentives rather than on investing in human capital. Moreover, childcare services have developed in response to rising demand, without the need for state intervention. Where the Nordic and the liberal regimes' route towards a post-industrial welfare state clearly differ is in the distributional dimension. Despite a renewed focus on fighting poverty in the late 1990s, levels of inequality are among the highest in the OECD and persistent social problems like child poverty remain at worrying levels (OECD 2008a).

Finally, Southern European countries seem to have shown less enthusiasm for active social policy. ALMPs and work–life balance policies are not entirely absent from their repertoires, but they are considerably less developed than in other countries. The same holds for market-based alternatives, such as privately provided childcare services. What is particularly striking is the contrast between the high levels of generosity found in some traditional social policies, above all old age pensions and the underdevelopment of the more active forms of social policy.

The clustering of countries that emerges from this mapping exercise provides some empirical elements that help us answer the question raised earlier: Is it justified to lump together different policies under the 'active social policy' label? The two seemingly unrelated areas, ALMPs and work–life balance policies, display patterns of cross-national variation, which are surprisingly similar. This comes out clearly also from spending figures, as apparent

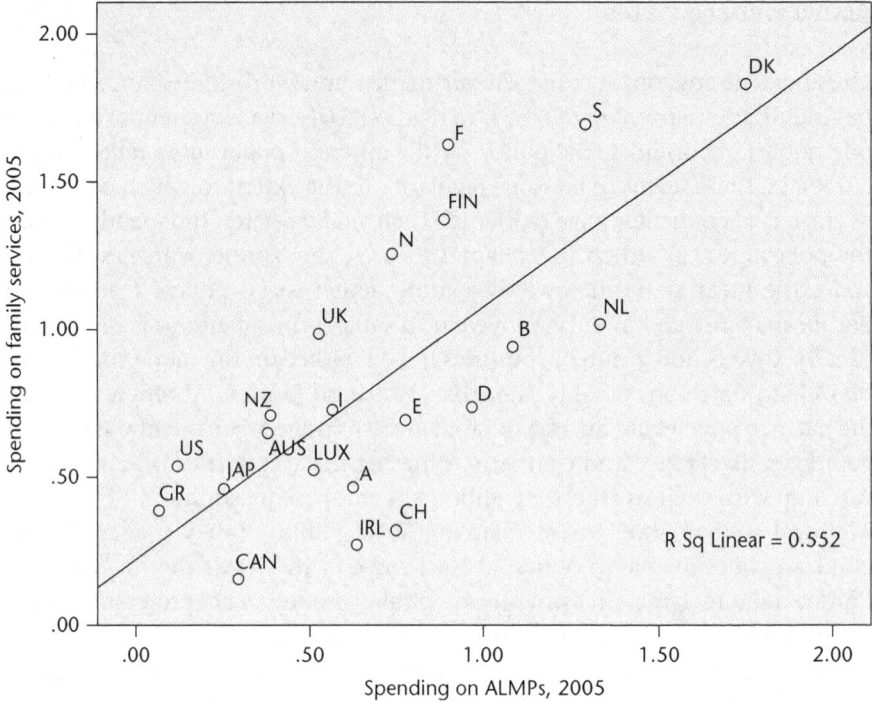

Figure 3.3. Spending on family services and on active labour market policies, 2005
Source: OECD *Stat*.

from Figure 3.3, which shows that spending on ALMPs and childcare are very strongly correlated. This result suggests that policies characterized here as active do have something in common. It is important to note that the very strong correlation between the two policy areas is more than the typical 'Nordic-countries-versus-rest-of-the-world' effect, which one finds rather often in cross-national comparisons of social policies. ALMPs and work–life balance policy efforts tend to co-vary also between and within other clusters of welfare states.

Four empirical conclusions

The objective of this chapter was to look at empirical evidence on the developments of active social policies across OECD countries. On this basis, a number of conclusions can be drawn.

First, active social policy is clearly an area of welfare state expansion, or at least it has been so over the past two decades in a majority of OECD countries.

True, in pure quantitative terms (i.e., measurements of spending as a proportion of GDP), the expansion is not huge. Despite increased spending in most countries and in both policy fields, ALMPs and childcare clearly remain low spending areas when compared to the established programmes such as old age or invalidity pensions. However, one should bear in mind that this expansion takes place in the current context of 'permanent austerity', in other words, of an economic environment characterized by constant pressures on government budgets and by the 'automatic' increases of spending on the age-related programmes such old age pensions and health care. Unlike in these fields, increases in spending on ALMPs and childcare are not the consequence of increases in the target population; most often they are the result of political decisions.

The extent to which active policies are expanding is probably underestimated by the spending figures and the other quantitative indicators shown in this chapter. First, policy changes take time before they show up in spending data. Second, in the field of ALMPs, the term expansion is not always appropriate. In fact, reorientation in the direction of a more 'active' active labour market policy (i.e., oriented towards promoting entry into unsubsidized market employment) may rely not only on the expansion of services for unemployed people, but also on stronger incentives, which may be the result of retrenchment. The case studies presented in Chapters 5 and 6 will show the various shapes that the reorientation has taken in different countries.

Second, this reorientation is taking place across welfare regimes despite the very different starting points. The type of divergence in responses to similar socio-economic problems seen in the 1980s seems to be a thing of the past. Countries are developing different responses, but they all tend to emphasize the promotion of labour market participation as the way to deal with social problems. While this approach may resonate in liberal and Nordic welfare states, it is completely at odds with the trajectory followed until the early 1990s in continental European countries.

Third, if the reorientation towards the active social policy paradigm is a general trend, one part of Europe, the South in particular, seems to be less enthusiastic about it. The data reported in this chapter show that Southern Europe is also following the same broad direction taken by other OECD countries, but at a lower pace.

Fourth, developments in the two policy areas studied are strongly associated with one another. Regimes and countries that have gone further in one of the two policies areas have done the same in the other one. What is more, as shown above, spending on ALMPs and on childcare tend to co-vary cross-sectionally. This is not simply a reflection of the fact that some countries are more inclined to develop big welfare states than other ones. One would not find the same level of correlation between spending on pensions and spending on ALMPs or between spending on healthcare and spending on childcare. How do we interpret this result? It is unlikely that in this case correlation indicates causality. Instead, what seems to be more plausible is that this correlation reflects the fact that the same or similar sets of determinants are impacting both policy areas, as will be discussed in the next chapter.

4

Explaining the Emergence of Active Social Policy

Political scientists tend to like accounts of policy change that emphasize one factor or one mechanism and play down everything else. While such an approach may more easily lead to elegant theorizing, it is unlikely to get us very far in understanding complex policy developments such as the one at stake in this book. On the other hand, analyses that conclude that everything matters are not very helpful either. For this study, I have chosen a strategy that falls somewhere between these two extremes. The theoretical framework I will develop next makes reference to a broad range of explanations based on socio-economic, political, institutional, and cultural factors. These explanations have two sources. In a few cases, I have been able to find them in the literature. This is the case, for example, of the adaptation of the power resources model made by Huber and Stephens (2001) and Huo et al. (2008), which found active social policy essentially to be a social democratic project.

Most of the time, however, I develop hypotheses on the development of active social policy on the basis of existing scholarship on general social policy-making. Fortunately, we can rely on a couple of decades of studies that have helped unravel the complex web of factors that account for the introduction, the expansion, and the transformation of welfare states. In general, one can expect the mechanisms identified by past research to play a role in the current transformation process. Obviously, however, the claims made by this large corpus of literature must be adapted to the problem investigated in this book: the emergence of active social policy. This is one of the objectives of this chapter.

More in general, the chapter puts forward a range of hypotheses that, theoretically at least, are capable of accounting for the reorientation of Western welfare states towards active social policy. These are the 'candidate explanations' for the reorientation of social policies. In Chapter 8, after having reviewed the empirical evidence, I will come back to these explanations and identify the most relevant ones.

Changing needs in competitive democracies

Early accounts of social policy development emphasized the role played by the emergence of new needs, resulting essentially from socio-economic structural changes (see, e.g., Wilenski 1975). Of course, needs alone do not create policies, but the emergence of a new problem experienced by large sections of the electorate can, in a well-functioning democracy, awake the appetite of vote-hungry political entrepreneurs and result in the bringing of the new problem in the political arena. Needs have been shown to matter also in more recent years. Scarbrough, for instance, argues that the resilience of welfare states in the 1980s and 1990s can be explained with reference to the emergence of new social trends such as 'divorce, single parenthood . . . rising part time and temporary employment . . . the growing number of outsiders' (Scarbrough 2000: 230–1). Econometric studies of changes in social expenditure over the same period have confirmed the importance of including social problems such as unemployment as independent variables of welfare effort (Siegel 2000; Huber and Stephens 2001).

But what are the needs addressed by active social policy? Active social policies can be seen as responses to two profound social transformations: deindustrialization and the massive entry of women into the labour market. Deindustrialization has resulted in high unemployment and high inactivity rates among the low skilled in most European countries. In the USA, it has contributed to sharp increases in inequality and poverty (OECD 2008a). This has been explained with reference to the strong skill bias in demand for labour in a post-industrial economy. Demand for low-skill labour has declined as low-skill industrial jobs have disappeared. At the same time, the new jobs created in the service sector tend to be high skilled (DiPrete 2005). Active social policy has been presented as a response to inactivity, but also as a response to poverty (i.e., by supporting households in increasing their labour market participation).

However, unlike in more traditional fields of social policy, demand for active social policy does not necessarily come from those who will receive it. This is clearly the case in the field of active labour market policy (ALMP). Demands for more activation in the 1990s did not come from inactive people. On the contrary, in many cases, representatives of various groups of non-employed people fought the activation turn. Arguably, active social policies respond to the expectations of groups that are much larger than those who directly benefit from them. As we will see below, this is a crucial feature for understanding the politics of policy-making in this field. Here, however, the hypothesis is that both the emergence of inactivity and increase in inequality that results from deindustrialization and the massive entry of women into the labour market can be necessary preconditions for the development of active social policy.

Active social policy as a social democratic project

The policy areas covered in this study, ALMP and childcare services, have often been considered as part of the standard social democratic social policy package. One influential strand in social policy analysis, known as the 'power resources' or 'politics matters' school, has gone as far as to argue that these policies represent the essence of the social democratic approach to dealing with social problems (Esping-Andersen 1990, 1999; Huber and Stephens 2001). In a nutshell their argument is the following:

> Active labour market policy, including training, retraining, and support for reloca-tion, was the cornerstone of this [social democratic] policy of labour mobilization, and public care facilities for children and the elderly became an additional com-ponent because they facilitated women's integration into the labour force. It is important to insist here on these central elements of the social democratic project in order to correct a widespread misinterpretation; the essence of the social demo-cratic welfare state is not decommodification, but rather high qualification for and participation in the labor market. (Huber and Stephens 2001: 184)

Huber and Stephens share my understanding of ALMPs and care services as being strongly related and part of a pro-employment orientation in social policy. However, most of the relevant literature focuses on one or the other policy field. This is why the two are discussed separately.

Active labour market policies

In the 'power resources' school's account of the development of different worlds of welfare capitalism, emphasis on ALMPs is considered to be one of the defining features of the social democratic welfare regime. The power resources of the Left allowed the labour movement to impose a costly but effective system of labour market policies, capable of securing full employ-ment in the context of a rapidly changing economic structure (Esping-Ander-sen 1990: 167–8; Huber and Stephens 2001: 184).

More recently this view has been taken up by Huo et al. (2008), who expect the Left to favour ALMPs on two grounds. First, social democrats have a preference for full employment, and ALMPs can contribute to this end.

Second, ALMPs are a superior way to passive benefits in guaranteeing wage-earners welfare. In their own words:

> The value of employment based human development, as a form of long-term insurance against social risk, serves to highlight the limitation of decommodification as a fundamental objective of social protection. (Huo et al. 2008).

Social Democratic parties, in sum, have promoted 'employment friendly' labour market policies. In this respect they are seen as different from Christian democrats, who have intervened in the field of employment by protecting jobs and by facilitating early retirement. Christian democracy, in their words, 'continues to have difficulty reconciling labour market activation and the principle that "labour is not a commodity"' (Huo et al. 2008: 17–18).

According to this view, partisan effects are responsible for the bifurcation between the Nordic countries on the one hand and continental and Southern Europe on the other. Countries where social democrats had the upper hand most of the time have developed comprehensive ALMP systems. In addition, one can say that the very idea of an ALMP is a product of the labour movement, as it was first developed in Sweden by two trade union economists, Gösta Rehn and Rudolf Meidner. In contrast, countries dominated by Christian democracy have turned to the traditional passive instruments of early retirement and employment protection legislation.

Though apparently plausible, this view has proved rather controversial. In relation to Sweden, it has been argued by Peter Swenson that in the 1950s employers were much more supportive of ALMPs than suggested by the power resources school. ALMPs were seen as a helpful tool in dealing with the main labour market problem at the time, labour shortage (Swenson 2002; see also Chapter 5).

A more general critique against the power resources account of the development of ALMPs has been made by David Rueda. First, he argues that social democrats in post-industrial societies are increasingly confronted with a dilemma. Recent socio-economic transformations have split the potential clientele of social democrats into two groups, insiders and outsiders. Insiders constitute the traditional constituency of social democracy: manual workers, low- to middle-paid wage-earners, public sector workers, etc. Outsiders are those who are experiencing disadvantage: unemployed people, atypical workers, or excluded individuals. Social Democratic parties can theoretically cater for both clienteles, but sometimes the interests of one group clash with those of the other one. In these circumstances, social democrats will tend to defend the interest of insiders, better organized and more likely to respond with electoral support than outsiders (Rueda 2007).

This is the case with ALMPs. Rueda argues that these policies are in the interest of outsiders because they facilitate the re-entry into employment, but they are also detrimental to insiders for two reasons. First, insiders, being protected by employment protection legislation against unemployment risk, are unlikely to see the point in co-financing these policies as taxpayers. Second, ALMPs stimulate labour supply and may create competition for (scarce) jobs or downward pressures on wages. As a result, Social Democratic parties are unlikely to support these policies. In his own words:

> ALMPs are designed to promote entry into the labour market of outsiders who will underbid insiders' wage demands. Since insiders are the core constituency of social democratic parties, my argument implies the absence of any government partisanship effects on ALMPs. (Rueda 2007: 74)

While plausible in abstract terms, this view implies that once 'activated', outsiders will be competing in the same labour market segment as the insiders. This, however, is rather unlikely. ALMPs, at least since the mid-1990s, are mostly targeted on the low-skilled, often long-term unemployed. These groups are unlikely to constitute a challenge for better educated middle-class workers. Insider opposition to ALMPs seems difficult to justify on theoretical grounds, at least in the current socio-economic context.

Surprisingly, both Huo et al. and Rueda find empirical evidence supporting their conflicting claims. Using Organisation of Economic Co-operation and Development (OECD) data and a pooled time series design, Huo et al. found that social democratic power is associated with higher spending on ALMPs. Using the same data, a pooled time series design, but different measurements for some of the variables and model specification, Rueda finds the opposite: either no left partisan effect or even a slightly negative association between left power and spending on ALMPs. In Chapter 7, where I present my own pooled time series analysis of spending on ALMPs, I will come back to the methodological issues brought up by this inconsistency.

Difficulties in identifying likely partisan effects on ALMPs are compounded by the ambiguity of the dependent variable. As seen in Chapter 2, the label ALMP may refer to very different policies in different countries. Some of these policies, especially in continental European countries, may not be so much geared towards promoting labour market re-entry. Their main objective is, instead, to provide an alternative to market employment. In the typology presented in Chapter 2, these ALMPs are labelled as 'occupation'. Occupation ALMPs are perfectly compatible with the passive orientation in employment policy adopted in Bismarckian countries during the 1980s—the so-called labour reduction route. By removing participants from market employment in the medium/long term, these programmes are more akin to other labour-reducing measures (such as early retirement) than to activation policies in the proper sense. However, these policies are costly, also because beneficiaries tend to remain longer in the programme. As a result, they will generate higher expenditure on ALMPs; moreover, analysis using simply aggregate expenditure levels will be unable to distinguish between these policies and the truly active ones. The breakdown of expenditure by type of ALMP is only partly useful because the same policy may be more or less geared towards promoting market employment depending on how it is implemented. Arguably, a more fine-grained qualitative approach, such as that adopted in Chapter 5, is needed here.

Identifying partisan effects on ALMPs is complicated, because of changes in the composition of the party constituencies. Both analyses discussed here consider Social Democratic parties as essentially workers' parties. In reality, Social Democratic parties in many European countries are better described as 'value coalitions' which obtain support from various social groups (mostly public sector workers, intellectuals, part of the urban middle class, etc.) and defend notions of equality, defence of the weakest, gender equality, and so forth (Häusermann 2010). If this is the case, then it is particularly difficult to develop hypotheses with regard to the position Social Democratic parties will adopt on active social policies. A preference for gender equality values may result in support for childcare. There is more uncertainty, however, in relation to the position on ALMPs.

The power resources approach has an additional limit for the study of active social policies. It implicitly considers the political impact of policy on the policy-takers only. With regard to ALMPs, however, the community of the policy-takers—composed of unemployed and especially long-term unemployed people—is small and not very influential. As a result, they are unlikely to have any political relevance. We are very far here from the numbers directly concerned by programmes like healthcare or pensions. As a result, it would be unreasonable to expect any relevant political effect of active social policy, if the support basis of policy were limited to the beneficiaries. In fact, as I will argue below, ALMP can be attractive for groups of voters that will probably never benefit from it, at least directly. In this they differ from policies like healthcare and old age pension that have been behind much welfare state theorizing.

Childcare

In relation to childcare one finds a surprisingly similar debate. Scholars belonging to the power resources school claim that investing in childcare is social democratic policy (Esping-Andersen 1999; Huber and Stephens 2000, 2001). Childcare plays an important role in gender equality policy, and social democrats have tended to pick up this issue faster and more comprehensively than other parties. In addition, the idea of subsidizing daycare services is at odds with the ideology of the two key historical competitors of social democracy. For Liberal parties, it represents an expansion of the states' reach, something that should in principle be avoided. For Christian democrats, childcare services may undermine the traditional family setup with a male breadwinner and a female caregiver. This may be at odds with deeply held values of these parties' core constituency (Morgan 2006).

Yet social democrats also have powerful reasons for opposing investing in childcare services. Childcare services have a positive impact on labour supply because they allow women with small children to be active in the labour market. True labour market segmentation limits the number of those who are affected by increased competition. However, unlike in the case of ALMPs, improved access to jobs is not limited to the low skilled, but can take place at all skill levels, representing thus a potential challenge for more numerous and possibly influential groups. We can as a result expect the representatives of wage-earners to be against or at least not to support an expansion of childcare services.

This hypothesis is likely to hold for traditional wage-earners organizations or representative bodies such as blue-collar, male-dominated unions or traditional Social Democratic parties. Things are going to be rather different for outfits whose membership includes a substantial proportion of women and parents of young children or individuals who have a stake in childcare. Our expectation on the position that unions will adopt in relation to childcare will depend on their membership composition. If the proportion of women/parents of young children is high, we can expect unions to favour childcare services; otherwise, unions are unlikely to make childcare a policy priority.

Social Democratic parties face a more complex dilemma. They may decide to support their traditional constituency (i.e., wage-earners) and decline to promote childcare services, or they may see themselves as the natural party of state intervention in the social sphere and the promoters of gender equality and take up the issue. This second choice presents the additional advantage of making Social Democratic parties attractive for women, especially at a time when their traditional base (i.e., industrial workers) is rapidly eroding because of deindustrialization. This kind of reasoning is perfectly compatible with the sort of reorientation undertaken by Sweden's Social Democrats in the 1970s, making policies for women a priority (Naumann 2005). Under these conditions, one can expect Social Democratic parties to favour childcare policy. In other words, it would be unreasonable to expect any Social Democratic party at any time to support policies that favour women's entry into the labour market. It is only in the context of a shrinking workers' base and of a strategy aimed at including female voters that this hypothesis makes sense. However, the incompatibility between the interests of (industrial) wage workers and working women remains, contributing to the well-known dilemmas Social Democrats are facing in the post-industrial world (Rueda 2007; Häusermann 2010).

Women's political influence and the development of childcare services

With regard to childcare, some studies have shifted their focus from the leftist's power resources approach to the discussion of the political influence of women. True, from a strictly rational choice perspective, one would expect parents in general to benefit from subsidized childcare, not only women. However, given the strongly unbalanced distribution of care-work within households in OECD countries, the issue of reconciling work and family life is considerably more pressing for mothers than it is for fathers. The development of a comprehensive childcare system impacts certainly more on the lives of women than on those of men, even though publicly financed childcare means a transfer to parents in general. Moreover, childcare availability impacts favourably not only on mothers, but also on women in general. In fact, employers may be more inclined to employ a younger woman if they know that having a child will not be an obstacle to her continuing participation in the labour market. This may not be the case in countries with shortage of childcare services. For this reason, I hypothesize an association between women's political influence and higher levels of childcare provision.

An extensive body of literature on the impact that elected women have on policies exists (see, e.g., Swers 2001; Lovenduski and Norris 2003; Poggione 2004; Schwindt-Bayer 2006). The most consistent finding emerging from this literature is that the presence of women in parliaments (or descriptive representation) matters in policy-making on issues that may be of particular interest to women, such as gender equality policies, reproductive rights, and policies that concern families and children. Female parliamentarians are clearly more supportive than men when it comes to developing these types of policies. A few single-country studies that have focused on childcare policies have shown that the presence of women in local/regional parliaments is associated with high levels of coverage. Consistent findings have been obtained in such diverse countries as Norway (Bratton and Ray 2002) and Spain's region of Catalonia (Gonzalez and Vidal 2004). It has also been shown that across OECD countries, women's descriptive representation in national parliaments is an important determinant of childcare expenditure (Bonoli and Reber 2010).

There are two problems with this hypothesis. First, it implies a link between women's presence in key democratic institutions and the effective representation of women's interests. Most elected women are not directly or indirectly accountable to a female constituency. In this respect, why elected women tend to support women's interests even when they are not elected by women remains a puzzle for traditional democratic theory. A more sophisticated understanding of actors' preferences is arguably needed here, making reference to gender identity (Swers 2005).

Political competition

Political explanations of social policy-making, in contexts of both expansion and retrenchment, assume that those who are on the receiving hand of policy change respond to it by modifying their electoral behaviour. Policy-takers are expected to reward or punish policy-makers depending on how they are affected by policy change. This mechanism constitutes a powerful incentive for election seeking politicians to adopt policy proposals that maximize the expected electoral returns. Active social policies, instead, are unlikely to be the result of the political mobilization of those who benefit from them only. In this respect, the political mechanism that links socio-economic transformations to policy is likely to differ from the one observed during the expansion phase of European welfare states. During the post-war years, cohorts of ageing workers were happy to support political parties that expanded pension coverage as well as other potentially beneficial branches of the welfare state. As a result, political parties had a strong incentive to champion welfare state expansion. That is one of the reasons why very few political actors openly opposed the development of social policies during those years (see, e.g., Alber and Flora 1981; Wilensky 1981; Ferrera 1993: 190–7).

In the current context, we can assume that the electoral incentive to develop active social policies will not come from those who will receive them. First, the groups directly concerned by active social policies, in other words, younger women or unemployed people, make up only a small fraction of the electorate. Small numbers scarcely constitute an incentive for political entrepreneurs to develop new policies. Second, especially in the case of activation, the receivers of the policy—those who rely on income replacement benefits—do not necessarily see reform to their advantage. Of course, the position of the policy-takers on activation reform is likely to depend very much on its detailed content. Reforms that strengthen work incentives by increasing pressure on beneficiaries are likely to be opposed, whereas those that provide them with training and employment assistance may be supported. However, as will become clearer in Chapter 5, the initial stimulus for activation reform always came from above (i.e., governments). Nowhere do we find any form of direct or indirect mobilization of the beneficiaries of ALMPs behind their development. Things are somewhat different in relation to childcare, where women organizations were one of the engines of change. However, women organizations do not only represent mothers of young children. The point here is that if we want to study the political implications of active social policy, we cannot restrict ourselves to a focus on the likely response by the policy-takers. Active social policy is likely to appeal way beyond the narrow groups it directly targets, whether we are talking about people on benefits or mothers of young children.

Active social policy has everything it takes to be attractive to middle-class constituents, who benefit the most from policy developments in both policy areas. In the case of ALMPs, members of the middle class, even those who are securely employed, are likely to support policies that promise to reduce inactivity by promoting labour market participation. Active social policy promises to reduce dependency and as a result reduce the cost of the welfare state to taxpayers. The middle classes are also more likely to benefit directly from childcare services (Cantillon 2010; Schlanser 2011). In short, if we assume a vote-seeking motive behind the development of active social policies, we must consider the electoral consequences on target groups that are very different and distant from the receivers of the policy.

This observation suggests that active social policies, even though limited in their impact to small groups of voters, may acquire far greater political salience. In particular, they may provide opportunities for credit-claiming exercises. Here I hypothesize that the reorientation of European welfare states towards active social policy follows a credit-claiming logic. The groups targeted by this credit-claiming exercise, however, are not limited to the receivers of the policies but are mostly geared towards the middle classes.

Getting policy right: sequences and learning processes

As Hugh Heclo famously argued, policy-makers do not only 'power' (i.e., impose policies thanks to favourable power equilibria), but they also 'puzzle' (i.e., look for solutions to what they perceive as key problems) (Heclo 1974: 305). For sure, a lot of puzzling must have taken place among policy-makers in the fields of social and labour market policies over the past two decades. Faced with apparently intractable employment problems, governments of different political orientation have experimented with all sorts of approaches. The convergence towards an active social policy can also be understood as the result of a long process of trial and error with a range of different tools, all of which are found suboptimal in at least some respects (Hemerijck 2012a).

This perspective tends to see policy-makers as problem solvers who will change policy when the available instruments do not deliver the desired results any longer. The process is one of trial-and-error, whereby the first attempts involve only moderate change in the established approach, typically a change in the settings of a given policy (for example, a reduction in the level of unemployment benefit). Only when these measures are proved to be ineffective will policy-makers turn to more radical reforms. Social learning processes have been highlighted in a number of empirical studies. Peter Hall, in his account of the shift in British economic policy from Keynesianism to monetarism, was able to identify different stages. Subsequent stages are characterized by a bigger degree of innovation relative to the established practice and gradually led the country of John Maynard Keynes' birth to embrace monetarism as its new economic policy doctrine (Hall 1993).

Looking at trajectories of adjustment since the employment crises of the 1970s and 1980s, one can see a similar pattern. In the first instance, countries respond with familiar tools. This results in a clear divergence, well reflected by Esping-Andersen's categorization of welfare regimes. By the 1990s, these initial responses had started producing problems of their own. The liberal response, consisting of labour market deregulation and welfare retrenchment, did result in higher levels of employment, but also in worryingly high levels of inequality and poverty. The strategy adopted in continental Europe—the reduction of labour supply though early retirement and other income replacement benefits—was also running into problems. It had failed to reduce unemployment and was proving way too costly. Finally, in Sweden, the use of ALMPs as an alternative to employment had managed to prevent the rise of open unemployment, but was also proving an excessive strain on public budgets. In the early to mid-1990s, OECD countries were facing problems that were largely the result of their initial responses to the crisis (see, e.g., Scharpf 2000; Palier 2010).

By the mid-1990s, these problems were generally recognized, and the idea of an active social policy as a solution to each set of problems was beginning to emerge. The reform of the main US social assistance programme of the mid-1990s can be seen as one of the first steps taken in this direction, together with the Danish 1994 unemployment insurance reform (see Chapter 5). In subsequent years, other countries followed suit, such as the UK, the Netherlands, and other continental European countries like Germany or France. In addition, the diffusion of the active social policy paradigm was strongly supported by international organizations such as the OECD and by the EU (Hemerijck 2011).

Social learning-based accounts of policy change tend to emphasize sequences of events. Policy change in one area may produce intentional or unintentional effects in a different area. These side effects may be problematic and require further policy change that may create new problems elsewhere and so forth. This 'spillover' effect is discussed by Hemerijck and Schludi (2000) in their study of sequencing in economic adjustment. They argue that policy-makers typically have short time spans and a vision of policy problems that is limited to their area of competence (the policies for which the relevant ministry is responsible). As a result, it is not at all surprising that decisions taken, in order to deal with a problem within a policy field, may generate new difficulties in other ones.

Sequences of reform driven by spillover effects can be identified in virtually any advanced democracy, but one of the best illustrations of this process is provided by macroeconomic policy adjustment in the Netherlands. The country responded to the oil shock with an expansionary fiscal policy which generated inflation. Through a mechanism of automatic wage indexation, inflation resulted in rising wages, which depressed employment in the second half of the 1970s. Decline in employment levels resulted in a dramatic increase in the number of invalidity benefit recipients, which in turn made the scheme financially unsustainable. Invalidity benefits were subsequently made less accessible, and in some cases, even removed. This meant that the labour market had to be deregulated in order to be able to absorb the excess labour that had previously been channelled onto invalidity benefit. This led to a series of reforms. In particular, labour market law was meant to facilitate job creation, especially part-time work. This extremely stylized account of economic adjustment shows how solutions to one problem can create a new problem in a different area of the political economy. This is arguably also an important mechanism of change (Hemerijck and Schludi 2000).

The social learning perspective implies also that countries learned from each other. Policy-makers confronted with a new problem are on the lookout for innovative solutions and thus likely to 'shop around' for best practices. There are several examples of studies showing the influence of foreign experiences on national policy trajectories in the field of social and employment policy (Dolowitz and Marsh 2000; Orenstein 2003; Seeleib-Kaiser and Fleckenstein 2007). The study of German employment policy by Seeleib-Kaiser and Fleckenstein brings together the two approaches, social learning and policy diffusion. In this study, they showed how German policy-makers, confronted with an apparently intractable problem of high level of unemployment, turned to the UK and the Netherlands in their search for solution. Policy-makers at various levels looked deliberately for models elsewhere in order to deal with seemingly unsolvable problems.

The social learning perspective provides useful insights into processes of policy change. If one assumes that the active social policy paradigm is a step towards a new equilibrium, it can help us to understand why this approach is being adopted across regimes and countries. From an empirical point of view, this assumption fails on at least two counts. First, it does not tell us why Southern Europe 'isn't learning', despite the persistence of labour market problems and of the international pressures (especially from the EU). Second, it also fails to account for why some countries were so much slower in adopting the active social policy paradigm. Its key weakness, however, is arguably linked to its core assumption that policy-making is about solving problems. It emphasizes 'puzzling' over 'powering'. Political scientists have shown that politicians' motivations are at least more complex and diverse and include also the fulfilment of electoral aspirations (Müller and Strøm 1999).

Public opinion and societal values

In informal, non-academic discussions, 'mentality' or 'culture' is often referenced as a key distinguishing characteristic of human societies likely to impact policy. In more formal terms, one can hypothesize that cross-national variations in the orientation of social policy may also be related to differences in mainstream societal values or dominant normative perceptions. Societal values are shaped by national histories, politics, religion, and so forth. In the context of a well-functioning democracy, citizens' preferences can be expected to impact policy outcomes. The reorientation of mature welfare states touches on some very deep beliefs, pertaining to the areas of work and, especially, the family. Should mothers of small children be in full-time employment? Are small kids well taken care of in a daycare centre? Should non-working disabled people be required to take up employment? How the median voter will answer these questions in different countries will contribute to determining how easy or difficult it will be to develop an active social policy.

The impact of normative perceptions on policy is a notoriously difficult field of study. There are serious measurement problems, and it is ridden with reverse causality and chicken-and-egg problems. In order to deal with these problems, one would need to study the impact of public opinion changes on policy, using longitudinal analysis. Public opinion data are helpful in this type of analysis, but surveys are typically carried out at large time intervals (4 to 6 years), making it difficult to find a sufficient number of time points in order to carry out meaningful longitudinal analysis. These difficulties notwithstanding, there have been a few attempts at assessing the impact of people's social policy preferences on actual policy, using both quantitative and qualitative methods.

A recent strand of literature, under the heading of 'policy responsiveness', has attempted to link variation in public opinion on welfare to levels of social spending, both across countries and across time (Brooks and Manza 2007). Taking aggregate public opinion data (at the national level) as their independent variable and using a time-series cross-sectional design, Brook and Manza show a relatively robust relationship between the policy preferences expressed by interviewees in various surveys and the level of social expenditure, controlling for a range of other political, economic, and institutional variables. They conclude that their evidence reveals 'a strong relationship between the policy preferences of national publics and welfare spending effort. The magnitude of these effects is substantial, even when compared to the effects of factors established by previous scholarship' (Brooks and Manza 2007: 48).

The existence of a strong association between preferences for more or less social spending and social spending itself is undisputed. The more difficult question is whether one can infer a cause–effect relationship from the simple statistical association. According to John Myles, the small number of time points available in the database (depending on the country, between two and three) does not allow the author to infer a causal relationship between the two variables. The observed effect is essentially cross-sectional and not longitudinal (Myles 2006). The causal relationship may well run in the opposite direction: Individuals who have grown up and have been socialized in high spending welfare states are more likely to support the generous type of provision they have become accustomed. The fact that public opinion data are available at few time points makes it difficult to ascertain the direction of causality in a convincing fashion. From a theoretical point of view, either effect seems plausible.

Moreover, it is rather difficult is to know what is exactly measured in public opinion surveys. Cross-national differences within mainstream or average opinions may reflect very different things, including religious traditions or historical legacies, but also political equilibria. In order to turn the 'policy responsiveness' hypothesis into a theoretically sound and heuristically helpful proposition, one would need a clearer understanding of the ontological status of public opinion data (Myles 2006).

Finally, from the point of view of this book, Brooks and Manza's analysis presents the additional problem of lumping together different categories of social expenditure, in particular spending on traditional social protection programmes and spending on more active ones. The hypothesis that some publics are more receptive to the active social policy ideology than other ones is not tested in their work.

Other authors have dealt with the issue of people's preferences in a different, qualitative fashion. Vivien A. Schmidt has argued that the capacity of governments to carry out welfare reform will depend crucially on whether these 'resonate culturally'. She looks at two decades of reforms across OECD countries and finds some consistency between the ethos of the traditional post-war settlement and the options that are chosen for reform. In particular, the justifications used for similar reforms, often unpopular, differ across countries or welfare regimes. In her analysis, public preferences are only one variable among many and often not the most important one (Schmidt 2002).

Studying the impact of public opinion on policy is a difficult exercise. The existence of feedback effects and reverse causality problems makes it extremely difficult to go beyond the observation that there seems to be a relatively strong relationship between what people say they want and what they get in social policy. Some of these problems may be dealt with in historical studies where countries are compared at different points in time in relation to mainstream values that are relevant for the expansion of active policies. For example, the preference for the traditional family model, based on the male breadwinner, is arguably an obstacle to the development of childcare services. Are there differences today across countries? Have these differences existed before, especially before the current re-orientation movement began in the 1970s? Chapters 5 and 6 attempt to answer these questions as well as to deliver some insight on the relevance of the public opinion/ societal values hypothesis.

Institutional opportunities and obstacles

In his already-mentioned seminal work on the politics of social reforms, Hugh Heclo observed that when policy-makers are confronted with a new problem, the question they ask is not *where do we go?* but *where do we go from here?* (Heclo 1974: 16). New policies are not adopted in a vacuum. Existing policies, traditions, and world-visions exert a crucial influence upon decision-making. The reorientation of mature welfare states is certainly no exception in this respect, and we can expect older policies that may already have had a pro-employment flavour to be a more promising ground on which to build an active welfare state than those based on the sheer protection of non-working individuals.

Political scientists, and more specifically neo-institutionalists, have written extensively on the mechanisms that connect existing institutional structures to new policies (see Thelen and Steinmo 1992; Pierson 1993; Hall and Taylor 1996). This literature is extremely rich and complex, but one can identify two main phases in its development. First, scholars emphasize the role played by existing institutions in limiting the room for manoeuvre available to policy-makers. Initial decisions and decisions taken at key moments, or 'critical junctures' in the developmental path of a policy, severely constrain the scope for future change. Often with reference to the notion of path dependency, several studies aimed at explaining the persistence of inefficient policy solution despite a better one being technically available (Myles and Quadagno 1997; Pierson 2000; Wood 2001).

This approach was later criticized for overemphasizing policy stability and failing to grasp the mechanisms that produce change (Streeck and Thelen 2005). More recent studies have shown that while existing institutions may limit the menu of available options, policy change does happen, even in areas that were considered as extremely resistant to change, such as old age pensions (Hinrichs 2000; Bonoli and Palier 2008), or in countries characterized as 'frozen' such as France or the Bismarckian welfare states (Palier 2010). In a useful attempt to reconcile the two perspectives, Streek and Thelen have identified a number of mechanisms that within institutional constraints can produce even substantial policy change (Streeck and Thelen 2005). Some of these mechanisms, which appear to be relevant in the current process of reorientation of mature welfare states, are discussed below.

There are at least three different ways in which earlier policy decisions can impact on the way in which welfare states can be reoriented towards active social policy: (1) early development of active policies; (2) the presence or absence of convertible institutions; and (3) existence of institutions embodying values that are compatible or incompatible with the active social policy idea.

First, even though most countries developed protective welfare states during the post-war years, in some cases policies that produce investment in human capital and encourage labour market participation existed well before the current reform movement. One of the first instances of active labour market policy is the Swedish labour market regulatory regime that emerged in the early post-war years, generally labelled as the Rehn–Meidner model. This approach entailed substantial investment in the training and the retraining of workers, and was set up in the early 1950s. It is considered as possibly the earliest clear example of active labour market policy and the reason why Sweden still boasts as one of the world's most developed systems of ALMP (Swenson 2002).

In addition, early examples of active social policy do not necessarily belong to the realm of welfare state. Such examples are found in the field of education and training. The German apprenticeship system is probably one of the best tools ever developed for securing a smooth transition from education to the labour market for young people. It is no recent invention, although its origin goes back to the late eighteenth century (Thelen 2004: 38). Combining education provided in state schools and on-the-job vocational training within firms, the German apprenticeship system fulfils all the criteria of modern active social policy. Active social policy is not an invention of the twenty-first century, and we can expect that the early adoption of active policies constitutes an advantage in the current reorientation movement.

While some countries may have developed policies of the active type well before the current wave, they may also have developed other policies that are particularly antithetical to the idea of an active social policy. One good example here is a peculiar Italian institution for temporary unemployment benefit (*Cassa integrazione*), which provides income replacement to redundant workers. Recipients of this benefit are not dismissed but continue to be technically employed by their employers. While *Cassa integrazione* is in theory temporary, in practice—especially in contexts of industrial restructuring—redundant workers tend to stay on it for lengthy periods (up to 5 years and even longer in some cases, see Barbier and Fargion 2004: 445 and Chapter 5 below). The fact that redundant workers are still tied to their last employer severely limits the extent to which ALMPs that encourage mobility can be developed.

Second, we can expect some earlier protective policies to be more easily turned into active ones. Streeck and Thelen identify a mechanism of institutional change labelled 'conversion'. They describe it as the 'redeployment of old institutions to new purposes' (2005: 31). They show that instances of conversion are frequent in the history of public policy. Their general focus, however, prevents them from identifying more specific mechanisms that make some institutions more 'convertible' than other ones. Of course, the potential for conversion depends on the nature of the original and of the target institution. Here we are particularly interested in existing policies that may not be directly aimed at promoting labour market participation, but also are not clearly incompatible with these aims and can more or less easily be turned into active social policy tools. The best example here is perhaps the well-known system of pre-schools that exist in France. These were set up in the context of a struggle between the state and the Catholic Church. Their more or less explicit aim was the early socialization of very young French citizens to republican values. In the 1970s, when demand for childcare services started to emerge, pre-schools could be easily turned into providers of care for working mothers (Morgan 2002).

Third, new social policies may find fertile ground in countries where they are more or less consistent with broadly accepted norms and values, especially those that are embodied in welfare institutions. Active social policies emphasize labour market participation of groups that were in the past exempted from this requirement, such as mothers of young children. Political support for policies like childcare may be related to the attachment to gender egalitarian values, which is likely to vary cross-nationally. Societal values that are relevant in accounting for success or failure of active social policies may be embodied in the welfare institutions that were built during the post-war years. In this respect, we may find that countries having developed family policies in a way that supports and reinforces the traditional male breadwinner family model may have more difficulties in turning to the active social policy paradigm.

The origins of social policy, the existence or the absence of antecedents and of convertibility of institutions may play an important role in shaping the opportunities for reform. At the same time, this approach is not very helpful in accounting for why, suddenly, a new course of policy is adopted. A focus on institutional inheritance can be only helpful in conjunction with other hypotheses.

Centripetal forces

Active social policies have a distinctive win-win and cross-class coalition flavour (see also Bonoli 2005). Both ALMPs and childcare policies are at least in theory capable of attracting the support of both capital and labour. This distinguishes them from the more traditional socially protective policies, which were sometimes imposed by powerful labour movements upon reluctant employers, such as employment protection laws (Emmenegger 2009). True, both labour and capital face dilemmas when having to take a position on active policies. For labour, as argued above, helping disadvantaged people and promoting gender equality may conflict with the objective of sustaining wages for core workers. For employers, the employment-promoting character of active social policies needs to be weighed against the increased need for public funds in order to finance them.

To an extent, active social policy may be seen as the second best option for both employers and workers. As a result, one can hypothesize that when acting under centripetal pressures—or pressures to compromise and find consensual solutions—employers and workers tend to converge on active social policy as opposed to either traditional protection policies favoured by workers or a laissez-faire approach, as preferred by employers.

When are these sorts of centripetal pressures likely to be strongest? We can identify at least two such situations. Centripetal pressures are likely to be strong in polities where power tends to be fragmented or when countries are strongly exposed to international economic competition and cannot afford conflict (Katzenstein 1985). These two situations are discussed next.

Fragmented political institutions

Several studies have shown that political systems that are dense with veto points tend to produce more consensual and centrist policy solutions than those characterized by strong power concentration with the executive branch of government. This is due to the fact that within an institutionally fragmented polity, a minimum level of consensus is needed in order to legislate. Alternatively, the political machine is unable to deliver, being blocked by intersecting vetoes. The best example of this type of polity is Switzerland, where the law-making process must go through a series of hurdles, at each of which a suitable coalition can stop the adoption of the relevant piece of law. These veto points include a symmetrical, bicameral parliament, a strict separation of powers between executive and legislative branches, a written constitution, and, for Switzerland, an easily accessible referendum system.

At the opposite extreme, one finds the Westminster type of political institutions. Here power is concentrated with the executive branch of government. The separation of powers between the executive and the legislative branches is purely a formal aspect. In reality, the executive dominates parliament. The second chamber of parliament has only symbolic powers, and there is no written constitution (Lijphart 1984; Immergut, 1992; Bonoli 2001; Armingeon 2002; Tsebelis 2002).

This understanding of the role of political institutions in shaping policy-making processes allows us to formulate fairly straightforward hypotheses. Basically, in relation to political institutions, one can expect countries where power is fragmented to be more inclined to turn to active social policy, the 'second best' solution to social problems for both capital and labour. In contrast, countries where institutions concentrate power tend to deal with new social problems through policies of a clearer liberal orientation when the Right is in power and through traditional protective policies when the Left is.

Exposure to international economic competition

Peter J. Katzenstein argued in the 1980s that the reason behind the very strong development of Nordic welfare states was the high level of exposure to international markets, inevitable for these small countries. Strong dependence on international markets has arguably led to a consensual approach to political differences, exemplified by the major social pacts adopted in the early years of the twentieth century. This consensual approach to economic and social policy has translated into generous welfare arrangements. Exposure to international competition, the argument goes, increases levels of economic insecurity for workers. They, as a result, turn to the state to get social protection. Katzenstein discusses the welfare state being a compensation mechanism for the high degree of economic uncertainty experienced by states participating within the global economy (Katzenstein 1985; Garrett 1998).

Katzenstein does not distinguish between traditional protective and active social policies. However, from the early days of post-war social policy, most notably with the adoption of an ALMP, Sweden and to a lesser extent other Nordic countries have developed social protection systems based much more on active policy tools relative to their continental and Southern European counterparts. Small countries strongly exposed to international competition have tended to compensate workers with social policy, but not with any kind of social policy. In order to succeed in the international economy, policies that could have burdened national producers were ruled out most of the time. These include employment protection laws, early retirement, and other costly passive benefits, which in contrast became standard policy in continental and Southern Europe.

Exposure to international competition may be seen as a development that fosters centripetal pressures. Workers need protection from economic uncertainty, but their representatives (the unions and left-wing parties) cannot afford to adopt solutions that impact negatively on their country's position in highly competitive international markets. The notion of active social policy provides the focal point where both the interests of labour and employers can converge. This view is compatible with the renewed and generalized interest in active social policies since the 1990s, a decade characterized by strong intensification of economic internationalization and competition (Scharpf 2000).

Timing and the crowding-out hypothesis

The trends responsible for the emergence of demands for active policies have progressed at a varying pace within different countries and regions. Broadly speaking, the Nordic countries and parts of the English-speaking world (USA, UK, and Canada) have been the first group of nations to enter the post-industrial age in the 1970s. They were followed by continental European countries about a decade later and by Southern Europe in the late 1990s. The claim made here is that differences in the timing of key post-industrial socio-economic developments will not only generate a catching-up phenomena, but may also result in long-lasting differences in the degree of development of active social policies (Bonoli 2007).

This claim is based on the following argument. Within countries that have entered the post-industrial age at relatively early points, new demands generated by the ongoing social transformations found comparatively little competition. Sure, those hit by these transformations had to fight in the political arena to obtain better provision, but they could also rely on the broad support of those actors generally in favour of welfare expansion, such as the Left and the trade unions. In contrast, within countries that have more recently developed into post-industrial societies, demands for the expansion of active social policies are in strong competition with demands for the preservation of the current level of protection provided by industrial welfare states, despite population ageing. The latter requires enormous resources and can rely on a substantial level of popular support, most notably by the large cohorts of baby-boomers who are approaching retirement. In contrast, those who stand to gain most from active social policies (i.e., women, younger people, immigrants, and in general labour market outsiders) are notoriously politically weak, both in terms of presence in key democratic political institutions and in terms of participation in elections (Norris 2002; Bonoli 2005).

One consequence of the unbalanced power relationship between the constituency of the post-war welfare state and those who are hit by current social transformations is that incentives for vote-maximizing political actors are clearly geared towards the defence of the industrial welfare state rather than towards the development of active social policies. Such incentives are further strengthened by demographic trends and by differentials in turnout between age groups. Over the next few decades, older, pension system-dependent voters will make up an increasingly large proportion of Western electorates. At the same time, as it has long been known by political scientists, turnout levels tend to increase with age (Norris 2002). These developments concur in setting extremely strong incentives for rational vote-seeking politicians to present themselves as the defenders of the pension system rather than the champions of childcare, negative income taxes, or ALMPs.

The presence of competing claims for different sets of social policies affects incentives across the whole political spectrum but can have a particularly strong divisive effect on labour movements and traditional pro-welfare constituencies, such as left-wing voters and parties. This is visible in the increasingly strong cleavage between modernizers and traditionalists that characterizes the Left in many continental European countries.[1]

Timing is a crucial element in this argument. Whether countries manage or fail to reorient their welfare states in a way that reflects changing socio-economic circumstances depends on the relative timing of key socio-economic trends in interaction with existing welfare state structures. The key developments are post-industrialization and the increase in the cost of the industrial welfare state resulting from the combination of demographic ageing and the maturation of generous pension entitlements. These two developments must not happen simultaneously if a welfare state is to be successfully reoriented.

Putting theory to the test

This chapter puts forward a broad range of hypotheses that either are found in the political science literature on the welfare state or can be built on the basis of existing scholarship. From a theoretical point of view, we can expect the

---

[1] See, for example, in Germany the fight within the SPD on social and economic policies (Hering 2004), or in Italy the strong division between the Centre Left and the refunded Communist Party (Ferrera 2000).

factors they focus upon to have played an important role in determining the reorientation of social policies. What needs to be done next is to test them against the empirical evidence that is available to us. This is the task of Chapters 5 to 7. Each of the hypotheses put forward here is discussed again in Chapter 8, this time on the basis of the empirical evidence presented in the book.

5

Active Labour Market Policies in a Comparative Perspective

Introduction

The objective of this chapter is to provide some of the empirical material needed to test the hypotheses put forward in Chapter 4 in relation to active labour market policies (ALMPs). This is done by presenting narrative accounts of relevant policy developments in seven Western European countries, selected so as to be as similar as possible in terms of problem pressure and at the same time maximize variation on the various independent variables considered in Chapter 4. The sample cases display also a fair degree of variation in relation to the dependent variable. It includes two Nordic countries with highly developed systems of ALMPs (Sweden and Denmark); three continental European countries which have invested much less in this field of policy (France, Germany, and Italy), and two countries which have turned to ALMPs only rather recently but have done so rapidly and to a broader extent than most other Western European countries (the Netherlands and the UK).

ALMPs constitute a component of a broader system of labour market regulation and unemployment compensation. The 'active orientation' of labour market policy depends not only on the efforts made in the policies explicitly labelled as 'active'. It also has much to do with how income replacement benefits are organized and with the type and degree of protection that exists against dismissal. These elements of labour market policy are also included in the narrative accounts below, at least insofar as they impact the overall active orientation of policy.

As will be shown in this chapter, each country follows a unique trajectory in labour market policy. However, there are some historical moments when most countries make crucial decisions concerning the future shape of their labour market policy. One can identify at least four such moments since the emergence of industrial economies. These are used to structure the narrative accounts below.

First, of great importance for subsequent developments, are the early steps taken in labour market regulation. The first instances of labour market regulation go back to the early days of capitalism (Polanyi 1957 [1944]). ALMPs were not at that time a popular policy solution to labour market problems, but some of the decisions taken then may have contributed to shape industrial relations and employment regulation systems in subsequent years. What seems to be particularly crucial for further developments is whether countries develop more in the direction of an adversarial system of industrial relations or one based on collaboration. It is also important to look at the role of the state, whether it intervenes in the labour market sphere. Countries that develop collaborative systems of industrial relations may in fact have an advantage in developing extensive ALMP systems. As shown by Colin Crouch, Western European countries developed different ways of sharing public space before World War II (Crouch 1993).

A *second* crucial stage is the early post-war years. This period was decisive in terms of determining a labour market regulatory system. Divergence at this stage is rather substantial and can be explained with reference to the structures that were in place before the war and the type of war experience the country had. In the UK, the early post-war years were particularly fertile for the adoption of highly redistributive policies. In Germany, a key preoccupation was to avoid excessive state intervention in the economy, while at the same time develop a system capable of maintaining social stability in uncertain economic times. In Italy and France, the early post-war years were characterized by a strong Communist movement (both in politics and labour relations), which had gained much popular prestige through its involvement in the underground resistance movement against the Nazis. The regulatory frameworks adopted after World War II evolved during subsequent years. In several countries, towards the end of the 1960s and early 1970s, labour market regulation was made stricter. Reform came largely as a result of a radicalization of the labour movement and of the Left, resulting in the adoption of more interventionist rules throughout the continent (Emmenegger 2009).

Post-war models were seriously questioned as a result of the employment crisis of the 1970s and 1980s, marking the *third* critical juncture. Virtually all Western European countries had to confront mass unemployment, but they dealt with it in radically different ways, to a large extent reflecting the labour market and welfare institutions already in place. Led by the UK and the USA, several OECD countries embarked in more or less ambitious labour market deregulation and welfare retrenchment programmes. Continental Europe, instead, turned to the so-called 'labour reduction route' while the Nordic countries expanded public employment (see e.g. Esping-Andersen 1990).

Finally, the *fourth* important period for the development of ALMPs is the recent 'activation turn' which has taken place since the 1990s. The countries covered in this study embraced the activation paradigm at different moments. Denmark, the UK, and the Netherlands were among the first to clearly move in that direction during the early to mid-1990s. Sweden, Germany, and possibly France subsequently followed. Italy, in contrast, has not so far experienced this type of transformation of labour market policy.

The relevance of these key moments also differs across countries. For example, in Italy, late to industrialize, developments before WWII may be less important than in Sweden or in the UK. By the same token, the activation turn that takes place from the 1990s onwards is more visible in some countries than in other ones. The individual narrative accounts of labour market policy presented in this chapter reflect these differences, and use an adapted version of the sequence described here.

Sweden

Many consider Sweden as the birthplace of ALMPs. The notion features prominently in labour market policy since the 1950s. The fact that the development of ALMPs in Sweden has be orchestrated by the hegemonic Social Democratic Party, often on the basis of initiatives coming from the trade unions, has prompted many to argue that Sweden provides proof of the left-wing nature of ALMPs (see Chapter 4). In fact, the development of ALMPs is rather more complicated, and the Swedish Left did not always support an active approach in labour market and unemployment policy.

Antecedents: developing cooperative industrial relations

Historical accounts of Swedish labour market policy point to a number of developments during the twentieth century that played a role in shaping the country's trajectory. The early years of the new century were characterized by strong levels of unrest in industrial relations, with employers and unions playing a game of cat and mouse with strikes and lock-outs. Domestic social issues, the rise of the labour movement and of the Social Democratic Party, together with the pre-World War II international tensions, paved the way for a new types of politics and industrial relations, dominated by a cross-class alliance (Swenson 2002: 74). The key event in the establishment of this cross-class alliance in Sweden was the famous *Saltsjöbaden* agreement between trade unions and employers (LO and SAF), signed in 1938. Basically, employers accepted the legitimacy of the unions as a labour market actor, and the idea of a strong welfare state in return for labour peace, preservation of private

71

control over property and the capital market, and trade openness (Katzenstein 1985: 141).

An additional important precedent was, according to Rothstein, the establishment of labour exchange offices at the municipal level in the early years of the twentieth century. These were composed of equal numbers of worker and employer representatives and played a neutral role in managing labour market disputes. This is very different from the role played by the equivalent state-controlled institutions in countries like Germany and the UK, which were essentially used to police the unemployed (Rothstein 1985: 156). This type of corporatist arrangements provided a fertile ground over which to build a more comprehensive system of labour market regulation outside of the state.

The post-war model

The next important development was arguably the setting up of a National Labour Market Board (AMS—*Arbetsmarknastyrelsen*) in 1948. After the end of WWII, there was widespread agreement that the labour market regulatory system in place during the war, which had made full employment possible, was to be in some ways retained. The proposal of a regulatory authority placed outside the direct control of government must be understood in this light (Rothstein 1985: 158-9). Staffed by employers and trade union representatives, the AMS had the important task of securing the smooth functioning of the labour market by administering the labour exchange system. According to Swenson, AMS became a tool that employers used in order to ration labour in the context of chronic labour shortages in the post-war years (Swenson 2002: 280). AMS, as we will see, played a crucial role in the development of the ALMPs in Sweden.

There is a general agreement in the literature that the idea of an active labour market policy initially came from the Swedish trade unions. This strategy was first put forward in a report published in 1951 by two LO economists, Gösta Rehn and Rudolf Meidner. In it, ALMPs were presented as an element of a broader economic policy approach, which became know as the 'Rehn–Meidner model' and would influence Sweden's economy for several decades to come. The essential objective of the model was to achieve sustainable full employment, that is, full employment that would not generate inflationary pressures. Its main ingredients were restrictive fiscal and monetary policy and wage moderation. Wage moderation was to be enforced through a solidarity wage policy, which basically meant a strong egalitarian pressure in the wage distribution. The egalitarian wage policy had both intended and unintended effects. Among the intended effects was a strong incentive for Swedish producers to invest in productivity-enhancing technologies. If productivity lagged behind imposed wage growth, companies would find it difficult to compete. This, in Rehn and Meidner's view, constituted a strong push for the modernization of Swedish industry.

But of course, not every industry would be able to keep up with the pace of wage increases agreed centrally. Low productivity industries were to be priced out of the market as collectively bargained wages increased. It is to deal with the workers that would as a result find themselves unemployed that Rehn and Meidner conceived ALMPs. As less productive companies were pushed out of the market, the surplus of workers were to be retrained and made available for expanding high productivity industries (see, e.g., Mabbet 1995: 141ff.; Benner and Vad 2000: 401; Swenson 2002: 275; Anxo and Niklasson 2006).

The idea of an ALMP came from the trade unions, but was clearly acceptable to employers. According to Swenson, it was probably them who suggested it in the first place (2002: 275). On the basis of extensive historical research, he concludes:

> Employers warmly endorsed activist training and mobility measures even before the labor confederation included them as the centerpiece of their plan for economic stabilization and industrial development (the 'Rehn-Meidner Model').... Organized employers were not merely resigned to hegemonic Social Democrats and hoping to appease them for special consideration on particular details, for nicer treatment in other domains, or to avoid public disfavor. They knew what they wanted. Sometimes they liked best what they got and got what they liked best. (Swenson 2002: 11)

The development of a comprehensive system of ALMPs was orchestrated by AMS. It's independence from the state might have played a role in it, since the resources used by AMS to finance the expansion of ALMPs were not subjected to the same kind of limitations and control applied to standard government expenditures. Over the years, AMS came to be seen as one of the most powerful institutions in the country, attracting by the same token, criticism, especially from the bourgeois parties (Rothstein 1985). In this favourable institutional context, ALMP expenditure increased from the 1950s onwards and reached a staggering 2 per cent by the 1970s (Swenson 2002: 274). During these years, it should be noted, ALMPs consisted essentially of a system of industrial retraining. Such policies are very different from the sort of active labour market policy that have been introduced in the late 1990s and early 2000s.

The end of the golden age

The Swedish response to the economic crisis of the 1970s was based on three key actions. First, public employment was expanded dramatically. Between 1970 and 1995, the proportion of working age individuals employed by the government skyrocketed from 15 to 25.7 per cent (OECD. *Stat*). This was partly an unintended consequence of the Rehn–Meidner model operating in an increasingly service-based economy. As pointed out by several authors, many service sector jobs offered very limited scope for increases in productivity (Iversen and Wren 1998; Pierson 1998; Esping-Andersen 1999). Most particularly, this is the case in low value-added services, such as catering, retail trade, and cleaning, but also care (both health and social care). The Rehn–Meidner model would price these services out of the market, as it did with less than average efficient industries. At the same time, full employment could not be achieved in a post-industrial context without expanding employment in these areas. The only way to do this, however, given the high level of wages imposed by centralized bargaining, was by expanding public employment (Iversen 1999: 171). This is precisely what happened from the late 1960s onwards.

Second, the 1970s saw a reorientation of ALMPs. It is noteworthy that the crisis years (mid-1970s to the late 1980s) did not result in open unemployment in Sweden. This was partly the result of the expansion of public sector employment, but also a consequence of a rather generous use of ALMPs. In fact, by providing an occupation to otherwise jobless persons, ALMPs allowed Sweden to keep unemployment at pre-recession levels (Mjoset 1987: 430). This was obviously a new function for ALMPs, which was adopted by default in the context of a stagnating economy with little net job creation outside the state sector. As a result, ALMPs were effectively turned into a tool for reducing labour supply and open unemployment and somewhat lost their original function of promoting mobility and upskilling.

Third, under the pressure of a strong and radicalized labour movement, Sweden turned to employment protection legislation (Emmenegger 2009). In 1974, an employment protection act was adopted. Among other things, it introduced rules concerning grounds for dismissal, notice periods, consultation with the trade unions, and priority rules for dismissals (and re-employment) in case of redundancies. Age and length of service criteria had to be applied in identifying the employees to be dismissed (referred to as the last-in-first-out principle; see Neal 1984).

The 1970s can be characterized as a period of departure from the post-war Swedish model, with the country adopting many of the policy options that were being developed in continental Europe, such as employment protection and labour supply reduction. The extent of the shift was nonetheless limited by what was happening in other policy fields, most notably the development of a childcare system resulting in a massive expansion of female labour supply (see Chapter 6).

Things were to change with the recession of the 1990s. The severity of the downturn, the loss of confidence of international investors which culminated in the 1992 devaluation of the krona (by some 20 per cent), and the degree to which the post-war model had already been overstretched to deal with previous recessions allowed no room for manoeuvre. The government put more and more people into employment programmes (in 1994, 6 per cent of the active population, Anxo and Niklasson 2006: 357). In the end, however, Sweden had to abandon this costly strategy, and allow open unemployment to rise from 1.6 in 1991 to 8.1 per cent in 1996 (OECD *Stat.*).

What role did ALMPs play during those years? To find out, we must turn to the evaluation literature. As seen in Chapter 2, the qualification of ALMP sometimes covers totally different types of interventions. In the Swedish case, from the 1970s onwards, ALMPs increasingly resemble alternatives to market employment. On offer one finds essentially training programmes and relief works, in other words, temporary jobs arranged mostly in the public sector. Typically, these jobs were used to renew entitlement to unemployment insurance (theoretically limited to 14 months). The emphasis had shifted from investment in human capital towards occupation as the main objective of active ALMP. In other words, supply-side measures were gradually replaced by demand-side interventions, in other words, the job creation programmes (Anxo and Niklasson 2006: 360). Micro-level evaluations pointed out that most of these schemes were rather ineffective in terms of favouring labour market re-entry (Calmfors et al. 2001). The original aim of ALMPs, to upskill workers so that they can enter more productive occupations, had somewhat fallen out of sight.

Reorienting ALMPs towards activation

Since the mid-1990s, however, ALMPs have adopted a more pragmatic orientation, favouring labour market re-entry for excluded individuals. For instance, the number of labour market programmes was increased, and more was done also in terms of experimenting (Kautto 2001). Work requirements were strengthened so that those still jobless after 100 days of unemployment may be required to accept a job anywhere in the country and a wage up to 10 per cent lower than the unemployment benefit (Clasen et al. 2001: 211).

The unemployment insurance reform of February 2001 further strengthened the pro-employment orientation of ALMP. This was done through a number of measures. First, the possibility of renewing entitlement to unemployment insurance through participation in labour market programmes was abolished. This practice was identified in several studies as detrimental to the re-employment chances of the long-term unemployed, who were de facto encouraged to spend their life between labour market programmes and open unemployment. Second, the reform introduced an 'activity guarantee' for long-term unemployed people or people at risk of becoming long-term unemployed.

This consisted of more individualized activities clearly geared towards re-employment (Swedish Government 2002; Timonen 2004).

Some commentators have interpreted this reorientation of ALMP in terms of a return to the original model. According to Anxo and Niklasson:

> The reorientation of ALMP in the early 1990s towards more supply-oriented programmes may be seen as a return to the initial conception of ALMP interventions, and better able to meet the increasing demand for skill upgrading. In fact, the primacy of demand-side measures during the 1970s and 1980s may be viewed as a deviation from the original ALMP strategy initiated during the late 1950s. (Anxo and Niklasson 2006: 360)

What is important is that Sweden has turned towards the same mix of positive and negative incentives in labour market policies that characterizes most countries today. Though tempted in the 1970s and particularly in the 1980s to use ALMPs as a de facto 'labour reduction tool', Sweden managed to return to a more employment-oriented use of labour market programmes. This was not done without difficulties. For example, the practice of considering participation in labour market programmes as equivalent to an entitlement was not phased out until 2001, considerably later than in Denmark which took this decision in 1994. Politically, the reorientation was led by the Social Democrats in power without interruptions from 1996 to 2006.

Denmark

Together with Sweden, Denmark is a country that today stands out as a major spender on ALMPs, and the two countries are similar in many respects. Yet, their labour market policy trajectories have converged only in the past few years, after following pretty distinctive paths. A strong emphasis on ALMPs is a relatively recent development in Denmark. In 1980, Denmark spent only 0.4 per cent of GDP on ALMPs, as much as the OECD average and a third of Sweden's spending at the time.

Denmark is also rather unique in having maintained a relatively unregulated labour market, combined with one of the most generous systems of unemployment compensation, which has made the country one of the most often quoted examples of a 'flexicurity' approach to labour market policy.

Antecedents

Denmark chose the road of cooperative industrial relations even earlier than Sweden and other Nordic countries, as the Danish tradition of social partnership goes back to the 'September Agreement', jointly signed by representatives of employers and workers in 1899.[1] In this agreement, which came after a period of sustained industrial unrest, employers committed themselves to respect employees' right to organize into trade unions. In return, they obtained the respect of 'managerial prerogatives', in other words, employers control over the organization work in private companies. This entailed a great degree of freedom in hiring and firing (Einhorn and Logue 2003: 278; Emmenegger 2009: 135). From this point of view, Denmark embarked on a path that was very similar to the Swedish one, characterized by cooperative industrial relations and regulation of the labour market by collective agreements as opposed to direct state intervention through legislation.

The post-war model

Like other parts of Western Europe, the post-war years in Denmark were characterized by strong economic growth, with rates hovering around 4 per cent most of the time. What distinguished Denmark from other countries, including Sweden, was the persistence of a current account deficit, which often forced the government to slow down the economy through higher interest rates and taxes (Benner and Vad 2000: 408). In addition, after World War II and until the 1960s, Denmark faced comparatively high rates of unemployment of around 4 per cent between 1948 and 1960, a level twice as high as in Sweden (Esping-Andersen and Korpi 1987: 56), In this context, labour shortage, one of the key reasons behind the emergence of ALMPs in Sweden, did not develop into a major problem.

In addition, Danish industrial policy was less oriented towards economic modernization than in the Swedish case. In contrast, it was much more based on a laisser-faire attitude (Benner and Vad 2000: 409). In sum, at least some of the conditions that prompted the development of a system of ALMPs as early as the 1950s in Sweden were simply absent in Denmark. This may help understand why the active approach to labour market policy was developed considerably later. Finally, Social Democrats were less powerful in Denmark than they were in Sweden. Between 1940 and 1971, the Danish Social Democrats received an average share of the vote of 39.3 per cent while the same figure for Sweden was 47.6 per cent (Arter 1999: 71).

As for labour market policy, the Danish post-war model was characterized by relatively liberal employment protection policy and a generous unemployment compensation system. With regard to employment protection, the basic elements of the 1899 September Agreement were maintained. There were,

---

[1] In subsequent years, similar agreements were signed in the other Nordic countries: in Norway (1935), in Sweden (1938, the Saltsjöbaden agreement, see above), and in Finland (1944) (Einhorn and Logue 2003: 287).

however, some attempts by the trade unions to limit the 'managerial prerogatives' as they were guaranteed by the agreement. In 1947 the unions, in the context of the introduction of co-determination structures in Danish enterprises, unsuccessfully tried to push through a reduction in employers' ability to hire and fire. They were more successful a few years later in 1960, when in a revision of the September Agreement, the unions obtained the inclusion of a clause protecting workers from arbitrary dismissal (Emmenegger 2009: 137).

In subsequent years (1964 and 1968), the Danish unions tried again to make advances in curtailing the managerial prerogatives of private companies and institute some form of economic democracy. The adoption of stricter employment protection legislation (EPL), however, featured less prominently in their agenda than was the case with their Swedish counterparts. Instead, the emphasis was on joint decision-making within private companies. According to Emmenegger, this was due to the different structure of the Danish labour movement, often dominated by craft unions. In Sweden, the labour movement represented mostly blue-collar workers, who had made stricter EPL a priority, because protection against dismissal was particularly important for easily replaceable low-skill workers. For the more skilled members of the dominant Danish craft unions, EPL was less important (Emmenegger 2009: 146). In the end, even though they managed to obtain some concessions, the Danish unions were largely unsuccessful in developing democratic decision-making practices within private companies.

Responding to the employment crisis

Like in other countries, Denmark saw the emergence of serious labour market problems in the 1970s. Unemployment, which had remained around 1 per cent until the early 1970s, jumped to over 7 per cent by 1978. Unlike in Sweden, job losses in Denmark were not absorbed by ALMPs and resulted in open unemployment. The initial response of the Danish Social Democratic-led government to the employment crisis was rather passive (Benner and Vad 2000: 436; Thorgaard and Vinther 2007) and produced poor results as the unemployment rate continued its climb until 1983 when it reached 10 per cent.

An active policy was not on the agenda in the early days of the crisis. Instead, Denmark turned to typically 'continental' solutions to employment problems. In 1978–9 an early retirement scheme was adopted (Benner and Vad 2000: 437). This made Denmark an outlier in the Nordic world and more similar to continental European welfare states (Ebbinghaus 2006).

Towards the end of the 1970s, some programmes labelled as active were introduced by the Social Democratic-led government (1978–9). These consisted of standard measures such as help with job search, training, and support for those wishing to become self-employed. The system put in place at the time, however, remained geared towards the coverage of temporary unemployment and was considered inadequate to deal with the kind of massive long-term unemployment the country experienced in the 1980s and early 1990s. The system also proved rather ineffective (ILO 1999).

Amid public discontent for the failure to tackle economic problems effectively, the Social Democrats resigned in 1982 and were replaced by a coalition government headed by the Conservative Party, which remained in power with different coalition partners until 1993. The rate of unemployment declined in the second half of the 1980s but rose again with the recession of the early 1990s, reaching a staggering 12 per cent in 1993. Despite this development, during the decade of Conservative government, not much was changed in the field of ALMPs. The system set up by the Social Democrats was essentially kept in place with minor adjustments, for example, putting more emphasis on access to education for the unemployed (Madsen 2002). There were also attempts by Conservatives to move in the direction of American-style workfare programmes, but these failed to gain enough support to be passed by Parliament (Torfing 1999).

In reality, labour market policy experienced a 'continental drift'. The public employment service set up in 1969 remained marginal as only 15 per cent of external vacancies were mediated there (Esping-Andersen and Korpi 1987: 59). In addition to early retirement, Denmark used to run a job offer scheme. This allowed unemployed people whose right to unemployment benefit had expired to be employed in the public sector for a period of time sufficient to rebuild entitlement to unemployment benefit. In this way, it was possible to remain trapped in a cycle of unemployment benefit or job offer scheme for rather long periods of time. According to Esping-Andersen and Korpi writing in the late 1980s, ALMP in Denmark played a marginal role in comparison to other Scandinavian countries (Esping-Andersen and Korpi 1987: 59).

The activation turn

Things were to change dramatically with the return to power of the Social Democrats in 1993, which resulted in a series of reforms that transformed the Danish system of unemployment compensation. The 1994 reform removed the possibility of re-gaining entitlement to unemployment insurance through participation in labour market programmes. It also set a 7-year limit to unemployment benefit. This period was subdivided in two phases: first, a passive period of 4 years and then an active period of 3 years. Work availability requirements were also strengthened and individual action plans were introduced (Madsen 2002; Kvist et al. 2008: 243). Some early retirement measures were also abandoned in 1994. In addition, the reform introduced the decentralization of employment services, making it possible for labour offices at regional level to develop labour market programmes suitable for their area.

The 1994 reform clearly signalled a change of direction in Danish labour market policy. It contained many of the features that have since become typical of activation systems throughout OECD countries. At the same time, with a 7-year entitlement period to unemployment benefit, pressure to re-- enter the labour market remained relatively low compared to current stand- ards. The reform was based on the recommendations made by a tripartite outfit known as the Zeuthen committee, consisting mostly of representatives of both the trade unions and employer organizations. The social partners obtained important concessions, such as an important role in the implemen- tation of labour market measures. At the same time, however, they agreed to reorient unemployment policy in the direction of activation (Kvist et al. 2008: 245).

Subsequent reforms further strengthened work incentives and activation elements. The duration of the entitlement period was reduced first to 5 years (1996) and then again to 4 years (1998). The 'passive' period was also shortened to 2 years and to 6 months for unemployed people younger than 25. After this period, claimants had both a right and an obligation to partici- pate in a labour market programme.

The 1998 reform meant a further acceleration of the trend towards acti- vation. First, policy for unemployed youth took a strong step towards stronger work incentives and investment in human capital. Measures adopted included a 6-month limit on standard unemployment benefit for the under 25 and the obligation to participate in training for 18 months, with a benefit equal to 50 per cent of the standard unemployment benefit. Second, with the adoption of a 'law on active social policy', the principle of activation was extended to social assistance claimants (Kvist et al. 2008: 241–3). Like in past reforms, together with incentive-strengthening measures, more supportive instru- ments were also adopted. This is the case of a programme known as flexjobs, which subsidizes up to two-thirds of labour costs for disabled people without time limits (Hohnen 2000).

Meanwhile, the labour market situation had improved dramatically. The unemployment rate, which had peaked at over 12 per cent in 1993, was down to 4 per cent in 2001. Some of the most costly labour market measures were discontinued, no longer deemed necessary in the more favourable labour market context.[2] A more favourable labour market and the election of a new

---

[2] This was the case, for example, of an ingenious scheme leave or job rotation scheme. People in employment were given the opportunity to take paid leave for training purposes or parental leave or for a sabbatical (the latter possibility was quite quickly abolished). Employers were encouraged to

Liberal–Conservative coalition government in 2002 did not change the over-all policy orientation which continued to be characterized by a strong prefer-ence for activation. Reforms adopted by the Liberal–Conservative government have continued to strengthen work incentives.

The Netherlands

Of the countries studied in this chapter, the Netherlands is the one that experienced the most dramatic turnaround in terms of labour market policy and outcomes. In the early 1980s, the country came to be considered 'the sick man in Europe', a metaphor which captured both its poor economic and labour market performance and the fact that large parts of the working age population were dependent on sickness or disability benefit. This dismal situation was the result of a very generous Bismarckian welfare state and a severely troubled economy plagued by wage drift problems. By the late 1990s, the Netherlands had managed to profoundly transform its labour market and welfare regime. Labour market indicators had likewise improved dramatically. No longer seen as a sick man, the country suddenly became a model of successful adaptation for other continental European countries (Visser and Hemerijck 1997).

The process has continued through the 2000s. Overall, one can identify a rapid succession of sometimes radical reforms, which succeeded in transform-ing an essentially passive income replacement system into an activation machine. Of course, the excellent labour market performance achieved in the late 1990s and early 2000s cannot be ascribed to activation only. At the same time, it is difficult to imagine that it would have taken place in the context of the generous and easily accessible system of income replacement benefits prevailing in the early 1980s.

The post-war model

Throughout the post-war years, the Netherlands had built a classic, generous, and easily accessible system of income replacement. Based on the social insurance principle, the welfare state provided essentially passive earnings-related benefits. Before the reforms of the 1980s, unemployment insurance provided earnings-related benefits for 6 months with a replacement rate of 80 per cent. A lower but not means-tested benefit was available for another

hire an unemployed person who replaced the employee while on leave, thus limiting the risk of long-term exclusion from the labour market in the context of high unemployment.

2 years, and if still jobless after this period of time, a person was entitled to social assistance (Hemerijck et al. 2000).

Conditions were particularly favourable to beneficiaries of invalidity benefits. The replacement rate was of 80 per cent. Access to benefits was possible also for relatively minor disabilities. An impairment that reduced work capacity by 15 per cent was sufficient to open the access to a partial disability benefits.[3] Theoretically, those on partial invalidity benefit were required to look for jobs corresponding to their remaining work capacity and, if jobless, to claim unemployment benefit. However, the law also said that labour market prospects had to be taken into account when awarding an invalidity pension. In practice, those who were unemployed were generally not requested to register with the employment service in order to claim unemployment benefit. A full invalidity pension was provided instead. As a result, partial benefits were very seldom awarded (in 1980, 85 per cent of beneficiaries were on full benefits). Finally, the benefit was made even more attractive by collective agreements between the social partners. Often, such agreements contained provision for a top-up of state invalidity benefit so that for 2 years the replacement rate would be 100 per cent (van Oorschoot and Boos 2001; Hogelund 2003: 80).

Another distinctive feature of the Dutch post-war labour market regime was the strong degree of state involvement in wage formation. Between 1945 and 1963, collective agreements had to be approved by a board where the Ministry of Social Affairs played a very influential role. The system collapsed in the late 1960s under the pressure of tight labour markets and the resulting upward pressure on wages. This gave way to a series of wage hikes that were to make the country's economy vulnerable in the following years (Hemerijck et al. 2000).

Responding to the employment crisis

In the aftermath of the oil shock, there were a few attempts to develop an incomes policy, aiming at containing wage growth. These were generally unsuccessful. Instead, in the context of high inflation, collective agreements increasingly included automatic indexation clauses. In 1974, the state did the same and public sector salaries and social security benefits were in turn linked to private sector wage increases. The result was a situation in which high inflation, private sector wages, and state expenditures were spiralling out of control, the different trends mutually supporting each other (Hemerijck et al. 2000: 211–12).

---

[3] This is a rather low threshold in international comparisons. Most countries apply a reduced work capacity threshold of around 40–50 per cent (Hogelund 2003: 80).

The general economic climate combined with wage drift had a major impact on employment. Total employment dropped from 62 per cent of the working age population in 1970 to 51 per cent in 1984. At the same time, the numbers of those depending on the welfare state soared. The unemployment rate peaked at 11 per cent in 1983. More pressing was the hike in disability benefit recipiency. In 1970, 4.5 per cent of the labour force received disability benefit. By 1985 the proportion had climbed to 13.2 per cent: a figure unequalled elsewhere in Europe. In that year, a third of the Dutch labour force was dependent on welfare benefits (Høgelund 2003: 69).

Of course, all this had a major impact on public spending. In 1982, with 31 per cent of GDP assigned to the welfare state, the Netherlands was the biggest spender on social programmes among OECD countries. It was this combination of high wages, low employment, and high public spending that prompted policy-makers to radically rethink the post-war model.

According to many commentators, the turning point in recent Dutch economic history was the Wassenaar agreement, reached by the employers and the unions in 1982. The agreement came a few days after a newly elected government, led by the Christian Democratic Prime Minister Ruud Lubbers, declared that it would have dealt with the problem of high wage costs, with or without the approval of the social partners. In Wassenaar, the unions agreed to renounce automatic price indexation of wages and to reduce working hours in a cost-neutral way. The recommendation issued in Wassenaar proved influential. By 1985, automatic price indexation had virtually disappeared. At the same time, reductions in working hours were adopted in a majority of the new sectoral agreements (Hemerijck et al. 2000).

In parallel, the government was working towards reducing public spending by retrenching the over-generous welfare state. In 1983 and 1984, the minimum wage, which serves as a basis for the calculation of flat rate welfare benefits (such as pensions and social assistance), was first frozen and then reduced in nominal terms. In addition, the link between private sector wages and the minimum wage (and thus also welfare benefits) was suspended (Hemerijck et al. 2000). In 1985, benefit replacement rates for unemployment, sickness, and disability were reduced from 80 to 70per cent. In 1987, access to unemployment benefit was made more difficult, and its duration shortened. Invalidity benefit, given the widespread misuse of the scheme made in previous years, was also an obvious target for retrenchment. In addition, partially disabled people without a job, in most cases, were now to rely on a partial invalidity pension and claim unemployment benefit (if eligible) for their remaining work capacity. In 1987, some measures aimed at facilitating access to employment for disability benefit recipients were also adopted. These had a limited impact and were broadly regarded as insufficient (Høgelund 2003: 82–3).

In the early 1990s, the Lubbers government began to adopt elements of ALMP. Increasingly, high levels of inactivity came to be identified as the main culprit of the country's economic difficulties. A mechanism linking benefit indexation to the employment rate was also introduced (Hemerijck et al. 2000). The dominant flavour of government policy, however, remained retrenchment.

This reorientation of what had mostly been up until this point a passive Dutch welfare state took place in various areas. First, contribution exemptions for employers hiring long-term unemployed people were introduced in 1986. Second, employment services were reorganized in 1990, with a view to improve their efficiency. Third, the government changed the eligibility rules for unemployed youth in 1991 and introduced a 6 months' time limit on cash benefits followed by participation in a job experience scheme (Spies and Van Berkel 2001; Sol et al. 2008). Fourth, invalidity insurance was subjected to a rapid succession of reforms aiming at reducing the number of recipients. The 1992 reform introduced a bonus (malus) system for employers who hired (laid-off) disabled people. One year later, a new reform restricted the definition of disability used to determine eligibility for the scheme. In addition, benefit entitlement for those below 50 years of age was reassessed with the result that in 50 per cent of cases, the benefit was either suppressed or reduced. Finally, a time limit of up to 6 years was imposed on earnings-related invalidity benefits. After this period of time, a flat rate 'follow-up' benefit is paid (van Oorschot and Boos 2001). These more radical measures managed to stabilize the number of benefit recipients. However, the tools used had more to do with retrenchment than with active social policy. This was the perception of voters who, in 1994, inflicted serious losses on Lubbers' Christian Democratic Party (Hemerijck et al. 2000).

The activation turn

The Social Democrats (PvdA) emerged from the 1994 elections as the largest party, and its leader, Wim Kok, became the new Prime Minister, supported by a so-called 'Purple coalition' (Social Democrats and Liberals). The new government position in relation to retrenchment was to avoid reducing benefit levels and duration, shifting the emphasis in the government discourse from retrenchment to promoting employment. 'Jobs, jobs and more jobs' became Kok's famous motto (Hemerijck et al. 2000: 223). In reality, some retrenchment measures were adopted (Green-Pedersen 2002). However, activation became the leitmotif of social policy.

A job creation programme in the public sector for young and long-term unemployed people (known as Melkert jobs, after the name of the PvdA Minister of Social Affairs) was launched in 1994 (the programme was later discontinued in 1998). In 1998 activation was made compulsory for the young and long-term unemployed who could be assigned to one of different options such as training, subsidized employment, or social activation for those deemed unlikely to re-enter the labour market (Spies and van Berkel 2001).

In 2001, employment services were reorganized and replaced by one-stop shops called 'Centre for Work and Incomes'. At the same time, a competitive market for privately provided employment services was established (Sol et al. 2008). The process of reforming disability insurance continued. In 1998, a system of differentiated contribution rates was introduced. Under previous legislation, all employers paid the same contribution rate. Under the new system, contribution rates were related to 'risk' or to the proportion of employees experiencing disability. A new law on the reintegration of disabled people was also adopted in the same year (van Oorschot and Boos 2001). By the year 2000, the Netherlands had managed, through a series of reforms adopted in rapid succession, to transform one of the most generous and less demanding disability schemes in Europe to one of the most work-oriented ones. In its assessment of invalidity insurance reform, the OECD singled out the Netherlands as the country among those surveyed that had done more to reduce the income compensation function while at the same time strengthening reintegration efforts (OECD 2003).

In 2002, the Christian Democrats were back in power and ruled the country first in coalition with the Liberals and, since 2006, with the Social Democrats. Labour market policy continued on the course of an ever stronger work orientation, with a strong inclination to experiment with new tools. In 2004, a reform of the law on social assistance replaced the notion of 'suitable work' with the one of 'generally accepted work'. In practical terms this meant that the recipient's qualifications or previous work history was now disregarded. The new law also reduced the exemptions from the obligation to seek employment (Sol et al. 2008).

One scheme after the other, the whole of the Dutch social security system was transformed from a typical Bismarckian, income guarantee welfare regime to one of the clearest exemplar of active labour market policy. The road taken was clearly characterized by a combination of retrenchment in cash benefits and the expansion of services. Spending on ALMP increased only slightly between 1985 and 2005, but the unemployment rate nearly halved over the same time period, showing a considerable increase in the efforts made to re-integrate non-working people into the labour market.

Germany

The setup of the German welfare state contains elements that are likely both to be conducive to active social policy and to act as obstacles. A high level of involvement of the social partners in labour market regulation and vocational training may provide a fertile ground for developing the win-win solutions to labour market problems that go under the rubric of active social policy. At the same time, the strong emphasis on social insurance and the 'equivalence principle' may constitute an obstacle. The 'equivalence principle' states that social insurance should provide benefits that are related (equivalent) to the contribution effort made while employed. Under these conditions, it is obviously problematic to subject the receipt of unemployment insurance benefit to an additional requirement such as accepting a job offer or to participate in a labour market programme. In addition, entitlements to social insurance benefits are considered as equivalent to property rights by the Constitutional court (Eichhorst et al. 2008: 39). More in general, the conservative, status-preserving ethos embodied in German social institutions sits awkwardly with the flexibility that an activating welfare state requires from its beneficiaries.

These factors help to explain why labour market policy remained rather passive in Germany until recently. However, in the late 1990s and early 2000s, the country clearly embarked on the activation turn, epitomized by the Hartz reforms in 2003–4. The activation turn started under the Christian Democrats, but it was pushed through by the Social Democrats under Chancellor Schröder. During his tenure in office, the Chancellor made the reform of labour market policy a priority, and gradually moved away from the traditional corporatist approach to labour market regulation to impose measures inspired by countries like Britain, Denmark, and the Netherlands (Seeleib-Kaiser and Fleckenstein 2007). The shift was not easy. It took a series of successive initiatives and reforms. The result is a system of ALMP that is similar to that of activation pioneers like the UK and Denmark.

Antecedents: self-regulation, social insurance, and the dual vocational training system

Germany is a country with a long history of social policy-making, with decisions made towards the end of the nineteenth century having left a clear legacy to the present day. When looking for the antecedents of active social policy, self-regulation by labour market actors, the social insurance system, and vocational training are obvious candidates. All these policies were pioneered in Bismarck's Germany. They were adopted in the context of an authoritarian regime, which had to resist a major challenge mounted by the labour movement. This aspect helps to explain the choices that were made at the time and particularly the involvement of labour market actors in the administration of the relevant schemes.

Social insurance schemes were adopted in the 1880s and had a clear objective: to gain the political allegiance of workers. At the same time, Bismarck passed legislation that outlawed the political organization of workers, be it within the framework or political parties or trade unions (Alber 1987). The first step was the establishment of local sickness funds in 1883 administered by representatives of workers (subsequently, when they became legal, of the trade unions) jointly with representatives of employers. Sickness funds constituted the first instance of labour co-optation in *Selbstverwaltung*. It provided the movement with some organizational capability from a very early stage and initiated the process of integrating workers into the economic system (Manow 1997). Social insurance developed rapidly with the adoption of invalidity in 1884 and of old age pensions in 1889. Unemployment insurance, however, was not introduced until after World War I in 1927.

Self-regulation played an important role also in the provision of vocational training with the establishment of the well-known dual system. In Germany, training is provided by employers at the workplace, with trainees simultaneously attending public professional school. The system, which is largely considered a key contributor to German industrial success, dates back to the heydays of modern Germany and to the survival of pre-modern corporatist institutions. In Imperial Germany, the guilds were allowed to regulate training and certification in their professions. Legislation adopted in 1897 upheld this principle and granted professional associations extensive powers in the field of vocational training. According to Kathleen Thelen this choice was dictated by political strategy. The authoritarian Imperial regime was challenged by the rising labour movement. Artisans were seen as a key political ally in resisting this challenge. As a result, it was important for the rulers of the time to gain their allegiance. To preserve the key role in the provision of training was an effective way to do that. At the time, this move was opposed by the Social Democrats (Thelen 2004: 38–42). The system survived throughout the twentieth century, being of course modernized and standardized, but without losing its distinctive feature of being based on the provision of training in the workplace.

The post-war model

Many of these elements were essentially kept in place after World War II. Employment protection legislation, however, was maintained, and social insurance was expanded. In the case of old age pensions, for instance, the 1957 reform is widely regarded as a major watershed in the role played by social insurance in Germany. On that occasion, the benefit was increased from subsistence level to an amount meant to constitute the main form of income for retired people. The link with work was also strengthened by increasing the contributory character of the scheme and by indexing benefits on wage changes (Alber 1987: 22; Clasen 1997). The basic institutional structure, with joint employer and union management, and the social insurance character of the scheme were not changed. A similar reform had been adopted only a few years earlier in the unemployment insurance.

With regard to ALMP, an important step was the adoption of the 1969 Employment Promotion Act (*Arbeitsförderungsgesetz*). The law was adopted by the short-lived first 'Grand coalition government' in Germany's post-war history. The CDU–SPD coalition, led by the Christian Democrats, lasted only 3 years (1966–9), but played an important role in shaping post-war labour market policy. The coalition came against the backdrop of the 1966–7 recession, after a row over the budget broke out between the CDU and the FDP, the parties that formed the previous government. Its approach to social and economic policy anticipated many of the themes that have been popularized by political leaders in the 2000s. According to Alber:

> To combat the economic crisis, the new government intended to shift public expenditure from social consumption to social investment. Various transfer payments were curbed, and for the first time, educational issues were given priority. . . . As a first step towards a more active labour market policy, the competence of the unemployment insurance scheme was extended to include the promotion of vocational training. (Alber 1987: 14)

The law was largely based on a proposal prepared by the SPD in 1966, at the time in opposition. It emphasized a new, preventative role for labour market policy, based on the adjustment of the workforce skills to technological change. The new law instituted the Federal Institute of Labour (*Bundesanstalt für Arbeit*) responsible for unemployment compensation insurance, but also for continuing education, re-training, employment services for the disabled, job creation programmes, and training (Frerich and Frey 1993). At the same time, a new law on vocational training was adopted, which significantly consolidated the system put in place 70 years earlier (Thelen 2004: 241).

Responding the employment crises in the 1970s and 1980s

The centre-left SPD–FDP government in charge during the 1970s responded to the crisis first with traditional Keynesian tools, such as public investments. These efforts, however, were soon frustrated by the non-cooperative behaviour of the independent central bank, the Bundesbank, which at the same time increased interest rates, making it impossible for the government to sustain a policy based on fiscal expansion (Manow and Seils 2000; Scharpf 1991). As a result, the government was forced to turn towards austerity and adopt cuts in public expenditure across the board.

Even though Germany did not embrace Keynesianism as enthusiastically as some other Western European countries (see Hall 1989), its generous social insurance-based welfare state contained several 'automatic stabilizers' which de facto played an important role in sustaining demand, but at the same time reducing labour supply. One key element in this process was the availability of several early retirement options, some of which had been introduced just before the 1970s crisis. Early retirement was possible without benefit reductions after the age of 63. In addition, workers experiencing health problems could apply for invalidity benefit and have their claim examined also on the basis of the current labour market situation. Finally, for people on unemployment benefit, early retirement was possible at the age of 60. This resulted in the development of a practice known as the '59er-Regel'. This meant that as excess workers turned 59, they were laid off and would spend 1 year on unemployment benefit and then move onto early retirement at the age of 60. To make this option attractive for employees, their former employer would typically top up their unemployment benefit to the level of the former salary (Ebbinghaus 2006: 134). Access to early retirement was further extended in 1987 when the entitlement period to unemployment benefit was extended from 12 to 32 months for people older than 54. The result was labour market exit became possible at the age of 57, at virtually no loss for the employee (Manow and Seils 2000: 281).

Active labour market policy did not feature prominently in the early crisis years, particularly under Willy Brandt's Chancellorship (1969–74). Things were to change in the following years. With unemployment rising, Germany turned to ALMPs in the second half of the 1970s. The type of policy developed, however, was clearly oriented towards reducing open unemployment rather than promoting re-entry into the labour market. Between 1975 and 1977 about 190,000 jobs were created through public employment programmes, mostly in construction but also in the social services. These measures were based on the Employment Promotion Act of 1969. In a development reminiscent of the Swedish story, the objective of this law shifted from the general upskilling of the workforce to a tool aimed at reducing open unemployment. The experience, however, was rather short-lived. Budgetary problems and the adoption of a restrictive approach to budgetary policy resulted in a rapid decline in the size of these employment programmes. The number of participants went down from 51,000 in 1978 to only 29,000 in 1982, marking the end of the period of Social Democratic-led government in Germany (Manow and Seils 2000: 273; Seeleib-Kaiser et al. 2008: 43).

Active labour market policies were back with the return to power of the Christian democrats. The Kohl government elected in 1982 expanded ALMPs in the context of a 'qualification offensive' based on various labour market and training programmes. Between 1982 and 1987, the total number of participants in such programmes rose from 555,000 to 1.4 million (Seeleib-Kaiser et al. 2008: 43). During the second half of the 1980s, Germany had yearly expenses on ALMP of around 1 per cent of GDP, which was above the OECD average. The figure was slightly up from the first half of the decade (around 0.7 per cent of GDP, see Clasen 2005, Table 4.5). But how was this money spent? OECD figures provide a breakdown by broad types of ALMPs. In the second half of the 1980s, German ALMPs were strongly based on training and placement services. Job creation programmes played a smaller role.

Things were to change with unification in 1991. As former GDR companies underwent restructuring, redundant workers were given access to early retirement and labour market programmes, which again had the objective of limiting open unemployment. Spending on ALMPs peaked at 1.8 per cent of GDP in 1992. At that time, however, the lion's share of active spending went to job creation programme (Manow and Seils 2000: 293; Clasen 2005: 61–2). The move was effective in reducing open unemployment. According to estimates, of the 4 million workers who had lost their jobs during the first 2 years after unification, about 3 million did not end up on unemployment benefit (Clasen 2005: 68). This policy, however, was not able to prevent a massive surge in the unemployment rate following the recession of the 1990s.

The activation turn

It is generally assumed that Germany embraced the activation paradigm with the Hartz reform, which came into force in 2005. In fact, measures going in this direction were clearly adopted throughout the 1990s. Unemployment benefit was made less attractive through a series of retrenchment measures, targeting in particular long-term unemployment benefit (*Arbeitslosenhilfe*). The most important development was arguably the 1996 reform of the Employment Promotion Act. On that occasion, long-term unemployment benefit was further reduced and stricter availability and job search requirements were introduced. According to some commentators, this reform signalled a fundamental paradigm shift in the German approach to labour market problems. As a result of the reform, unemployed people were expected to accept job offers even if earnings and qualifications were lower than in their former job (Clasen 2005: 69).

These measures did not succeed in preventing further deterioration of labour market conditions in the country, with unemployment continuously rising until 1998. As a result, labour market problems were at the top of the agenda of the newly elected Social Democratic government lead by Chancellor Gerhard Schröder. The government turned initially to an ad hoc corporatist type of outfit, known as the Alliance for Jobs, which included representatives of employers and the unions. However, conflicting demands made the Alliance unable to produce adequate policy proposals. Employers were keen on wage restraint agreements, while the unions refused to include this item and wanted to focus the proposals on vocational training. Because of its inability to produce a proposal for a substantial labour market policy reform, the Alliance was eventually discontinued in 2003 (Aust and Bönker 2004). Nonetheless, several ideas that were introduced by this outfit, such as the motto '*foerdern und fordern*' (promote and oblige) were to become prominent in the following years (Clasen 2005).

The activation turn was further pursued with the adoption of the so-called Job Aqtiv Act in 2001, making Germany move in the direction of countries like Denmark or the UK. The reform included several of the measures that one finds in the standard activation toolbox: stricter monitoring of job search, the profiling of jobless people, reintegration contracts, and wage subsidies (Clasen 2005: 72). According to some commentators, this reform was the result of EU influence, notably through the European Employment strategy (Büchs and Friedrichs 2005).

These changes, however, were not regarded as going far enough by the Schröder government. In fact, only a few months after the adoption of the Job Aqtiv Act, a new commission was set up and given the task to make proposals for the modernization of labour market policy. The commission was headed by Peter Hartz, a former manager at Volkswagen, and its members had been selected directly by the Chancellor office. Notably different from past similar exercises, the commission did not include representatives of the main peak labour market associations, the BDA (employers) and the DGB (unions) (Aust and Bönker 2004: 9). The Hartz commission presented its report shortly before the October 2002 general election.

The proposals included several measures, ranging from support to unemployed people who want to set up their own business, to the creation of a 'personal service agency', a temporary placement service for unemployment people. However, the most visible and controversial proposal was the merger of long-term unemployment benefit and social assistance (the so-called Hartz IV reform). Under the previous system, jobless working age able-bodied people where covered by three different arrangements: unemployment insurance for those unemployed for less than 12 months, unemployment assistance for the long-term unemployed, and social assistance for those who were not entitled to unemployment benefit (i.e., because of a missing or insufficient contribution record). The system was widely regarded as inefficient. As a result, in an effort to improve access to labour market and placement services, a new benefit called Unemployment Benefit II was introduced. It replaced the former unemployment assistance benefit and social assistance for those deemed capable of working. The level of the new benefit reflected the amounts paid by social assistance, in most cases lower than what had been available before through unemployment assistance benefit (Fleckenstein 2008).

The various measures, though extremely unpopular with the workers' wing of the party, were implemented in the following years. This was done in the context of a programme for reform know as Agenda 2010, announced in early 2003, after the Social Democrats had been returned to power by a very narrow victory in the October 2002 election (Hassel and Schiller 2010). The reform proved very unpopular and certainly contributed to Gerhard Schröder's fall in 2006. If, like his peers in other European countries, Schröder wanted to use activation as a credit-claiming device, clearly something went wrong.

In a few years, Germany shifted from an essentially passive welfare state, emphasizing early retirement policy and using labour market programmes to reduce open unemployment, to one that aims to activate jobless people. The shift has certainly been guided by the persistence of problems, as the rate of unemployment remained high throughout the period during which reforms were adopted. Policy, however, was probably also guided by the belief, held by SPD modernizers, that activation was the right orientation for German labour market policy. It would otherwise be rather difficult to explain why reforms were adopted in such a rapid succession.

France

France is a typical continental welfare state, with a well-developed social insurance system of Bismarckian inspiration providing high cash benefits to those who are unable to work. As seen in Chapter 3, this qualification concerns most sectors of the French welfare state, with the exception of family policy, which, due to its relatively strong emphasis on services, puts France closer to the Nordic countries. In relation to active labour market policy, France stands out for being a latecomer in embracing the activation paradigm, a reorientation that took place in the mid-2000s. This is not to say that France did not invest in ALMPs before. On the contrary, the country is a big spender on this function of social policy, but most of the programmes are not oriented towards getting jobless people back into employment. Rather, in many cases, policy has aimed at providing an alternative occupation to market employment.

Like in other countries, the reorientation towards activation in France faced a number of obstacles. Among these, a crucial one is the high degree of involvement of the social partners in the management of social insurance schemes (Bonoli and Palier 1997; Palier 2002). Social security is run by funds administered by representatives of employers and employees, according to the parity principle (equal representation for each of the two actors). Throughout the post-war years, attempts by the government to strengthen the link between social security and the promotion of access to employment have often been frustrated by the resistance of the social partners. This situation changed only in the mid-2000s.

The post-war model

The modern French welfare state was institutionalized in the immediate post-war years. The blueprint for it was provided by a report by Pierre Laroque, a senior civil servant. The key element of the plan was the development of a 'general social security system' (*Régime général*) for private sector employees only, providing coverage against old age, sickness, and family benefits. Other occupational groups, some of whom were already covered by their own social security arrangements, were expected to join the general regime, which would then become a universal system. Crucially, the management of the system was assigned to the social partners. The trade unions, very influential at the end of World War II, clearly favoured this model over direct control by the state (Palier 2002: 88).

Unemployment insurance was not part of the system put in place after the war. A scheme known as UNEDIC was introduced in 1958 through a collective agreement between the social partners, a setup that provided unions and employers with even more autonomy than was the case within the social security system. Even though the social security system was managed by the social partners, the key parameters of the system such as contribution rates and benefit levels were set by parliament. In contrast, unemployment insurance was entirely under the jurisdiction of the social partners (Clegg 2005: 157).

This peculiar institutional setup was to prove a formidable obstacle to the introduction of an ALMP. In 1963, the Gaullist government embarked on a reform of unemployment policy that would have facilitated access to re-training for unemployed people. This proposal encountered nonetheless the strong opposition of the trade unions, who feared increased state intervention in the management of unemployment insurance (UNEDIC). The result was a watered-down version of the initial proposal. The episode highlighted the tension between an insurance-based unemployment compensations system run by the social partners and a public policy objective: the upskilling of unemployed people in the context of labour shortage.

A few years later, plans to set up a national employment office, which would have been responsible for unemployment benefit and placement services, were also rejected by the social partners, in particular by the trade unions. For this reason the government set up a state agency responsible for placement only (ANPE). The result was a division between the two key functions of unemployment policy: compensation and placement, which was to provide a constant source of tension in the following years. The social partners' and particularly the trade unions' narrow understanding of unemployment compensation as an insurance scheme severely limited the scope for injecting active and training measures into unemployment policy (Clegg 2005: 176–9).

Responding to the crisis

France's response to the employment crisis of late 1970s and early 1980s can be qualified as the textbook version of the labour reduction route. It consisted essentially of the provision of easily accessible early retirement. Schemes allowing older unemployed people to leave the labour market had been put in place in the 1960s.[4] These were expanded in response to the rise in unemployment in the second half of the 1970s. In 1979, the age limit to be eligible for early retirement was lowered from 60 to 55. In 1981, François Mitterrand, the leader of the Socialist Party, was elected President. Among the first series of measures meant to deal with mounting unemployment was a reduction of the age of retirement from 65 to 60. The result of these (and other) measures was a massive reduction in the employment rate of the age group 55–64 years, from 74 per cent in 1970 to 47 per cent in 1985. The same years also saw the reinforcement of employment protection legislation (Emmenegger 2009; Nickell 2003).

In parallel France developed instruments labelled as 'active labour market policy'. Starting from the mid-1980s, various tools sometimes targeted on different groups were adopted in a rapid succession. In general, their objective was 'occupation', in other words, providing an alternative to market employment to jobless people rather than labour market re-entry. Typically, much emphasis was put on the notion of 'social insertion' or the possibility of participating in society without being in paid employment (Dufour et al. 2003; Barbier and Fargion 2004). In practical terms, these measures consisted of subsidized temporary jobs in the public or in the non-profit-making private sector.

The development of French ALMP started in 1984 with the adoption of the Travaux d'utilité publique (TUC) for jobless youth by the Socialist

[4] For example, in 1963 a fund providing up to 90 per cent wage replacement for workers over 60 years old who were laid off as a result of industrial restructuring was introduced (Joint-Lambert 1994: 192).

government. These were soon complemented in 1986 with the *Programmes d'insertion locale* (PIL) targeted on long-term unemployed and introduced by a Gaullist government. By 1989, these were replaced by *Contrats emploi-solidarité* (CES). In 1988, the Socialist government back in power introduced a general means-tested benefit (*Revenu minimum d'insertion* (RMI)), which theoretically included an activation component in the shape of an insertion contract signed between the beneficiary and the authorities. In fact, as extensive evaluation of this programme has shown, its ability to move beneficiaries into the labour market remained extremely limited (Palier 2002: 302–3). During these years, the French approach to activation was characterized by a strong emphasis on occupation, accompanied by a strong rhetoric of social inclusion, or 'insertion'. Despite this rhetoric, little effort was made to move jobless people back into the labour market.

Other tools aimed at facilitating access to training for jobless people. In 1988, for example, a training benefit for unemployed people was introduced (*Allocation formation-reclassement* (AFR)). The scheme was available to unemployed people receiving the insurance benefit, financed jointly by UNEDIC and the government, and administered by ANPE (Joint-Lambert 1994: 240). Its role remained nonetheless marginal. In 1992 some 88,000 unemployed people were receiving AFR, around 4 per cent of the 2.3 million unemployed person at the time.[5] A second avenue followed by French policy-makers consisted in reducing contributions payable on low wage jobs. Since 1993, employers' contributions on jobs paying up to 1.3 times the minimum wage have been reduced on a sliding scale (OECD 2003: 124).

This trajectory was confirmed by the Socialist government of the late 1990s (1997–2002). While the rest of Europe embraced the activation paradigm in labour market policy, France remained committed to its own tradition in employment policy: labour reduction and social insertion. Beside the well-known law reducing the number of weekly working hours to 35, the government introduced new job creation programmes aimed at the young by subsidizing jobs in non-commercial sectors (state and associations) for up to 5 years (Clegg 2005: 222). The objective of the programme was to see the organization providing the job to pursue the employment relationship after the end of the subsidized period. This, however, did not happen as often as expected (Simonin et al. 2002).

While the Socialists stuck to the traditional French post-1970s approach well into the1990s, their right-of-centre successors were tempted by the liberal route of deregulation. France has a rather rigid labour market, with a high degree of legislative and contractual regulation of both hiring and firing and

---

[5] Figures concerning AFR recipiency are from Clegg (2005: 228; total unemployment from OECD *Stat*.

wage formation (Bonoli 2003). Right-of-centre governments took several initiatives aimed at reducing employment protection at the margin. Rather than reduce protection for core workers, new contracts have been introduced. Examples are the introduction in 1986 of the possibility of hiring on temporary contracts for up to 2 years, a contract type that has become the main source of job creation (Palier and Thelen 2010). On occasion, attempts at deregulation were frustrated by mass protest. Edouard Balladur, a Gaullist Prime Minister, was forced to withdraw plans to introduce an employment contract for young people, paying less than the statutory minimum wage in 1993. The same fate awaited a similar proposal made by another Gaullist Prime Minister, Dominique de Villepin in 2006.

The activation turn

By the early 2000s the idea of a more active unemployment policy had made its in-roads among French policy-makers. Diverse actors such as the Socialist Labour Minister Martine Aubry and the employer's association both insisted on the need to emphasize labour market re-entry as a key objective of unemployment policy (Clegg 2005: 254–9). Steps in this direction, however, were made difficult by the ever present tension between the government and the social partners each responsible for one of the two functions of unemployment policy (compensation and placement). For example, the Socialist government, employers, and the unions had to negotiate for over a year to agree on a new benefit, known as *Plan d'aide au retrour à l'emploi* (PARE). Its objective was to put more emphasis on job search for people on unemployment benefit. PARE included some of the standard tools of activation, an individualized action plan, an obligation to effectively seek employment and sanctions. Given the complex structure of French unemployment policy, PARE had to be introduced through an agreement between the social partners and the state. Its implementation, in turn, depended on the collaboration of the relevant institutional actors (Clegg 2005; Barbier and Kaufmann 2008).

In subsequent years, several initiatives aiming at strengthening the pro-market employment orientation of unemployment policy were adopted. In 2005, for example, the right-of-centre government passed a new law, which tried to institutionalize the coordination of the various relevant actors (UNEDIC, ANPE, and the national agency for further education). It also abolished the ANPE monopoly on placement services (Barbier and Kaufmann 2008). This trend culminated with the decision, taken in 2008, to merge the two key institutions, UNEDIC and ANPE into a single agency, known as Pôle Emploi. In the same year was decided the transformation of the main social assistance programme, RMI, into a *Revenu de solidarité active* (RSA), which contains a job search obligation for most beneficiaries (Barbier 2009).

The reforms adopted since the early 2000s have moved France closer to other European countries in embracing the activation paradigm. Two factors seem to explain the delay in the reorientation: First, the division between insurance managed by the social partners and employment services dependent on the state; second, the lack of enthusiasm for activation among the French Socialists. When in power, whether in the 1980s or between 1997 and 2002 (under Prime Minister Lionel Jospin), the Socialists did not, like Social Democrats in other European countries, champion the cause of ALMP. In this respect France is a clear outlier. In the late 1990s and early 2000s, the ideas popularized under the label of the Third Way in much of Europe were, in France, received as essentially neo-liberal and hence unsuitable for a Socialist party (Bergounioux 2001). France is exceptional in another respect. Of the seven countries covered in this chapter, it is the only one where the socialists were in power throughout most of the 1980s and responsible for the first retrenchment oriented reforms (Palier 2002). As a result, and unlike their European counterparts, the French Socialists were not under pressure to convince voters of their suitability to govern in difficult times. In contrast, they won the 1997 election on the basis of a rather traditional left-wing programme, and had no incentive to turn to active social policy. This may help to explain the reluctance to adopt Third Way discourse by the Jospin government.

Italy

Italy stands out in international comparisons as a country in which the approach to labour market policy has been and remains dominated by passive measures. Spending on ALMPs has been consistently far below the OECD average since the beginning of the data time series in 1980. This feature has also been pointed out by many commentators in qualitative studies (e.g., Ferrera 1993; Esping-Andersen 1996; Ferrera and Gualmini 2000). The recent and current popularity of activation as an adequate policy tool for dealing with unemployment has only had a very limited impact in actual policy, particularly at the implementation level. In 2008, after a decade of EU recommendations that Italy should do more in the field of activation[6] and several OECD reports praising active social policy, one leading Italian labour market expert observed that:

---

[6] Such recommendations have been consistently made through the European employment strategy.

> There is no relation between the payment of benefits and retraining or job search requirements. Active policies to support job searching and incentives to accept regular but poorly paid jobs, together with screening devices to detect moral hazard are usually lacking, especially in Southern Italy. (Samek Lodovici and Semenza 2008: 168)

Why did Italy not embrace ALMP in the post-war years? Why has it not moved in this direction in the 2000s? These questions require in-depth investigation and are strongly related to those being addressed by the whole book. In relation to Italy, however, one hypothesis can be ruled out from the outset: that Italian policy-makers did not and do not believe ALMP is good policy. In fact, the history of Italian post-war labour market policy is littered with failed attempts at introducing policy measures that were clearly in line with what was happening in Northern parts of Europe. Throughout the post-war years to the late 2000s, Italian governments of different political persuasion have attempted, generally through negotiations with the social partners, to introduce employment-related training, forms of flexibility that are promising for disadvantaged workers, and so forth. In most instances, however, the provisions adopted were hardly used.

The typical 'failure story' of Italian ALMP initiatives starts with a government proposal for a new law or a governmental invitation to the social partners to negotiate a collective agreement which may be turned into law. The social partners negotiate in a climate characterized by lack of trust. The unions expect employers to misuse the measures under discussion in order to exploit, underpay, or dispose more easily of waged workers. Italian unions, especially in the early post-war years, hold considerable political power, which allows them to impose strict conditions for employers wishing to make use of the new active instruments. The instruments are created, enshrined in labour law, but virtually never used by employers who find the red tape excessive. As will be seen below, this sequence of events reflects many an attempt by Italian policy-makers to shift the balance of labour market policy towards a more active approach.

The early post-war years

Italy, like many parts of occupied Europe, emerged from World War II with a balance of power strongly tilted in favour of the radical, essentially Communist, Left. This was partly a result of the leadership role played by underground Communist organizations in the resistance movement. Politically, this meant a strong Communist party (Partito Comunista Italiano, PCI), the largest in the West, and a powerful trade union confederation, the Confederazione General Italiana del Lavoro (CGIL), with strong ties to the PCI. At the end of the war, Communist resistance leaders decided to support liberal democracy. The first elections, held in 1948, were won by the Christian Democrats, but the influ-ence of the radical Left remained substantial.

The first steps in labour market policy were taken very early in the post-war years, and they were clearly influenced by this balance of power. In 1945, a moratorium on layoffs was adopted. It remained in force until 1947. In 1946, a mechanism providing the automatic indexation of wages to inflation came into force. Finally, the typical Italian institution of temporary unemployment benefit (*Cassa integrazione*), a state payment that provides a replacement income for workers who are temporarily laid off, was adopted in 1947 (Gual-mini 1998: 100–1).

In 1949, the state, now dominated by the Christian Democrats, took over from the unions the existing system of labour exchanges and developed a tightly regulated process of access to employment. Job seekers were prioritized according to 'need' (i.e., breadwinner status, age, length of the unemployment spell, and other income). In these early days (and until the late 1980s), employers who turned to labour exchanges had no choice on who they wanted to employ, except in some cases, such as management positions or specialized workers. The result was that during their first 40 years of existence, labour exchanges were most of the time avoided by employers (Gualmini 1998: 103–5).

The 1950s and 1960s were characterized by strong growth, a period Italians remember as the 'economic miracle'. Politically, the Christian Democrats remained in charge of government without interruption. Unemployment ceased to be a problem, also because of mass migration from the South to the North and abroad. A new labour market problem, however, was the provision of adequately trained workers to the expanding industries in the North. In order to deal with it, a law on apprenticeship was adopted in 1955. It made provision for on-the-job training and lower salaries for trainees. The law on apprenticeship is generally not considered as belonging to the realm of ALMP. Yet this initiative, just like the 1950s Swedish ALMP system, was chiefly designed to deal with a problem of labour shortage in expanding industries. The Italian approach, however, was less successful than the Swedish one. The scheme imposed strict limitations on employers' right to choose who they wanted to hire, as a result of which the scheme never really took off (Gualmini 1998: 108).

The end of the golden age

The late 1960s and 1970s saw a reinforcement of union and more in general of Left influence. The Socialist Party was invited to join the ruling coalition in 1962. In the following years, the economic crisis combined with a radicaliza-tion in politics resulted in an extremely tense political climate, characterized by frequent industrial unrest and, in the 1970s, the emergence of a terrorist organization, the Red Brigades. It was in this context that many initiatives in labour market policy were taken. These tended to imply the reinforcement of the route adapted in the early post-war years: social protection through employment protection.

Stricter EPL was a response to union demands, prioritizing employment protection after a wave of collective dismissals in 1964–5. One important piece of legislation was the 1966 law on individual layoffs, which introduced the legal notion of a justified dismissal, meaning that it was up to the employer to show evidence of wrongdoing by the employee. If the dismissal was found unjustified by a labour tribunal, the employer had to re-employ the worker or pay a penalty of up to 12 months' salary. In 1970, the rules governing individual dismissal were made even stricter. If a dismissal was found unjustified by a labour tribunal, the employer was forced to re-employ the worker, without having the option of paying compensation. These rules concerned (and still concern) only employees working in firms with more than 15 employees.

By forcing unjustly dismissed employees back onto the firm's payrolls, Italy has one of the strictest employment protection laws among OECD countries. From the employers' point of view, individual dismissals are a highly cumbersome procedure with an uncertain outcome. This explains their preference for non-standard, less well-protected, forms of labour contracts (Ferrera and Gualmini 2000; Samek Lodovici and Semenza 2008).

The 1970s also saw a reinforcement of temporary unemployment compensation (*Cassa integrazione*). The replacement rate of the benefit was increased to 80 per cent of earnings, and the duration extended to up to 5 years, although under particularly harsh labour market conditions it could be extended beyond that time limit. During this period of time, the beneficiary remains technically employed by his or her original firm, but performs no work and receives no salary, only the 80 per cent replacement benefit. Theoretically, once business picks up, beneficiaries are expected to go back to standard employment. However, in the context of industrial restructuring, in companies undergoing downsizing, this outcome seldom materializes. Only workers in firms with more than 15 employees have access to temporary unemployment benefit (Gualmini 1998: 115; Ferrara and Gualmini 2000).

The institution of temporary unemployment benefit is arguably a major obstacle towards the development of an ALMP. Jobless, former workers remain technically employed by their old firm and may be more inclined to wait for better times than to look for a new job. More in general, it seems difficult to reconcile the notion of a temporary unemployment benefit with that of activation. If unemployment is temporary, then activation is not needed. Policy-makers tried on various occasions to reform temporary unemployment benefit. In 1977, for example, temporary unemployment benefit was coupled with a 'mobility allowance', a measure encouraging recipients to look for a job elsewhere. Workers wishing to make use of this opportunity also had access to training. But this measure was hardly used, because of heavy bureaucratic requirements. Most excess workers remained indefinitely in *Cassa integrazione* (Gualmini 1998: 131–2; Barbier and Fargion 2004: 445).

The tense political climate of the 1970s was certainly not favourable to the development of an active and flexible regime of labour market regulation, which requires some degree of collaboration among the state, employers, and employees. Yet, even at the height of the crisis years some initiatives going in this direction were taken, like a new law on vocational training adopted in 1977. It contained incentives for employers who hire with 'training/work contracts'. The law was unsuccessful because employers did not use the new contract. Like in many past training initiatives, employers were not allowed to select candidates who were sent to them by labour exchange offices (Gualmini 1998: 130).

The 1980s: half-hearted deregulation and labour reduction

Like elsewhere in Europe, the 1980s in Italy were characterized by a reduction in the influence of the Left and of the unions. Even though the Socialist Party was part of the ruling coalition, its contribution to policy was less radical than in the past. Its overall orientation in labour market policy included elements that would in the late 1990s become part of the Third Way. The influence of the Socialist Party was highest during Bettino Craxi's term as prime minister. Under the rubric of deregulation one of the most significant developments was probably the abandonment of automatic indexation of wages in 1982. In addition, some of the cumbersome labour exchange regulations introduced in the early post-war years were undone, allowing, for example, employers to select candidates for work-training contracts. In 1987, regional employment agencies, which were meant to be more dynamic actors than the existing labour exchanges, were introduced (Gualmini 1998: 143).

Legislation on new forms of employment was also initiated during the 1980s, in general following the familiar pattern: a new tool was introduced but it was wrapped with so much red tape that it was hardly used. A good illustration of this mechanism is provided by part-time employment. A law regulating part-time work was adopted in 1984. Since the trade unions were fearful that part-time work could be used by employers as a tool to underpay regular employees, for example by adapting working hours to fluctuating demand, they fought for an extremely tough set of rules. The result was that part-time contracts had to specify when during the week the employee was supposed to work (e.g., which days or during which hours every day). Second, part-time workers were not allowed to do any overtime work and third, a company relying on part-time employment could not hire additional workers unless its part-time employees were not interested in increasing their working time. In addition, social insurance contributions were calculated so that two 50 per cent workers would generate total labour costs equivalent to 133 per cent of a full-time workers with the same salary (Gualmini 1998: 143; Redaelli 2006). Regulated in this way, part-time employment did not take off, reaching only 10 per cent in 1994 (OECD 2007b: 262).

Part-time employment was also at the centre of a union-sponsored initiative to deal with unemployment, the so called 'solidarity contracts' and included in the same 1984 law. These contracts were meant to encourage reductions in working hours by standard employees in order to avoid layoffs and/or make new appointments possible. The income lost by the employees working reduced hours was partly compensated by temporary unemployment benefit. The scheme was hardly used. In 1990, 6 years after its introduction, only twenty-five firms had developed this kind of contract (Gualmini 1998: 140–1).

Like elsewhere in continental Europe, in the 1980s, however, the main tool for dealing with labour market problems was the reduction of labour supply, through a variety of channels including invalidity insurance and early retirement programmes. Since 1981, for example, early retirement became possible for those who were jobless at 55 for men or 50 for women with no reduction in benefits.

The 1990s and 2000s: flexibility through labour market segmentation

The 1990s were characterized by the collapse of the post-war party system and by the emergence of new parties organized in a left and a right-of-centre coalition. Employers became more assertive in demanding labour market deregulation. The key political parties were also willing to pursue this type of policy because of the pressures coming from international agencies (i.e., EU and OECD) emphasizing the detrimental impact that a rigid labour law was having on Italy's labour market performance. The unions were more inclined to accept deregulation than in the previous decades, and together with the radical Left fought strenuously for the defence of core workers' entitlements, not only in the field of old age pensions, but also of employment protection legislation.

Since 1991 employers wishing to hire a person registered as unemployed could select candidates, as the priority list system based on need was entirely abolished. Other important elements of deregulation were introduced with the 1997 labour law reform, known in Italy as the 'Treu package', from the name of the then centre-left labour Minister Tiziano Treu. These included the deregulation of part-time employment, the abolition of state monopoly on employment services, and some human capital investment elements such as the setting up of a fund paying for the training of atypical workers financed by a levy of 5 per cent of total gross wages paid by temporary employment agencies and a revised regulation of employment/training contracts. The 1997 reform introduced also some of the least protected forms of employment such as fixed-term contracts, also known as 'project-based contracts', which basically treat the person who is hired for a fixed term as self-employed (Samek-Lodovici and Semenza 2008: 169).

Also noteworthy was the introduction in 1998 of a pilot scheme providing a last resort safety net on a national basis. Up to then, Italy did not have a general social assistance scheme available at the national level. Some municipalities did provide social assistance, but mostly in the North. The minimum income scheme was introduced by the centre-left Prodi government in thirty-nine municipalities, with the intention of extending it nationally. The programme was instead phased out by the next right-of-centre government in 2002, in the context of broader social pact with the unions (Barbier and Fargion 2004; Jessoula et al. 2010).

During these years, we see very little policy change that resembles an attempt to re-orient the welfare state towards activation. There are some declarations by centre-left political leaders that suggest a shift in this direction, but virtually no relevant development at the national level. Instead, the most fundamental labour market reform adopted since the turn of the century was the so-called 2003 Biagi Law.[7] Through this piece of legislation were introduced a number of different labour contracts that employers can use as an alternative to the overprotected standard open-ended contract. The aim of the reform was to facilitate access to employment for disadvantaged workers, to fight informal employment, but also to improve the protection of some of the most precarious contracts introduced in 1997. Some contracts introduced previously were subjected to somewhat stricter rules, adding up to thirty-five different types of work contracts.

The Italian route to labour market deregulation is clearly characterized by a strong dualization movement in the labour market. Labour market insiders continue to enjoy the full protection of the post-war model, whereas outsiders (mostly young workers, women, and immigrants) are employed on extremely precarious terms. Temporary employment is certainly a better stepping stone to an open-ended contract than unemployment, but the risk of being trapped in it for a long time is high (Samek-Lodovici and Semenza 2008). In a way, flexibilization at the margin has provided an alternative to activation in Italy. Highly flexible labour contracts have allowed job creation in the low-skill

---

[7] The law was named after Marco Biagi, an economist who advised the government at the time and was later killed by a left extremist terrorist group.

segment (but not only), contributing to a decline in the unemployment rate from a peak of 11.3 per cent in 1998 to a low of 6.1 per cent in 2007.

The United Kingdom

Labour market policy in the UK has always been characterized by a tension between an unregulated labour market, where wage formation is basically left to market forces and a means-tested welfare state. The combination of these two institutional features tends to generate poverty and unemployment traps, or situations in which economic incentives are not geared towards employment but de facto to encourage people with labour market problems to stay on benefits.

From the early days of British social policy, governments have tried, with different tools, to restore an incentive structure favourable to employment. The reorientation of the welfare state towards activation must be understood in this context. The activation paradigm provides a response to the incentive problems that have created tensions between the welfare state and the labour market since the early day of social policy.

Institutional antecedents

British labour market policies has always been characterized by a low level of regulation, especially in protection against dismissal and wage formation. Employment protection has always been minimal in comparison to other European countries. The reach of collective bargaining has also been significantly lower than in most other European countries, and encompassing agreements are not supported by law as much as is the case in other Western European countries. Except for a brief period in the 1970s, collective agreements have never been legally enforceable in the UK (Addison and Siebert 1993: 351). Wage councils, bodies set up in 1909 with the task of setting legally binding minimum wages in low-skill industries, constituted the exception. Their coverage has, however, been limited; in 1968 they covered 3.5 million workers and, in 1984, 2.7 million, mainly in catering, retail trade, and hairdressing, with about a third of those covered earning the minimum wage. Wage councils were weakened on various occasions by the Thatcher governments in the 1980s, and were finally abolished in 1993 (Addison and Siebert 1993: 372–3; Glennerster 1995: 216).

The origins of modern British social policy go back, at least, to the New Poor Law of 1834. In Polanyi's account of the establishment of a market economy in England, the New Poor Law was behind the emergence of a free market for labour. Because it abolished outdoor relief for the poor, the new law constituted the state's acceptance of non-interference in the functioning of the labour market, and as a result, its decision to limit social intervention to those individuals who were unable to earn a living through market exchanges (Polanyi 1957 [1944]: 78–84).

The 1834 law highlighted also a key problem in this liberal ideal of two separate institutions, the market and poor relief, coexisting without interfering with one another. In order to function, markets need incentives, and poor relief, or financial help given without requiring work, could encourage individuals not to participate in the labour market. That is why the New Poor Law had to conform to the principle of 'less eligibility', which stipulates that an individual should be given relief only if 'his situation on the whole shall not be made really or apparently so eligible as the situation of the independent labourer of the lowest class' (Poor Law Commission Report 1834, quoted in Rimlinger 1971: 52). The New Poor law temporarily solved that problem, by forcing individuals requiring relief into workhouses. However, to reconcile a free labour market with a social protection system based essentially on means-tested and subsistence level benefits has been a central concern to social and economic British policy-making to the present day.

The post-war model

The twentieth century saw the modernization and the expansion of social protection in Britain, but always with minimal direct interference with the operation of the market. This principle was confirmed after World War II with the adoption of Beveridge's proposals for the creation of a comprehensive welfare state. Social intervention, again, was limited to those who were unable to obtain their livelihood from market exchanges, a principle that affected the post-war institutional set up in two ways. First, intervention was to be limited to those individuals who because of old age, unemployment, sickness, and so forth were unable to participate in the labour market. The British post-war settlement included very little for those involved in the labour market: hiring and firing as well as wage determination were largely left to market forces. Second, the Beveridge ideal intentionally limited state intervention to meeting basic needs, as testified by the adoption of flat-rate benefits at subsistence level. Even though Beveridge chose the institutional format of contributory social insurance, British cash benefits fulfil a rather different function from their French or German equivalents. UK cash benefits are basically an instrument of poverty prevention, and fulfil increasingly less an insurance function. In recent years, in particular, as means-tested benefit packages, which may include housing benefit, tend to be more generous than the corresponding contributory benefits, the British National Insurance system has de facto lost much of its insurance character.

Responding to the employment crisis

In the late 1970s, Britain was facing several economic problems, including rising unemployment and intractable budget deficits. This situation lead to the demise of the up to then prevailing orthodoxy in economic policy: Keynesian demand management. Before the election of Margret Thatcher in 1979 as Prime Minister, the Labour government had already renounced the traditional tools of macro economic policy and embraced austerity (Hall 1993). In terms of labour market policy, the key decisions were made under conservative rule and were consistent with liberal ideology.

First, the level of unemployment benefit was reduced in various ways. The most significant changes were the abandonment of the earnings-related component of the benefit in 1981 and the abolition of child additions to unemployment benefit in 1984 (Erskine 1997; Clasen 2005). Unemployment benefit was further curtailed through smaller, less visible changes. Atkinson and Micklewright in 1989 identified seventeen changes in unemployment benefit adopted by conservative governments in the 1980s. Of them, only two were favourable to the unemployed (Atkinson and Micklewright 1989).

In parallel, the Conservatives developed measures that can be classified under the rubric of active labour market policy. According to Clegg, this development was particularly visible in the early 1980s. In contrast towards the end of the Thatcher/Major years (late 1980s, early 1990s), policy emphasized stronger work incentives. Programmes aimed at youth unemployed, including training and job subsidies, were developed and expanded in 1981 and 1983. By 1986, the UK was spending around 0.8 per cent of GDP on ALMPs, a level not so far from what one fond in France or Germany at the time (Clegg 2005: 189). In 1986, a new initiative was adopted under the name of 'Restart'. It introduced compulsory interviews for unemployed persons after 6 months of being out of work, as well as participation in job-search assistance activities. In 1989, proof of 'actively seeking employment' became a condition to receive the benefit, and after 13 weeks of unemployment, a lower wage could not be used as a reason to turn down a job offer (Clasen 2005: 78).

The early 1990s saw fewer reforms, most of them geared towards further tightening eligibility criteria and work requirements for unemployed people. Then, in 1996, more profound changes were adopted. Unemployment benefit, a contributory flat rate payment, and income support, a social assistance scheme, were merged into a new 'Jobseekers' allowance (JSA). This was divided into two components: a contributory benefit lasting 6 months (down from 1 year under the previous regime) and an income-related one. On the same occasion, additions for dependants were abolished, and the rate for younger unemployed lowered by 20 per cent. The reform coincided with the introduction of some typical activation tools, such as the requirement to sign a 'jobseeker agreement' and a pilot scheme known as 'Project Work', which was aimed at the long-term unemployed and provided intensive job search and work experience (Clasen 2005: 81 and 199).

These measures were meant, in part, to tackle what was seen as an incentive problem, sometimes referred to in terms of 'dependence' on state support. Together with these measures aimed at 'activating' unemployed people, the Conservatives acted also on work income, not by regulating wages, but by introducing an in-work benefit scheme: family credit. Introduced in 1986, this new cash benefit was paid to families with dependent children working at least 24 hours a week (reduced to 16 in 1992). The scheme remained nonetheless rather marginal, with only 5 per cent of families benefiting from it in 1991 (Glennerster 1995).

The activation turn

It is difficult to appropriately time the activation turn in the UK, as many elements described above were put in place by Conservative governments since the early 1990s. In fact, the New Labour's flagship programme, known as the New Deals, resembled closely the Conservative programme 'Project Work'. What is certain, however, is that with the Labour Party's accession to power in 1997, ALMPs became a high profile and highly publicized area of government policy. Already in the 1997 election manifesto, the Labour Party emphasized what was to become a mix of duties and responsibilities that would become a trademark of the Third Way: 'The best way to tackle poverty is to help people into jobs—real jobs. The unemployed have a responsibility to take up the opportunity of training places or work, but these must be real opportunities' (British Labour Party 1997).

In 1998, schemes known as the New Deals[8] were introduced for young and long-term unemployed people as well as for lone parents. These were complemented in 1999 with a New Deal scheme for partners of unemployed people and were subsequently strengthened on various occasions. The New Deals have been described as packages of interventions. Joining one of these programmes is compulsory for most unemployed people after a certain time spent out of the labour market (between 3 and 12 months). With some variation, these schemes involve the assignment of a personal adviser and the adoption of a 'personal action plan'. The first stage consists of more or less intensive interviews geared towards job search. It can also include, if deemed necessary, confidence-building measures or treatments to deal with social

---

[8] The New Deals were discontinued in 2011 and replaced by a new flagship ALMP known as the 'Work programme'.

problems such as substance abuse. If the jobseeker is still unemployed after this phase, then he or she will be assigned to a compulsory active labour market programme. For instance, in the New Deal for Young People, those who are still jobless after 4 months of job searching are assigned to either training, subsidized employment, voluntary work, or an environmental task force (Kluve et al. 2007).

Together with the emphasis on ALMPs, the newly elected Labour government developed other labour market policy tools, coherent with its objective of moving as many non-working people as possible into employment. The most important tools in this respect were a national minimum wage, first introduced in 1998 and increased in subsequent years, and a tax credit programme. The minimum wage was set initially at around 47 per cent of median earnings. It was increased in 2004 to approximately 52 per cent of median earnings (Brewer 2008). The tax credit programme, initially known as working families tax credits, replaced a previous programme introduced in 1986 by the Conservative government (see above) known as family credits. Tax credits are paid to households working at least 16 hours a week. The New Deals, the minimum wage, and the tax credits resulted in a coherent approach in social and labour market policy, designed to make work both attractive and possible for most non-working people (Rhodes 2000). Part of this approach was also the promotion of childcare services, a topic that is discussed in Chapter 6.

Since the 1990s, ALMP in the UK has been mostly based on employment assistance, as shown by both expenditure data and the narrative account presented here. Other tools of ALMP played a comparatively smaller role. It is more difficult to answer the question of who bears the political responsibility for the activation turn in the UK. The Labour government elected in 1997 clearly followed a policy line that had already been developed by the Conservatives in the early 1990s. What certainly changed was the scale of activation, and perhaps above all the hype associated with it (Clegg 2005: 195).

Active labour market policy across time and space

It is clear from the evidence presented in this chapter that the notion of active labour market policy can encompass very different policies, with respect to their objectives, the tools they use and the way they interact with passive unemployment compensation systems. The distinction between different types of ALMPs introduced in Chapter 2, however, makes it possible to track changes in the objectives and tools of ALMPs across countries and across time. A number of observations can be made on the basis of narrative accounts.

The first striking finding is that ALMPs tend to adapt to changing economic circumstances, to a large extent regardless of welfare regime. The main periods used to structure the narrative accounts are characterized above all by very different economic and labour market conditions. The first period, the 1950s and 1960s, was a time of rapid economic growth and labour shortage. Under these conditions, at least four out of the seven countries covered tried to develop an ALMP system geared towards upskilling the labour force, so as to provide adequately trained workers to expanding industries. Steps in this direction were taken by Sweden, Germany, Italy, and France, though only Sweden succeeded in developing a fully fledged re-training system.

In the second period (mid-1970s to mid-1990s), sluggish growth and industrial restructuring dominated the economic context. ALMPs turned into an alternative to market employment, and provided mostly occupation to jobless people. During this period, even programmes labelled as training tended to fulfil this function rather than genuine upskilling, as shown by the evaluation literature. Here too, welfare regimes do not seem to matter much. Instead, the existence of a tradition in ALMPs plays a more important role. The turn towards occupation concerns mostly countries that had developed ALMPs during the previous period (i.e., Sweden, Germany, and France), despite belonging to different welfare regimes.

Finally in the third phase (mid-1990s to late 2000s), better economic and labour market conditions pushed countries towards activation. This is also a development that spans across regimes. In fact, all the countries covered (except Italy) turn to the activation paradigm in labour market policy, emphasizing employment assistance and the reinforcement of work incentives.

Rather paradoxically, the laggards of the second phase become the leaders in the third one. The first countries turning to activation are Denmark, the Netherlands, and the UK, with high profile reforms adopted between 1992 and 1997. Other countries followed suit, but at a lower pace. In Sweden, the 2001 reform can be seen as a milestone in this process. For Germany, one could identify the 2003–4 Hartz IV reform as the tipping point. Quite clearly, countries without an extensive system of ALMPs in place in the early 1990s have an advantage when it comes to re-orienting policy towards the objective of re-entry into market employment. Using ALMPs as an alternative to market employment created expectations among actual and potential beneficiaries, for example in terms of the ability to renew the entitlement to unemployment insurance. These practices, which are incompatible with the activation paradigm, are difficult to abandon.

Shifts in the orientation of ALMP that partly reflect changing economic conditions are also visible in the spending data by type of ALMP. These data can be used to illustrate shifts in the emphasis of national ALMPs between the various types identified in Chapter 2: employment assistance, which includes the OECD spending categories 'public employment services and administration, employment subsidies, job rotation schemes, and start-up incentives'; occupation, which includes the category 'direct job creation'; and human capital investment, which includes the category 'training'. In this way, we are able to trace the evolution over a 20-year period of the relative effort made in the different components of ALMP.

ALMP spending profiles presented in Figure 5.1 reveal a number of important observations. First, there is obviously a cyclical effect (shown by the decline in overall spending between 1995 and 2005), which can be explained with reference to the decline in unemployment (especially in Sweden, Denmark,

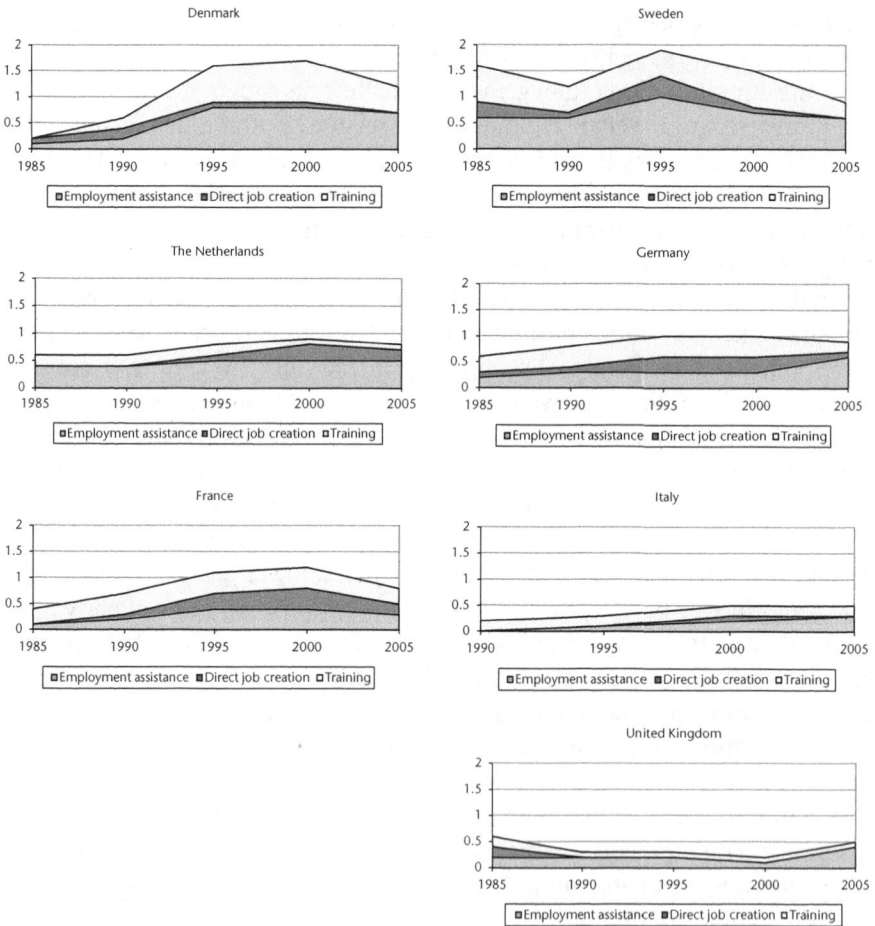

Figure 5.1. ALMP spending profiles in seven OECD countries. Spending as a percentage of GDP, 1985–2005

Source: Graphs constructed on the basis of data obtained from OECD *Stat*.

and France). The increase in overall spending in the UK calls instead for a political explanation, as this took place in the context of declining numbers of jobless. Second, if one compares trends over the 20-year period covered, there is clearly a reduction in the size of direct job creation, which is relatively important in France, Germany, and Sweden until the mid-1990s, but then declines everywhere. Third, over the same period of time, one sees employment assistance gaining importance everywhere except in Sweden where spending on this function is basically stable over time. Finally, spending on training does not show a clear trend over time (except in Denmark where it peaks in 2000). The biggest variation in relation to training is across countries, not time, with the Nordic countries being the biggest spenders, the UK the lowest, and the continental European countries somewhere in-between.

OECD spending data needs to be considered with caution since the distinctions adopted by the OECD do not always match national categories, and sometimes information is missing on given categories for several years. The results presented in Figure 5.1, however, are broadly compatible with the narrative accounts presented in this chapter.

Welfare regimes do not seem to matter much in this more recent period, as the trends identified span across of Western Europe (with the exception of Italy). However, it would be incorrect to simply argue that regimes are irrelevant. Nordic countries continue to invest considerably more in this field of policy than any other welfare state, and they continue to spend a bigger proportion on training. Nonetheless, we see a clear convergence towards the activation paradigm since the mid- to late 1990s.

In addition, the narrative accounts presented in this chapter highlight an institutional effect: the role of Bismarckian social insurance in slowing down though not preventing the development of an ALMP. In both Germany and France, features like the 'equivalence' principle of the joint management of insurance schemes by the social partners are widely seen as causes of the relative delay with which these countries embrace activation.

What about political determinants? The narrative accounts presented above show that there is little regularity across time and space in the political forces behind major ALMP initiatives. This is because, as argued in Chapter 2, there are many different approaches subsumed under the label of ALMP. Even within each period we find a mix of left-wing and centrist political parties among the initiators of ALMPs. On many occasions, a key role is played by the Christian Democrats, in Germany with the 1969 employment promotion act, and again during the 1980s and early 1990s. In Italy, the law on apprenticeship was adopted under a Christian Democratic-led government. Referring to the four ideal types of ALMP presented in Chapter 2, it appears that Social and Christian Democrats share similar preferences for two types of ALMPs: human capital investment and occupation. Conservative and liberal parties have often supported incentive reinforcement instead.

Employment assistance, a type of ALMP that emerged more recently as the cornerstone of employment policy, is much more associated with left power. The five countries that have most clearly adopted this policy paradigm (Denmark, the Netherlands, UK, Sweden, and Germany) did so under left-of-centre governments. I argue that this is not a simple coincidence. It can be understood instead as a result of the fact that budgetary problems and constraints imposed by economic globalization have severely curtailed the room for manoeuvre to introduce traditional left-wing labour market policies. An emphasis on employment assistance in the 1990s and early 2000s allowed left-wing parties to propose an option that was at the same time different from what their right-wing competitors were favouring (retrenchment and the reinforcement of market incentives) and compatible with budgetary and international economic constraints. This option proved particularly attractive to Social Democratic parties that had been out of power throughout the 1980s and had to simultaneously prove that they were capable of governing in difficult times and to pursue progressive policies. Activation provided them with a clear opportunity to do both.

6

Childcare Policy in a Comparative Perspective

Introduction

The field of childcare policy is closely linked to one of the most fundamental social developments occurring in the late twentieth century: the general shift in women's preferences away from homemaking and towards labour market participation. The shift seems to be fairly generalized across Western Europe (and beyond). Its timing differs, especially with Northern European countries which experienced the massive entry of women into labour markets a couple of decades before their Southern counterparts. Notwithstanding differences in timing, the dual-earner couple (or more often the one-and-one-half-earner couple) is becoming the norm across Europe.

In this context, work–life balance policies become indispensable. It has been pointed out that the shift in women's preferences towards employment does not mean that the aspiration to form a family has disappeared. Even though parents today may prefer slightly smaller families than their parents or grandparents, data on the number of desired children confirm a more-or-less constant and strong preference for having two children (Esping Andersen 1999). This suggests that the key problem facing policy-makers is how to make it possible for parents to be in the labour market and simultaneously have and care for their children.

Childcare, quite obviously, is the backbone of any policy aimed at facilitating the conciliation of work and family life. Other tools are also important, such as flexibility in working hours and arrangements, the availability of part-time work, and the availability and duration of maternity and parental leave. In addition childcare services can pursue many objectives. Besides allowing parents to work, childcare has been shown to impact positively on child development and school performance for disadvantaged children (Kamerman et al. 2003; Esping-Andersen 2009). Childcare, by facilitating parental employment, can also be part of a strategy to tackle child poverty, as was more or less explicitly done in the UK (Evers et al. 2005). In this chapter, in line with the focus of this book on active social policies, I concentrate on the 'reconciling work and family life' dimension of this policy.

Publicly subsidized childcare may also be of interest to employers. In the context of the shortage of skilled labour that results from population ageing, having the possibility to recruit female employees without needing to provide costly childcare facilities is certainly appealing to employers. For this reasons, the political game around subsidized childcare may differ somewhat from that of the traditional redistributive social programmes. In particular, cross-class or productive coalitions are more likely (Ballestri and Bonoli 2003; Bonoli 2005; Hausermann 2010: 210–15).

As for active labour market policies (ALMPs), it is possible to identify an ideal-typical sequence of phases in the development of childcare policy within a country. This can be seen as a rough guide that will help structure the narrative accounts of childcare policy in the seven countries.

Important antecedents of childcare policies can be found at the end of the nineteenth century and the beginning of the twentieth century. In many countries, services providing care for young children emerged for two rather different purposes. First, early steps in childcare policy were part of the rudimentary anti-poverty strategies of the time, allowing poor mothers to work while ensuring decent living conditions and food were available for their children during the day. Several of the countries studied in this chapter started childcare policy along these lines. The second important antecedent concerns the middle classes. As pedagogues in different countries recognized the important role of early socialization and education for child development, childcare and early education institutions sprang up in several European countries. The objective of these institutions was clearly not work–family reconciliation, so they tended to have short opening hours. Institutions of this kind were widespread in Denmark, the Netherlands, Germany, and Italy. France, finally, followed a unique trajectory in the early days of childcare policy by developing a fully fledged pre-school system very early on towards the end of the nineteenth century.

Like in other important areas of social policy, the second important phase for childcare was the post-war period. The early post-war years can be characterized as the golden age of the male breadwinner model. Throughout Europe, female employment remained low. Working women tended to be childless, and as women got married they tended to exit the labour force. The fact that maternal employment was increasingly less needed on economic grounds was part of the growth dividend of those years. In a country like Italy, as male wages grew in line with the economy, the female employment rate actually dropped, as can be seen in Figure 6.1 for the period 1960–8.

As seen in Chapter 5, the post-war years were also characterized by labour shortage in much of Western Europe. In some countries, employers and the

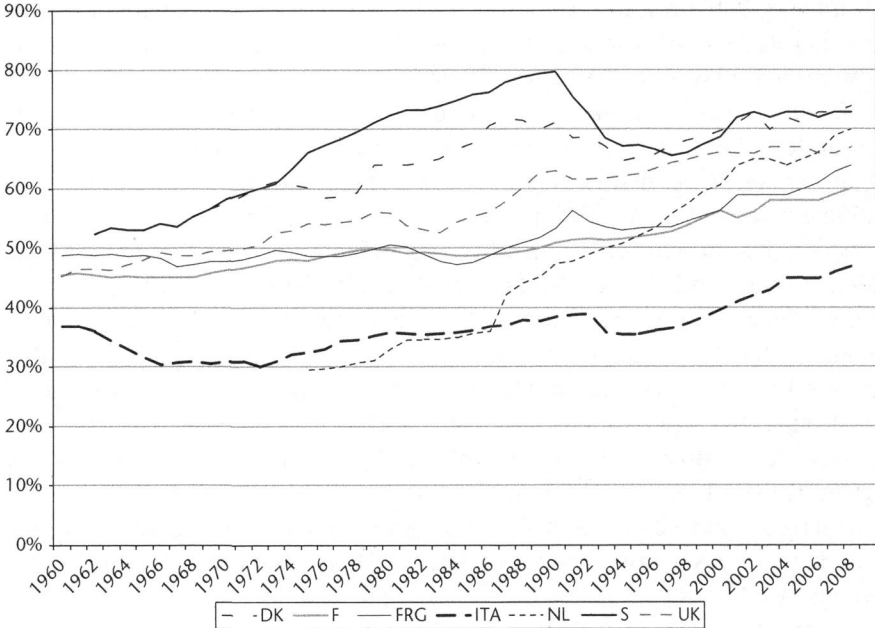

Figure 6.1. Female employment rate in seven European countries, 1960–2008
Source: OECD *Stat.*

unions considered expanding female employment in order to ease a tight labour market. This was clearly the case in Sweden, even though by the time the political system was ready to implement a strategy aimed at bringing women to the labour market in the early 1970s, the recession made labour shortage a thing of the past. Decisions taken in the context of labour shortage of the 1960s may nonetheless have impacted subsequent developments.

The third phase is the take-off in female employment. Some have wondered whether women were attracted to the labour market by easily available child-care facilities, or childcare facilities were developed in response to women's changed employment preferences. Qualitative studies, including this one, leave little room for doubt. While there may be some reverse causality going on as well, the typical sequence is that women *first* hit the labour market and *then* childcare services developed, always with a time lag, as illustrated by various indicators of unmet demand, such as waiting lists (see also Leira et al. 2003).

As already mentioned, the take-off takes place at different moments in different countries. Taking a female employment rate of 55 per cent as a benchmark, the seven countries covered in this study reach it at very different moments in time: Denmark in 1967, Sweden in 1968, the UK in 1978 and, after a drop, again in 1985, the Netherlands in 1997, Germany in 1998, and

France in 1999. Italy, in the context of comparatively lower employment rate for all categories of working age people, has not reached this threshold. One can nonetheless see a clear upward trend since the mid-1990s.

During the take-off years, pressures to provide childcare services are strong, regardless of when it happens. Leira and colleagues show how similar were the experiences of the first cohort of women to hit the labour market in three different countries. Whether in Norway, Italy, or Spain, the supply of childcare was insufficient for the growing demand, and mothers had to find solutions to their childcare needs (Leira et al. 2003). Naumann (2006) provides a very similar account of Sweden in the early 1970s. It is nonetheless in such a context that the most far-reaching policy initiatives are adopted. Typically, countries pass legislation providing central government subsidies for local authorities that are generally responsible for the implementation of childcare policy. Alternatively, or subsequently, legislation may introduce rights or guarantees in terms of availability of childcare places. Concretely, however, the setting up of a comprehensive childcare system takes a long time, and the gap between higher demand and lower supply persists in most countries for about two decades.

As mentioned above, this is an ideal-typical path in the establishment of a system of subsidized childcare provision. In fact, as will be shown below, individual countries follow different trajectories.

Sweden

When it comes to childcare services, Sweden is often considered as a leader in Europe. The country was among the first to develop a comprehensive system, and the provision of childcare is a highly valued government function. Childcare is also part of a broader family policy package that aims at encouraging female and more specifically mothers' employment, using a broad range of tools including parental leave and individual taxation. The development of family policy and in particular of childcare services in Sweden has been investigated in several studies. The key factors identified in order to account for this rather exceptional trajectory include the strength of the Social Democrats, labour shortage in the 1960s, the role played by the feminist movement, and concern with population issues in the 1930s. They are all covered in the narrative account below.

Antecedents

Many accounts of family policy in Sweden begin with a mention of the work of two well-known academics: Gunnar and Alva Myrdal. An economist and a pedagogue, they wrote a number of influential books and reports on population issues, where the idea of publicly provided childcare was strongly advocated.[1] The main reason behind this position was a concern for child development. According to the Myrdals, the best conditions for child development were achieved in two-earner families with access to quality childcare (Sainsbury 1999; Daune-Richard and Mahon 2001; Naumann 2006; Morel 2007: 271–6).

Their ideas were certainly innovative for their time, and continued to influence debates well into the 1950s. Their impact on policy and people's behaviour was nonetheless limited. Myrdals' view was picked up in an official report published in 1938, but the position defended in it was that childcare should be provided part-time, complementing rather than replacing maternal care (Naumann 2006: 136). True, in 1943, a law was passed establishing subsidies for childcare services provided by the municipalities. These were nonetheless modest, amounting to some 10 per cent of running expenses (Naumann 2006: 137; Morel 2007: 279). In addition, throughout the early post-war years the dominant family model was clearly that of the male breadwinner. Until the mid-1960s, Swedish women were not more likely to be in employment than their German or French counterparts. Maternal employment was the exception rather than the rule, and it was generally acknowledged, including in a governmental report published in 1951, that given the choice, mothers would prefer to be full-time carers (Morel 2007: 280).

The early post-war years saw a return to the traditional family, but the innovative views of the Myrdals had not entirely disappeared. A subsequent governmental report, published in 1955, argued for the increase in state subsidies for daycare centres (Naumann 2006: 138). These recommendations, however, were not followed by facts, at least in the short run.

The 1960s: childcare is back but with new actors

The issue of women's role in the labour market was brought back onto the political agenda in the early 1960s. Two totally independent developments converged to focus public attention on women's place in the labour market. First, the early 1960s saw the emergence of the feminist movement. A number of influential authors wrote in favour of women's integration into labour markets. Important texts included a book co-authored by Alva Myrdal and Viola Klein in 1957, a book by Eva Moberg published in 1961, and a book edited by Edmund Dahlström. These publications were rather influential and broadly discussed. They all supported the idea that it is both society's duty

---

[1] The most important of which was 'Crisis in the Population Question', published in 1934.

and in society's interest to facilitate women's access to employment (Morel 2007: 285ff).

The second development concerns the labour market. As elsewhere in Western Europe, in Sweden the 1960s were a period characterized by strong economic growth and labour shortages. As seen in Chapter 5, labour shortage was a major problem in Sweden's post-war economic history. It was addressed with a range of tools, one of which was the support for publicly subsidized childcare. According to Swenson: 'employers keenly favored this development to dislodge mothers from their homes and mobilize them for industrial work. Institutional childcare was less labor-intensive, after all, than home care, promising at least a modest net gain in the female labor supply' (Swenson 2002: 306; Naumann 2006: 153).

Swedish employers, in addition, were not alone in advocating higher levels of female labour market participation. The issue was brought up in a brochure on 'The daycare question' published in 1962 by the large blue collar union LO. The union strongly favoured investment in services supporting maternal employment. This brochure represented a clear break in LO policy concerning women. Although its women's branch had pushed in this direction, official LO policy up until this time had been to make sure that male workers had access to adequate wages, sufficient to support a dependent wife who would take care of young children.

One reason behind LO's change of orientation might have been a government report published in 1962 which proposed two possible ways to deal with the problem of labour shortage: facilitating women's participation in the labour market through subsidized childcare or increase massively the recruitment of immigrant workers. According to Naumann the LO chose what it regarded to be the lesser of two evils. A massive inflow of poorly organized foreign workers would have jeopardized the solidaristic system of wage bargaining. Swedish women were seen as a lesser threat to the post-war achievements of the labour movement (Naumann 2006: 154).

The conjunction of the claims made by influential feminist thinkers, of employers' demands, and of the shift in LO's policy on women's employment created a new set of conditions that was extremely favourable to the rapid development of childcare services. It was in this new context that in 1966 a new law on childcare subsidies was adopted, increasing the proportion of daycare facilities' running costs covered by the central government from 10 to 25 per cent (Naumann 2006: 159; Morel 2007: 297).

The issue of women's employment had made its way into the political arena. Childcare and other tools that facilitate women's employment would become flagship policies of the Social Democrats, but according to Naumann, the first party to openly side with women's demand were the Liberals. In the 1961 election campaign, they clearly targeted women voters with proposals such as individual taxation, equal wages, and women's right to choose between employment and homemaking (Naumann 2006: 156). Political parties had clearly spotted the potential for credit claiming represented by subsidized childcare services.

1970s: the Social Democrats step in

Despite the measures taken in the 1960s, demand for childcare services was far from being met in the early 1970s. Accounts of Swedish families' actual experience with childcare showed that large numbers of women were failing to obtain access to the services they needed. Childcare policy took off when the Social Democrats (SAP), Sweden's natural party of government, decided to make of it a key priority. An important step in this direction was the publication in 1969 of a report by a joint SAP–LO commission, entitled simply 'Equality'. The commission, headed by Alva Myrdal, promoted a new understanding of the childcare issue that was likely to resonate among Swedish Social Democrats. The issue of female employment was now framed in terms of gender equality, and the traditional SAP–LO emphasis on the promotion of vertical equality was extended to equality between men and women (Naumann 2006: 164). The same year saw the election of Olof Palme as Sweden's Prime Minister, who made gender equality and the expansion of childcare services key priorities of his government's political platform.

Reforms were adopted rapidly. In 1971, Sweden was one of the first OECD countries to adopt individual taxation, and paid parental leave was introduced in 1974. An important step in the field of childcare was the 1975 law, which included quality requirements for childcare services and targets for the municipalities (Morel 2007: 299). Access to services remained problematic, though. In the late 1960s and throughout the 1970s, lack of childcare places and waiting lists were recurrent themes in the media. Feminist movements were actively organizing protests and mobilizing within existing organizations, such as political parties and trade unions (Naumann 2005: 58).

The Social Democratic governments that successively ruled the country confirmed and strengthened their commitment to childcare, essentially by increasing the amount of funds transferred from the central government to the municipalities for the provision of services. In 1976, for instance, block grants were wage indexed so that every increase in the grant would produce a net increase (Morel 2007: 300). Between 1966 and 1980, the proportion of cost covered by the central government doubled to 50 per cent (Morel 2007: 306).

By the late 1970s, Swedish childcare policy was firmly set on course to universal coverage. This will be de facto achieved considerably later, in the 1990s (see Figure 6.2). However, the 1970s were clearly the crucial decade insofar as childcare policy in Sweden is concerned. Over the following years,

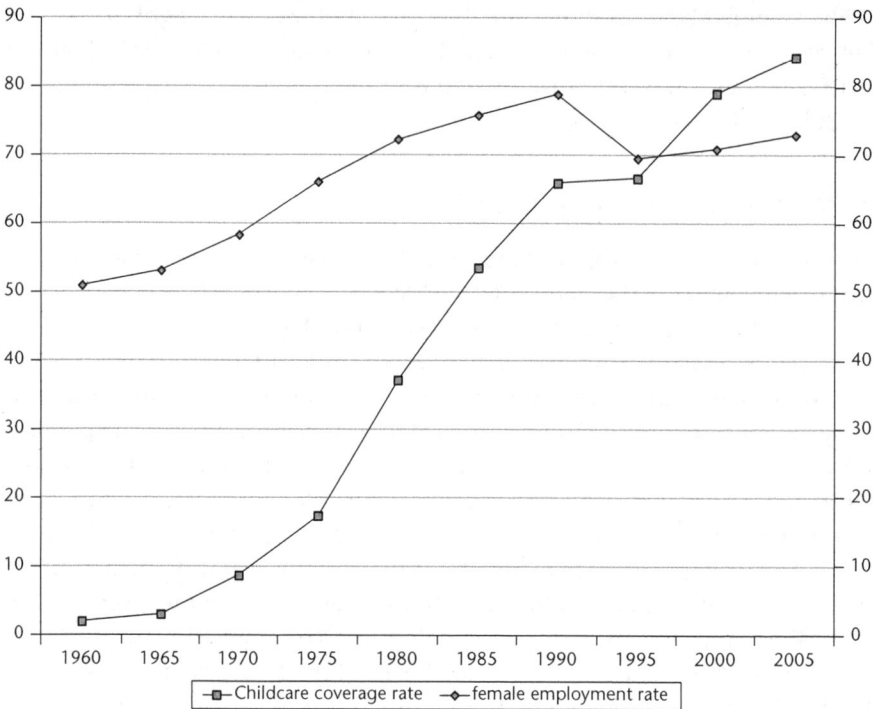

Figure 6.2. Coverage of childcare services (number of places divided by children aged 1–7), and female employment rate, Sweden 1950–2005

Source: Employment rate: OECD *Stat*. Childcare data were kindly provided by Nathalie Morel.

the right to publicly provided childcare was never really challenged. In contrast, a formal obligation for municipalities to provide childcare to those parents who request it was introduced in 1995 (Morel 2007: 325ff.).

Childcare policy after the take-off

The broad acceptance in Swedish society of the state's role in the provision of childcare did not mean absence of debate and controversy. These were mostly of an ideological nature and concerned the role of the private sector in the provision of childcare, gender, and vertical equality. An example is the debate and the repeated legislative changes generated by the 1983 decision of a municipality in the Stockholm area to subcontract the provision of childcare services to a private for-profit company, Pysslingen. This initiative provoked a major controversy between the employers' confederation (in favour of private providers) and the Social Democratic government, who was against it. This resulted in a new law, adopted in 1984, which explicitly forbade the payment of subsides to commercial providers, a law known as

Lex Pysslingen. The law was then repealed by the bourgeois government, elected in 1991 (Morel 2007: 311).

Other recent reforms have aimed at facilitating access to childcare services, particularly for disadvantaged children. Since 2001 municipalities are obliged to provide childcare also to parents who are unemployed (up to then the entitlement was available only to working parents) and in 2002 a ceiling of 3 per cent of household earnings is introduced on childcare costs, known as *Maxtaxa* (Morel 2007: 332).[2]

Current Swedish childcare policy clearly faces problems that are very different from those that dominate the agenda in other European countries, who struggle with how to extend coverage. In this country, the battles on the respective role of the state and the family in the provision of childcare services took place in the 1970s, a very different economic and social context from today's. In the political arena childcare was clearly a tool for credit claiming, as it became later on in other Western European countries.

Denmark

Where care services for children are concerned, Denmark has been leading the way, even among the Nordic countries. State subsidies for childcare services were institutionalized as early as in 1919. At the time, state intervention in this field was motivated by social concerns, more precisely by the wish to limit the consequences of poverty on child development (Rostgaard and Fridberg 1998). The sort of provision introduced in 1919 was far away from the type of universal services one finds in the present day, but it may have facilitated the expansion of childcare in subsequent years.

Today Denmark stands out as the OECD country with the most developed childcare system, at least insofar as its coverage rate is concerned. Perhaps surprisingly, the development of the Danish childcare system was not the result of political battles. Instead, it was gradual and consensual. In this respect, it is noteworthy that the key legislative act paving the way for universal childcare was passed by parliament in 1964 with the support of all the main political parties.

Antecedents

Like other European countries around the end of the nineteenth century, Denmark developed pedagogical institutions for pre-school children, known

---

[2] The 3 per cent ceiling concerns the first child. Subsequent children cannot generate costs over 2 per cent (second child) or 1 per cent (third child) of parents' earnings.

there as kindergartens. Initially, these were mostly used by middle-class parents and on a part-time basis, but they gradually took on a social policy function as well as a pedagogical role. As a result, opening hours were extended so that they could also be used by working-class parents in need of childcare during working hours. Kindergartens, with their pedagogical objectives, provided good quality childcare and were as a result costly to run for private organizations. It was in this context that in 1919 a law providing public subsidies to childcare institutions was adopted (Rostgaard and Fridberg 1998).

During World War II, childcare services were extended in order to allow mothers participation in the labour market. However, by the 1960s, Denmark was not different from the rest of Western Europe, and the male breadwinner model was the norm. Interestingly, the Danish female employment rate, at 43 per cent in 1960, was lower than France's 45 per cent or Germany's 49 per cent. However, female employment took off during the 1960s so that by 1970 it reached 58 per cent, the same level as Sweden.

The 1964 law and the early development of childcare services

It was in this context of rising female labour force participation that a law on childcare services was adopted in 1964. Subsidies that were limited to facilities catering for the poor were now being made available on a universal basis. The principle that childcare costs had to be split equally between parents, the municipalities, and the central state was adopted on that occasion. The law provided subsidies for various types of childcare facilities: daycare centres but also private childminders. The 1964 law was adopted under Social Democratic-led government, but the political actors that fought most to put the adoption of a new law on the agenda were the well-organized childcare professionals (Borchorst 2002: 274), in the context of an alliance with women's organizations (Bertone 2003). What is particularly striking in this reform is the fact that the 1964 law was supported by all the main parties represented in parliament. Very little controversy surrounded the notion of subsidizing formal childcare services. Bourgeois parties accepted the idea, although they had a somewhat stronger preference for childminders (Borchorst 2002: 274–5).

The 1964 law transformed childcare from a residual state service targeted on the poor into a universal one. It can be regarded as a key event in the development of the Danish childcare system. The act was adopted in a consensual manner, and many of the arguments that fraught similar attempts made in other countries decades later, such as value judgements on the role of mothers, financing issues, or divisions within the feminist movement, were not so prominent. With regard to financing issues, the timing of the development seemed crucial as the budgetary problems that framed similar initiatives taken in countries like Germany or Italy in the 1990s were inexistent. As noted by Borchorst, the ideas that inspired the social pedagogues in their support for subsidized childcare had been around for a while, but they had to wait for the favourable economic context of the mid-1960s to become politically feasible (Borchorst 2002: 274).

With regard to women's organizations, Bertone points out that in the 1960s these organizations, like elsewhere in Europe, were divided with regard to the ordering of priorities between support for housewives and women working outside the home. They found a common terrain in the support of good quality childcare. To some extent the potential conflict between the two components of the feminist movement was defused by focusing on the interest of children. This in turn meant a strong degree of professionalization of the service, which of course facilitated the alliance with those working in childcare institutions (Bertone 2003).

Controversy was relatively limited and concerned what for an external observer looked like relatively minor questions. One key question was the role that private childminders (also known as day mothers or family daycarers) would play in the new system. Childcare professionals and women organizations were against supporting this type of provision, on grounds that it did not offer the same guarantees in terms of quality and pedagogical development as collective daycare facilities. Of course for professionals, the danger was also the prospect of facing competition from childminders with lower costs. On the other hand, the right-of-centre parties—with a strong, popular base in the countryside—supported childminders arguing that in rural areas with more dispersed populations, it would have been problematic to set up an adequate supply of collective services. In the end, a compromise was reached and both types of services were declared eligible to receive public subsidies (Kremer 2005).

The services provided by the childminders within their private homes were subsequently further institutionalized. In 1971, under pressure from the public sector unions, a collective agreement providing for relatively good wages for childminders was adopted (Kremer 2005). Today, childminders are employed by the municipality and subjected to rather strict rules concerning number of children, approval of premises, and so forth (OECD 2000a).

From the end of the 1960s onwards, the supply of childcare services increased steadily with the support of state subsidies. At the same time, female employment was also rising, which meant that demand for services generally exceeded supply. Women were providing the additional labour needed by the expanding economy so that Denmark did not turn to immigrants during these years (Borchorst 2002).

The 1980s and the 1990s: the take-off of childcare provision

By the early 1980s, female employment had clearly taken off, reaching 64 per cent in 1980. The supply of childcare followed suit. In 1982, the coverage rate of the various types of care for pre-school children (aged 0–6) exceeded 50 per cent.[3] As seen in Chapter 5, the 1980s in Denmark were a period characterized by serious economic and employment problems. These difficulties notwithstanding, the supply of childcare places continued to increase throughout the decade, reaching over 60 per cent of the age group 0–6 years in 1990 (Rostgaard and Friedberg 1998).

It was in this context that parental leave was introduced, first by the Conservatives in government between 1982 and 1993. In 1992, a 36-week transferable leave for parents was introduced, mainly as a labour market measure. Parental leave came on top of maternity leave, available only to mothers and partly compulsory. By encouraging parents to temporarily withdraw from the labour market, it was hoped to ease the unemployment problem. The Social Democrats, in power again since 1993, stepped up provision for parental leave by extending it to 1 year for each parent (of which 6 months subjected to employer approval). The new scheme, which was also renamed 'childcare leave', provided each parent with an individual right to time off work. With a replacement rate of 80 per cent, the new childcare leave proved extremely popular, with very high take-up rates in some occupational groups such as nurses. Partly as a result of its success, the amount of the benefit was subsequently reduced to 70 and 60 per cent of earnings (Rostgaard and Fridberg 1998; Kremer 2005: 134). Parental leave was later reformed in 2001 by the newly elected bourgeois government. The duration was shortened to 32 weeks, and the leave was made transferable. At the same time, the replacement rate of the benefit was harmonized with that of unemployment, which meant a slight increase (Kremer 2005: 134).

One of the most comprehensive childcare systems

Despite this legislative activism and the continuous expansion in childcare services, demand clearly exceeded supply well into the 1990s. In 1993, 59,000 children were on a waiting list (Kremer 2005: 149). In this context of shortage of childcare places, the Social Democratic-led government introduced the so-called 'childcare guarantee'. Municipalities are encouraged to adopt the guarantee, meaning that they assure every resident child aged 0–9 of a childcare place. By 2000, some 90 per cent of municipalities had implemented the guarantee (Borchorst 2002: 279). In 2006, under a bourgeois government, the guarantee became compulsory for all municipalities so that by 2008 over 90 per cent of children older than 1 were in care. The maximum parental

---

[3] The coverage rate is calculated by dividing the number of full-time equivalent places by the number of children aged 0–6.

contribution has been lowered from 33 to 25 per cent (Danish Government 2007: 48).

The Danish trajectory in childcare policy is rather unique. Denmark was one of the first countries to adopt a law on subsidized childcare, at a time when the male breadwinner model was still dominant. In addition, Denmark, unlike Sweden, did not have a problem of labour shortage in those years that could justify the support of women's employment on macroeconomic grounds. With regard to the political determinants of childcare policy, it is important to point out that the Danish Social Democrats have traditionally been less strong than their Swedish counterparts. Yet it is in Denmark that notions of institutionalized care for children and the promotion of female and maternal employment have gone further (Borchorst 2002: 270). The expansion of childcare services found little opposition in Denmark, suggesting once again that this exercise was highly popular and that political parties had no interest in opposing it.

The Netherlands

In European comparisons, the Netherlands stands out as a country where women's employment expanded particularly late. In 1975, the female employment rate was at 30 per cent among the lowest in the OECD world and far lower than that of neighbouring countries like France (48 per cent) or Germany (49 per cent). It was only towards the end of the 1980s that female employment clearly took off, in conjunction with decisions taken by the social partners to develop part-time employment (see Chapter 5). One explanation given for the late emergence of dual-earner couples in the Netherlands makes reference to pillarization, or the segmentation of institutions and social organizations (above all education) into four pillars: Catholics, Protestants, Social Democrats, and Liberals (Lijphart 1968). Authorities within each of society's pillar defended their own value system. Although they were different, they had in common a preference for the traditional male breadwinner family model (Kremer 2005: 69–70). What is clear is that until the 1980s the notion of a dual-earner couple was much less socially acceptable than in many other European countries (Plantenga 1996: 67; Morgan 2006: 164).

Dutch exceptionalism in the field of women's employment can probably be ascribed to a conjunction of factors, the timing of which played an important role. Possibly because of the influence of the moral authorities behind the pillarization system, the value change that led to the massive entry of women into the labour force took place somewhat later than in other countries, and it coincided with the worst employment crisis the country had seen in the post-war years. As a result, the overall social and political climate was not particularly favourable to the development of childcare services. The take-off in women's employment had to wait for the improvement in labour market conditions, something that took place in the 1990s. Furthermore, it happened to a very large extent through part-time jobs, which contributed to maintaining demand for childcare services relatively low. It is only since the early 2000s that the supply of childcare provision has really taken off.

Antecedents

With regard to the early steps in the field of early education and childcare policy, the Netherlands is no exception to the boarder continental European trend. One finds antecedents in both anti-poverty and early education policy. In the nineteenth century care facilities for disadvantaged children were available. At the beginning of the twentieth century this residual form of childcare provision was complemented by early education institutions, or kindergartens, which had a clearly pedagogical objective and targeted the middle classes. Kindergartens expanded rapidly in the post-war years but remained focused on preparing children for school rather than providing childcare for working parents. In the 1960s, in response to feminist mobilization, a new form of childcare called playgroups emerged. Playgroups were often initiated by groups of mothers, but as they became more popular, they were turned into institutionalized structures, with professional staff. The extent to which playgroups could provide childcare for working parents was, however, extremely limited, as they were typically open for only 2 half days a week (Vedder et al. 1996: 11–2).

The post-war years

Throughout the post-war years, the provision of childcare and early childhood education remained a marginal affair. In 1963 there were only about 30 day-care centres in the whole country. By 1975 their number had increased to 167. Playgroups were more widespread (1,589 in 1975), but their very limited opening hours made them unsuitable as providers of childcare for working parents (Kremer 2005: 193). In addition to limited childcare supply, the education system provided pre-school services to children aged 4 and 5 years. Coverage was rather high, exceeding 80 per cent in the early 1970s. The objectives of pre-schools were essentially pedagogical, and the opening hours were not suitable for working parents (Morgan 2006: 72–3).

During the post-war years, the tax treatment was not particularly favourable to dual-earner couples. In 1984 taxation of married couples was transformed so as to comply with European Union treaty articles on gender equality. The result, rather paradoxically, was a new tax system that imposed very high marginal tax rates on second earners. Based on the principle of a personal transferable tax allowance, the new rules were particularly advantageous for high-income, one-earner families (Kremer 2005: 93–4).

In the early 1980s, amidst the very serious employment crisis the country was going through, dual-earner couples were not necessarily valued by society. With so many jobless households around, the priority seemed to be access to employment for them, rather than for spouses of working men. A debate emerged with regard to the appropriateness of the state supporting dual-earner couples, which were thought to be advantaged and as a result could be asked to make a bigger fiscal effort in the context of severe austerity. These positions were defended above all by the Christian Democrats, as the Social Democrats were clearly struggling to reconcile the two policy objectives of gender and class equality. This dilemma was illustrated by the debate on whether Mrs Philips, the imaginary wife of the electronics conglomerate's boss, had to be supported by the state (Kremer 2005: 94).

Childcare policy per se remained a marginal field during those years. The only notable development in the 1980s was a modest childcare benefit introduced in 1987, which paid parents (i.e., mothers) who provided care to young children. Recipients of the benefit had subsequently access to unemployment insurance, so that the benefit was presented as a bridge to employment for mothers (Kremer 2005: 104–5). In reality, it probably gave married women an additional incentive to withdraw from the labour force. The ongoing reorientation of the Dutch welfare state towards the promotion of employment had not reached women yet even though they were one of the groups least likely to be in the labour market.

In this context, the expansion of childcare provision was slow. True, playgroups and other forms of limited care supply had grown significantly since the 1970s. However, proper childcare (i.e., formal care that allowed both parents to work) was extremely limited until the end of the 1980s. In 1989, some 17,000 children, or 1 per cent of the relevant age group, were cared for in this kind of facilities (Plantenga 1996: 64).

The take-off of women employment through part-time work

In this context, Dutch women turned to part-time employment as a convenient solution for reconciling work and family life. Part-time employment was also encouraged by the social partners, who a few years earlier had agreed on wage moderation in return for shorter working hours (see Chapter 5). The reduction of working hours took several forms, and one of them was an impressive expansion in part-time employment. Between 1983 and 1997, two million new jobs were created, prompting some to talk of a Dutch 'employment miracle'. Three-quarters of these jobs were part-time, and the majority of them were taken up by women (Visser 2002). Part-time employment doubled to over 20 per cent of the working age population between the early 1980s and 1997. During the same period of time, female employment rose from 33 to 56 per cent.

According to Jelle Visser this dramatic expansion of part-time and female employment was the result of the coincidence of various developments. These included the late entry of Dutch women into the labour force, the lack of childcare provision, and the commitment by the social partners to reduce average working time (Visser 2002: 25). By the end of the 1990s, the Netherlands had clearly caught up with, and in some cases overtaken, its European neighbours in relation to women's employment and the adoption of social norms regarding labour market participation of mothers of young children. Thanks to the strong reliance on part-time employment, the Dutch female employment rate in 2000 (61 per cent) was higher than those of France and Germany (both at 56 per cent).

Probably because of the strong incidence of part-time employment among parents, parental leave was not perceived as a particularly crucial issue in the Netherlands. An individual right to a 6-month parental leave was introduced in 1990. The leave is unpaid, but collective agreements can include compensation of earnings during parental leave.[4] In 1997 the structure of parental leave was made more flexible, for example, allowing the combination with part-time employment or the 'saving' of holidays so as to gain entitlement to a longer paid period out of the labour market (Kremer 2005: 131–2).

Since the early 1980s, when the reorientation of the Dutch welfare state was initiated, the context had changed dramatically. As a result, policy in the broader field of reconciling work and family life took a new more modern spin. The 2001 tax reform, for instance, introduced individual taxation and replaced transferable allowances with non-transferable tax credits. These can also be paid out in cash for those who have no income from work. The result was a sharp reduction in the marginal tax rate faced by second earners and the introduction of an implicit subsidy for dual-earner couples. One key objective of the reform was to 'make work pay', or improve incentives to increase households' labour supply. In fact, the big winners of the 2001 reform were dual-earner couples (OECD 2002: 161).

In 2005 the Christian Democrat-led government adopted a new law on the financing of childcare provision. As a result, childcare facilities are not subsidized directly, as used to be the case in the past; instead, parents receive a tax credit that they can use to buy childcare services. The tax credit is income

---

[4] In 2002 this was the case only for 5 per cent of private sector agreements. Public sector employees are instead entitled to a wage replacement benefit corresponding to 75 per cent of previous earnings.

related, its amount declining as household income increases. The result of the 2005 law has been an expansion of the role of private commercial providers and a reduction in the proportion of costs paid by parents overall. Since 2007 employers are also required to contribute one-third of the overall costs of childcare, through an addition onto the unemployment insurance contribution (OECD 2008b).

Of the countries covered, the Netherlands is probably the one that has undergone the most rapid and substantial transformation in the field of work–life balance policies and female employment. The 2005 and 2007 innovative laws on childcare are only an illustration of this development. Even before the adoption of these key legislative acts, spending on childcare rose fast. Of all the countries surveyed in Table 3.5, the Netherlands is the one which between 1998 and 2007 has seen the strongest increase in spending on childcare, from 0.7 to 1.4 per cent of GDP. During this period, the Christian Democrats were in government most of the time.

Germany

From the point of view of family policy and social values, Germany is generally considered as a typical example of a strong 'male breadwinner model' (Lewis 1992, 2006). Throughout the post-war years, policy has supported one-earner families through a wide range of tools from joint taxation to long parental leave schemes and contribution credits for carers. Extensive provision of childcare services became a policy objective comparatively late, in the early 2000s. Another peculiar feature of German family policy is the Nazi antecedent. During Nazi rule, family policy had an overtly pronatalist orientation motivated purely by military considerations. In reaction, post-war Germany made non-intervention in the family sphere a sacrosanct principle of government policy. This view delayed the development of policies that could be interpreted as 'state intervention' in the very private sphere of the family, such as childcare services (Schultheis 1996). It is only towards the early 2000s, in the context of mounting concern over population ageing (and pension financing) that a link between family policy and demography has been made in the public sphere (Clasen 2005: Ch. 6).

The post-war years

In the early post-war years, denazification was a key priority in the newly born Federal Republic. In the field of family policy, this implied the abolition of legislation introduced by the Third Reich, the clear assertion of the subsidiarity principle, and the recognition that family affairs are private affairs. The

1949 Basic Law sanctioned the state's protection of marriage and the family and parents' exclusive right to educate their children (Naumann 2006: 106). As a result, family policy remained a marginal field of public policy throughout the post-war years. In 1953, a Family Ministry was created, interestingly against the background of demographic concerns and after controversial debates. However, its role in the years to come remained marginal (Schultheis 1996).

The post-war years were characterized in Germany by a general consensus in support of the traditional, male breadwinner model. This can be explained with reference to the dominance of the Christian Democrats in the political arena (in government between 1949 and 1969) and through them, the influence of the Catholic Church and its social doctrine. However, Christian Democrats and Catholics were not the only supporters of a traditional vision of the family. Like in other Western European countries at the time, there was a clear consensus on the desirability of distinct gender roles within couples. Other political parties, the SPD and the FDP, agreed with the CDU that the objective of policy was to make sure that married women would not be forced to work out of economic necessity (Naumann 2006: 111).

The same vision was shared by the trade unions. In 1961, the peak federation DGB published a study on the double burden their women members were facing, having to work both in the labour market and at home. One conclusion was that more investment in childcare was needed, but more emphasis was put on the idea that mothers should have the opportunity to spend their time caring for their children and not have to work out of economic necessity (Naumann 2006: 149).

Like other Western European countries, Germany experienced labour shortages in the 1960s. However, unlike in Sweden, German employers and unions did not consider the option of turning to women to solve their problems. Instead, the strategy adopted was to deal with labour shortages through immigration (see, e.g., Manow and Seils 2000: 273).

Largely failed SPD efforts at progressive family policy

After a short-lived experiment with a grand coalition between 1966 and 1969, West Germany saw the accession to power of the first government headed by the Social Democrats. This signalled an important change in the orientation of policy towards families, though it produced rather little results. In 1972 after an election victory, the SPD-led government tried to push through a bill that would have entitled children aged 3 to 6 years to pre-school education. The proposal was met with resistance by the *Länder*, which would have born responsibility for implementing the scheme. The idea was finally abandoned in 1974 when after the oil shock, Germany's public finances deteriorated, and the SPD's junior coalition partners, the Liberals, vetoed new public spending (Naumann 2006: 208–9). Instead, the government adopted a less ambitious programme, which aimed at organizing a system of childminders, or 'day-mothers'. The project, known in German as '*Tagesmütter*', was implemented at the municipal level and consisted merely in the coordination of supply and demand of childcare services by childminders and working parents. Perhaps unexpectedly, the scheme provoked massive public outcry, as many saw the state's involvement in providing care outside of the family as illegitimate (Naumann 2006: 213).

In the following years, certainly also as a result of feminist mobilization within and outside of the party, the SPD developed a policy on gender equality, stating explicitly the policy objective of facilitating access to employment for women. This objective was to be achieved above all by expanding childcare services. Support for the reconciliation of work and family life was expressed also by the trade unions, who emphasized policies such as a 3-year parental leave, contribution credits for time spent out of the labour market to perform care, and childcare services (Naumann 2006: 203–4). However, as the 'day-mothers' scandal had shown a few years earlier, mid-1970s Germany was not yet ready to accept mothers' participation in the labour market as the norm.

The SPD–FDP coalition did manage to obtain some victories in family policy, such as the replacement of regressive tax deduction with child benefits or the introduction of 4 months' maternity benefit in 1979 (Clasen 2005: 154). Overall, however, especially insofar as childcare policy is concerned, very little changed during those years.

Christian Democratic rule and the promotion of choice

Back in power with the Liberals in 1982, the Christian Democrats presented a somewhat updated discourse in relation to gender equality and family issues. The party's position was to favour choice for mothers between labour market participation and caring for children (Bleses and Seeleib-Kaiser 2004). Political leaders insisted also on the fact that women's unpaid home-based caring work should have received more recognition (Aust and Bönker 2004: 36). Severe budgetary problems in the early 1980s, however, made it impossible to expand family policy for the new government.

Things changed in the second half of the 1980s. Two important changes were adopted in 1986: parental leave and contribution credits for old age pensions for those providing care. The type of parental leave introduced by the Christian Democrats, however, was rather different from what the Nordic countries had introduced over a decade earlier. First, parental leave benefit was available to all parents: those who prior to giving birth were in employment and those who were not. This aspect was presented as an element of equal treatment between full-time mothers and those who had a job. The leave could be taken for up to 36 months. The duration of the cash benefit was shorter. The benefit, set at a rather low level, was universal for the first 6 months, means-tested against household income for the next eighteen, and phased out thereafter. At the end of the 36-month period, parents were guaranteed a job with their previous employer (Bleses and Seeleib-Kaiser 2004: 83; Clasen 2005: 156–7).

Pension contribution credits for those raising children were introduced in the same year. For each child, parents not in paid employment (i.e., mothers) were to receive a pension contribution credit equivalent to 1-year employment at 75 per cent of average earnings. Parents who remained in employment received a reduced rate. Pension credits were subsequently increased (Clasen 2005: 158–9).

The CDU–FDP government had managed to develop a new orientation in family policy that was consistent with the party line in several fields of policy. First, by more or less explicitly targeting women, it allowed the party to respond to concerns that female voters were beginning to abandon the CDU (Aust and Bönker 2004: 35). Second, the line adopted was perfectly consistent with how Germany had responded to the employment crisis of the late 1970s/early 1980s, in other words, by reducing labour supply. By providing support for mothers who remained outside of the labour market, family policy reinforced the negative impact on labour supply that had been produced by early retirement and other labour market measures. Finally, even though framed in terms of choice, the CDU family policy provided above all support to families opting for the traditional male breadwinner model, something that could resonate with the value orientation of the conservative wing of the party.

German re-unification in 1991 provided new impetus in childcare policy. East German women had been used to remaining in employment after childbirth, and to using state-provided childcare services. This put additional pressure on policy-makers to develop services for families. Ironically, this allowed the Christian Democrats to succeed where the SPD had failed in 1973–4. In 1996, the government adopted a new law introducing a right to a place in a kindergarten for children aged between 3 and 6 years. The law was adopted after lengthy debates in parliament and had to overcome resistance from the *Länder*, who had to pay for the costs. In addition to re-unification, a number of other factors facilitated its adoption. First, the law was adopted in the context of a reform of abortion regulation. As Naumann points out, an expansion in childcare services was one of few points on which pro-choice and pro-life activists could agree in the debate that proceeded the adoption of the new abortion law (Naumann 2006: 214). Second, it came as a result of an initiative staged by female members of parliament of all political parties in favour of a right to childcare for every child (Aust and Bönker 2004: 44–5). Finally, since the SPD attempt of 1973–4, kindergartens had expanded significantly in West Germany, and by 1994, 72 per cent of children aged 3 to 6 years already had a place in one (Aust and Bönker 2004: 45).

Towards an adult worker model

In 1998 the Social Democrats were back in power; this time in a coalition government with the Greens. Initially, family policy continued to support traditional German families (Clasen 2005: 163). It is only after 2001–2 that the government headed by Gerhard Schröder gave priority to the expansion of childcare services and to policy supporting working parents. In 2001, parental leave was reformed with the adoption of higher cut-off points for the receipt of the benefit and the introduction of possibly taking a higher benefit for a shorter period of time (12 months instead of 24). The German parental leave became slightly more similar to the Nordic variant. These measures were complemented by a right for parents to work part-time (Clasen 2005: 210). In 2002, in the context of the Hartz reform of the labour market, new federal funds were made available to the *Länder* for developing childcare services, this time for the age group 0–3 years (Aust and Bönker 2004: 48; Clasen 2005: 165). In 2004, a new law on childcare, meant to create 200,000 new subsidized childcare places, priced at 1.5 billion Euros (Zylka 2004a), and a target (to be achieved by 2013) of 20 per cent coverage for children aged 0 to 3 years were adopted. By that time, family policy, particularly childcare, was framed also in terms of demographic concerns. The government supported a 'sustainable family policy' with reference to the option of using family policy in order to limit population ageing and decline.

The reorientation of family policy towards an adult worker model was confirmed by the CDU–SPD coalition government elected in 2005. In 2007, a reform of the parental leave system completed its transformation into a Scandinavian-like scheme. Parents are entitled to 14 months' paid leave with a replacement rate of 67 per cent (with a ceiling). One parent can take up to 12 months' leave, with the remaining 2 months being 'reserved' for the other parent, in most cases for the father (Leitner 2008:106). In relation to childcare, the CDU–SPD coalition-led government adopted a more ambitious target than the previous government, 35 per cent of children aged 0–3 years in care until 2013. Furthermore, the Federal government, not directly responsible for the implementation, provided substantial funds to the *Länder* (Leitner 2008: 115).

The German story is reminiscent of that of another welfare state strongly influenced by Christian democracy: the Netherlands. Both nations, some 30 years after the Nordic countries, re-oriented family policy towards the promotion of parental and maternal employment. The German U-turn in family policy may have been less dramatic than the Dutch one, since rates of female employment had traditionally been higher. However, considering the fact that until the late 1980s German policy favoured strongly one-earner couples, the shift is rather significant. It is difficult to assign political responsibility for this re-orientation in family policy, as it has been a rather gradual development. Clearly, the Social Democrats initiated it, but the Christian Democrats pursued the effort largely in the same direction.

France

France stands out among continental European welfare state as a country where women's employment has traditionally been relatively high and policy has consistently supported mothers' double role of workers and carers. In the 1950s, with an employment rate of 30 per cent, French mothers of young children were twice as likely to be in employment as their Swedish counterparts (Morgan 2006: 71). Various factors help to explain this apparent anomaly.

First, the French approach to women's employment has always been driven by pragmatism, leaving little space to the upholding of traditional family values (Morgan 2003). At the end of the nineteenth century, protective legislation for maternal employment was clearly geared towards allowing mothers to participate in the labour market without endangering themselves or their babies. This approach resulted very early, in 1913, in the adoption of a compulsory 16-week paid maternity leave for those working in industry (Jenson 1989: 241). In subsequent years, policy always tended to value women's contribution to the economy, especially at times of labour shortage.

Second, in contrast to other conservative welfare states, traditional family values played a limited role in shaping public policy also because the political representation of Catholic values has been weak throughout most of France's recent history. The most influential party of Catholic inspiration, the Mouvement Républicain Populaire (MRP), played a relatively important role only during the first decades of the post-war years. With the advent of the Fifth Republic, the party dissolved into the conservative coalition historically dominated by the Gaullist movement. The latter, though clearly a conservative party, has always taken a very pragmatic line when it came to promoting the country's modernization, including in support of women's employment, if need be (Morgan 2003, 2006).

Third, it has been argued that the early development of a comprehensive pre-school system, even though not intended to provide childcare for working parents, did facilitate women's entry into the labour force (Morgan 2003). Whether the existence of a widely accepted pre-school system facilitated the development of childcare services for younger children is an open question.

The fact that Italy (see below) has had a similar pre-school system (though for a shorter period of time) and has remained a laggard in provision of care for the age group 0–3 years suggests that other explanations may be needed here.

One consequence of the French approach is that unlike in other countries, female employment and childcare policy are relatively unconnected to the debate on gender equality and the development of gender egalitarian values in society. The pragmatic approach to women's employment has meant that during times of labour market problems women, especially those with low skills, were encouraged to leave the labour market (Morgan 2003, 2006). This view is also confirmed by the relatively slow progress of gender equality in other important fields, such as politics (Siaroff 2000).

The development of a pre-school system

France was the first country in Western Europe to develop comprehensive pre-school coverage as part of the national education system. Pre-schools were institutionalized at the end of the nineteenth century against the background of an ideological and power struggle between Republicans and Catholics, played out in the field of early childhood education. The previous decades had seen the development of preschools at the initiative of religious organizations, and the stepping in of the state can be interpreted as part of a strategy for protecting and promoting republican values of separation between state and church. A law institutionalizing '*école maternelle*' was adopted in 1881. It created a non-compulsory, free of charge and non-religious (*laïque*) public service for children aged 3 to 6 years. From the beginning, *école maternelle* was fully integrated in the state education system, with the same opening hours, and source of financing (OECD 2003: 14). This was a very different start in early childhood policy from what happened in other parts of Europe, where the early steps taken in this field were typically part of anti-poverty policy or left to the private initiative of pedagogues.

The post-war years

The early post-war years, or the golden age of the male breadwinner model, saw the adoption of measures geared towards supporting full-time motherhood. Cash family benefits, which had been introduced in the 1930s with an overtly pronatalist objective, were increased on various occasions and were complemented by a subsidy for one-earner families (Morgan 2003: 264, 275). By the end of the 1950s, however, concerns about labour shortage had prompted economic planners to advocate investing in childcare facilities so as to allow a larger number of women to enter the labour force and fill the growing demand for labour in industry. As it turned out, unrest in North

Africa (namely Algeria) led to mass immigration, which basically solved the labour shortage problem so that the expansion in childcare coverage did not take place. The episode, nonetheless, provides an additional illustration of the pragmatism in French policy towards female employment (Morgan 2003).

The 1970s and the 1980s: daycare as an opportunity for credit claiming

Childcare was back on the political agenda in the early 1970s, this time not as a result of economic pragmatism but in response to women's demands. The investment of state funds in childcare began under a Gaullist prime minister in 1970, but the issue was subsequently picked up by other political actors. In 1972, the target of 1,000 new daycare centres was mentioned in an electoral agreement co-signed by the Communist and the Socialist parties. In the 1973 election campaign, the Gaullist candidate promised twice as many new crèches, 2,000 (Morgan 2003).[5] In the following years, under the centre-right president Giscard d'Estaing, a series of important initiatives were adopted. In 1976, childcare expenses were made deductible from taxable income. In the following year, a law regulating family daycare was adopted. Its main innovation was to assign an educational role also to individual childminders. In 1977 unpaid parental leave was adopted and the subsidy for one-earner families was converted into an additional family benefit available to all families, regardless of parents' employment status (Leprince 2003; Morgan 2003). These developments did impact on the overall supply of childcare places, which increased from 69,000 in 1975 to 119,000 in 1983 (Leprince 2003: 20).

The expansion of services concerned also the pre-school system, even though in this field significant steps had already been taken in previous years. In 1970–1, 87 per cent of 4 year olds and 100 per cent of 5 year olds were attending *école maternelle*. Pre-schools were also made accessible to children aged between 2 and 3 years. Among this group, coverage was also increasing rapidly from 10 per cent in 1960–1 to 18 per cent in 1970–1. The coverage for 2 year olds has stabilized at around 35 per cent since the 1980s (OECD 2003: 43).

The 1980s and the 1990s: pragmatism under economic constraints

The Socialists, in power throughout most of the 1980s, did not fundamentally alter the course of policy towards women's employment, maintaining the pragmatic approach. True, during the opposition years, the French Socialists

---

[5] As it turned out, the figure of 2,000 was the result of a mistake. In reality the plan was to build 200 new daycare centres. The Gaullist prime minister, however, stood by his word and maintained the higher figure, failing nonetheless to implement such a big plan in the following years (Morgan 2003: 283).

had strongly emphasized gender equality as a policy goal to be pursued once in government. However, the road taken in labour market policy in response to the unemployment crisis of the 1980s clearly impacted on family policy. Rather than facilitating women's access to paid work, the main thrust of the new initiatives taken was the provision of subsidies for parents who quit the labour market to care for their children. A key step in this direction was taken in 1985 with the adoption of *Allocation parentale d'éducation* (APE), a cash benefit paid to parents who withdrew from the labour market after the birth of a third child. Even though framed in gender neutral terms, APE turned out to be a major disincentive for women's employment, especially for low-skill women whose wages could not exceed the modest amount of the benefit by much (Jenson and Sineau 1995). The number of childcare places continued to expand throughout the decade (Leprince 2003: 20), but it fell short of both the electoral promises made by candidate Mitterrand in the 1981 presidential election campaign and parents' demands (Jenson and Sineau 1995: 256). The emphasis was also put more on childminders rather than on daycare facilities (Daguerre 2006: 218).

According to Jenson and Sineau the gap between the Socialists' electoral promises and their actual policies can be explained with reference to the economic and labour market difficulties that France experienced in the early 1980s, which forced the Socialists to take a neo-Liberal turn (Jenson and Sineau 1995). Subsequent years were characterized by continuity, with most policy efforts going in the directions of both expanding daycare places and subsidizing childcare provided by parents. Vouchers to pay for childminders were also introduced and developed. Childcare benefits paid to parents were often criticized because of the negative impact they had on maternal employment. Although this was probably an intended effect, perfectly consistent with the 'labour reduction route' taken in labour market policy, attempts were made to soften this negative impact. In 2004, a new benefit for parents providing care was introduced, with a structure that makes it convenient to combine care work with a part-time job (Daguerre 2006: 219).

As argued earlier, France is a rather unique case within the seven-country sample covered in this book, and arguably more generally. Unlike in most other countries, childcare policies are relatively unrelated to the gender equality debate. This was clearly the case with the early steps taken in the field by establishing a comprehensive pre-school system at the end of the nineteenth century, and in subsequent years, when the target was the younger group. When the gender dimension is taken into account, policy is considerably more ambiguous, relying on benefits that are available to both working and non-working parents. Politically, the expansion of childcare services did not depend on the Left's influence. Instead, the story of childcare policy in France highlights well the potential for credit claiming embodied in this social policy tool.

Italy

The story of childcare in Italy is intriguing in many respects. The country is generally considered to be a laggard in this field, as shown by low coverage rates for the age group 0–3 years, low rates of female employment, and low fertility rates, suggesting huge problems for women in reconciling work and family life. Given the above, it may come as a surprise that Italy was one of the first continental European countries to move forward as far as formal legislation is concerned. In 1968, pre-school for the age group 3 to 6 years were institutionalized under the Ministry of Education. In 1971, a national law making provision for central government subsidies for childcare services was adopted.

To find out why a country dominated by Christian democracy and with a very low female employment rate is among the first to move in continental Europe one must look at antecedents from the fascist period and at radicalization of politics over a rather short period of time (late 1960s to the early 1970s) when a number of improbable laws were adopted.

What is also puzzling in the Italian case is the fact that despite these innovative laws being in place, childcare provision did not take off. In fact, the new laws were adopted in a context in which work was not yet an aspiration for a majority of women. Expanding childcare, therefore, was not an attractive political option for elected politicians. Later on, when Italian women did massively enter the labour market, they tended to turn to more informal solutions, such as the grandparents and immigrant care workers. This reduces the extent of unmet demand for childcare services and, as a result, the incentives for politicians to invest in childcare as well.

Antecedents

Like in other countries, in Italy one finds two types of very different antecedents to childcare policy. On the one hand, childcare has been available to disadvantaged people since the end of the nineteenth century, often within factories employing female workers as part of an employer-paternalistic approach to social policy. On the other hand, more or less simultaneously, one also sees the development of pre-school facilities, largely under the influence of pedagogues such as Maria Montessori, where emphasis was placed on child development and early education. Montessori's own kindergarten in Rome served as an example for the whole country. According to Saraceno: 'Her model was aimed towards developing early learning and logical capabilities. It soon became the standard for elite pre-school throughout Italy, which were attended by the privileged children regardless of the work situation of the mother' (Saraceno 2003: 154–5). With the exception of these elite pre-schools, childcare at the turn of the century had a bad reputation, often associated with poverty and with women who had to work out of economic necessity.

Like other totalitarian governments, the fascist regime in power between 1922 and World War II had a strong penchant for heavy intervention in family policy. Essentially for strategic reasons, like in Nazi Germany, family policy had a strong pronatalist bias. These measures, which included a tax on celibacy and a family benefits system with the level of the benefit increasing with each additional child, provided strong financial incentives to have children (Saraceno 1990). While fascist family policy clearly had a pronatalist orientation, it did not necessarily oppose or discourage female employment. Women were also needed in the factories, and policy had to make sure that high fertility and employment could be combined. As a result, legislation forcing companies employing more than fifty married women to provide childcare facilities and 'breastfeeding rooms' was passed. The fascist government was also responsible for the creation in 1925 of Opera Nazionale Maternita e Infanzia (ONMI), a national institution providing counselling and childcare for working-class mothers (Saraceno 2003: 157).

These policies combined a strong conservative value orientation in relation to marriage and gender roles with the efficiency requirement of an economy that was preparing for war. These decisions proved important for Italian family policy. Unlike in Germany, where the end of World War II coincided with a complete regime change in policy towards families, in Italy many institutions set up during the interwar period outlived the fascist regime.

The post-war years: the rise of the male breadwinner model

During the post-war years, Italy experienced strong economic growth. With rising male wages, the number of women who had to work out of necessity declined sharply. In fact the female employment rate declined quite substantially until the early 1970s. OECD data, available only since 1960, show a reduction from 37 per cent in 1960 to 30 per cent in 1970. It was in those years that the male breadwinner model emerged as dominant in Italy. The model was also institutionalized in several policy domains. For example, in unemployment policy, fathers with dependent children were given priority by the labour exchanges over other categories of unemployed people (see Chapter 5).

Institutions inherited from the fascist period were updated. For example, in 1950, the obligation to provide childcare for companies was based on the number of all female employees and not only of married women as it used to be the case. This provision was eventually scrapped in 1971. Its effect was to discourage smaller employers from hiring women. By linking women's presence in the firm with childcare services, this provision emphasized women's primary responsibility for childcare. Childcare was as a result only available to female staff. The law was scrapped under pressure from the trade unions and the feminist movement in an effort to transfer responsibility for childcare services from employers to local governments. (Saraceno 2003: 77–8).

The post-war years were also characterized by the continuous expansion of pre-school facilities, especially in the North and in urban areas. Pre-schools were not meant to provide childcare for working parents. Their role was mostly pedagogical. The service was provided by the municipalities, by religious outfits, or by organizations inspired by a given pedagogical method (e.g., Montessori or Steiner schools). In 1968, in the context of a broader reform of the education system, pre-schools were taken under the responsibility of the state.[6] As a result, coverage of pre-school services for the age group 3 to 6 years increased fast, reaching 60 per cent in the early 1970s (Saraceno 2003: 165).

The 1971 laws

The late 1960s and early 1970s were characterized, in Italy as elsewhere in Europe, by a strong radicalization in politics and by the rise of the feminist movement. The latter in Italy was divided along ideological lines, reflecting the key players in the party system. One key actor, Unione Donne Italiane (UDI), was close to the Communist Party and the Communist trade unions; alongside it, one found also various Catholic women's organizations. As a result, the feminist movement was profoundly divided, but towards the end of the 1960s, both of its components saw support for childcare as an opportunity to differentiate themselves from their male-dominated reference organization: the Communist Party and the Catholic Church, respectively (Bertone 2003).[7]

This convergence among women's organization on support for policies helping women reconcile work and family life, such as childcare and maternity leave resulted in the adoption of two important pieces of legislation, both passed in 1971: a law on childcare and one on maternity benefit and parental leave.

Through the new law on childcare, the central government provided subsidies to the municipalities, both for setting up childcare facilities and towards running expenses. The development of services was facilitated by the dismantling of ONMI, an institution providing childcare to disadvantaged families that had been set up during the fascist period. Its premises could now be used

[6] The central government took direct responsibility for the provision of kindergartens along with the municipalities which already offered this service.

[7] As pointed out by Bertone, for the UDI a focus on childcare was part of a strategy aimed at making the organization more autonomous from the positions of the Communist Party. Quite similarly, Catholic women saw an opportunity to gain some independence from the Christian Democrats and the Catholic Church. They emphasized the fact that work outside the home (like childrearing) was also a contribution to society (Bertone 2003: 242).

to provide modern universal childcare services. The 1971 law included also a target: 5 per cent of 0 to 3 year old children within 5 years. In reality, the target will be reached some 20 years later (Saraceno 2003: 158).

In the same year the government adopted also a new law on maternity leave. The leave consisted of two parts, a compulsory one of 5 months and a voluntary one, of up to 9 months. During the compulsory 5-month leave, a benefit of 80 per cent of earnings (or 100 per cent for public sector employees and those working for large companies) was payable. For the additional 9-month voluntary leave, the benefit level was of 30 per cent during the first 6 months. The voluntary part of the leave could be taken by the father, as long as the mother renounced her right (Saraceno 2003: 80–1).

The laws of 1971 were a rather unlikely development. With government solidly in Christian Democratic hands (in a coalition with three centre-left smaller parties) and with a female employment rate of 31 per cent (compared with 60 per cent in Denmark or Sweden in the same year), reconciling work and family life was hardly at the top of the government's list of priorities. It can be understood with reference to feminist mobilization, but also to the rise of the Communist Party at the time. The PCI, although out of government, was quite influential in those years. The Christian Democrat-led government acted pre-emptively and adopted policies such as stronger employment protection legislation, childcare, and parental leave (see also Chapter 5).

The fascist legacy, however, arguably played a role too. The availability of an infrastructure of the ONMI—and the rather heavy requirement put on employers to provide childcare services if they wanted to employ women—can be seen as factors facilitating the adoption of a childcare law that was certainly innovative for the time.

Sure, the 1971 laws, especially the ones addressing maternity and parental leave, had a strong Christian Democratic flavour, despite its generosity. For example, the compulsion element in the leave was meant to protect the child before and after birth, and the fact that a father could take part of the leave only with the approval of the mother upheld the traditional division of roles. Access to childcare services is often based on priority lists, with a point system which is determined at the local level and generally considers single parent status, family income, number of children, and the fact of having or not having the grandparents living in the same area. In a way, the latter criterion institutionalizes the role of the family as a provider of childcare, which has been considered as a defining feature of the Southern European model of welfare by various authors (see, e.g., Ferrera 1998)

Notwithstanding these peculiarities, by the early 1970s Italy had in place a legislative framework for childcare, reconciling work and family life that was not so different from what one found in the Nordic countries. What was different was the context: female employment in Italy was not ready for take-off yet.

141

Developments since the 1980s

Despite the innovative legislation adopted in 1971, the coverage rate of child-care services for the age group 0–3 years did not take off. The coverage rate for children under 3 years increased very moderately, reaching 5.8 per cent in 1992 and 7.4 per cent in 2000. These rates, as one would expect, conceal huge regional variations, ranging between around 2 per cent in some southern regions to 18 per cent in the central-northern region of Emilia-Romagna. Things were different for pre-schools, which after the 1968 reform were part of the state education system. By the mid-1970s, coverage reached 70 per cent of the age group 3–6 years and 90 per cent by the early 2000s (Saraceno 2003: 160).

Under the influence of EU legislation, in particular the parental leave directive adopted in 1992, the Italian parental leave system was updated in the 1990s. On top of maternity leave (5 months) each parent is now entitled to a 6-month leave, with a 30 per cent income replacement benefit. The total duration of the leave, which must be taken before the child is 3 years old, cannot exceed 10 months. An additional month is granted if the father takes at least 3 months' leave.

In more recent years childcare has not featured prominently in social policy debates, concerned more with pension reform and employment protection. A very large role in terms of provision of care is played by the extended family, especially by the grandparents, and, increasingly, by immigrants, often undeclared (Da Roit and Sabatinelli 2005). As a result, pressure on the government to develop a comprehensive publicly financed childcare system is probably lower. In such circumstances, incentives for credit claiming are weak.

The United Kingdom

The UK is a country that has tended to neglect policies helping parents reconcile work and family life until very recently. Coverage against the loss of earnings due to maternity has existed since 1946, but more advanced instruments have only been introduced much later. Childcare, in particular, has remained underdeveloped by comparative standards until the beginning of the twenty-first century. One should also note that in the UK, primary education begins at the age of 5, or 2 years earlier than in the Nordic countries. This may help to understand why demand for early childhood education and care was less present on the policy agenda for much of the post-war years.

The post-war years

World War II provided a missed opportunity to develop a comprehensive childcare system. In fact, in order to allow women to work in the armament and other industries, war nurseries were set up throughout the country, providing extensive coverage. At the end of the war, however, these were dismantled apparently in the face of little protest, partially because there was a generalized expectation that these would be replaced by the expansion of nursery education (Riley 1983).[8]

The absence of significant policy efforts throughout the post-war years in the field of reconciling work and family life has been explained with reference to the pervasiveness of an 'ideology of motherhood', which understood the role of women, and mothers, as carers as opposed to carers and workers (Lewis 1980). But the prevalence of societal values that ascribe a domestic role to women is, historically, hardly a British specificity. In addition, a strong ideology of motherhood can be considered an obstacle to the development of a childcare policy but should be associated with a preference for policies that allow women who work to spend more time with their children, such as parental leave. In Germany, as seen above, this was precisely what the Christian Democrats did.

Others have explained British reluctance to intervene in the broad field of family policy with reference to the liberal tradition in policy-making, which has resulted in political actors developing the belief that the care of children is a private matter and that the state should not interfere in this sphere. The fact is that throughout the post-war years, the consensus was that mothers of small children should stay at home rather than being involved in paid employment, a view that was shared by actors of different political orientations including the Labour Party and various unions (Randall 1995: 342).

The conservative governments of the 1980s and early 1990s

As a result, well into the 1980s and early 1990s, Britain remained a country with an underdeveloped policy in the field of reconciling work and family life. Childcare coverage for small children remained low and financial help for families in paying for this service virtually nonexistent. The Conservative governments of the 1980s clearly considered the provision of childcare as a private matter, as testified by the 1992 election manifesto, which refrained from committing any public money to the provision of childcare.[9] It is only towards the mid-1990s that the Conservative government headed by John Major introduced a voucher scheme enabling parents to pay for part-time

[8] In the British context, a distinction is made between childcare, or daycare, which simply implies looking after children so that parents can attend to other activities, and nursery education, which is often provided on a part-time basis and has above all a pedagogical objective.

[9] The manifesto made reference to the role that the private and voluntary sector were encouraged to play as providers, with local authorities being expected to supervise quality (Kremer 2005).

nursery education for 4 year olds (Randall 2000: 359). Parental leave was not developed either. The EU directive on parental leave, which came into force in 1996, did not have any legal impact on the UK given that this country had negotiated an opt out from the social chapter of the Maastricht treaty (Treib and Falkner 2004).

Childcare policy under New Labour

The New Labour government elected in 1997 found itself in a situation that could be characterized by an almost total absence of public provision in the work–life balance policy field, and by strong expectations from working women and families for more to be done. Such a situation contained strong incentives for the new government to act according to a credit-claiming logic. As a matter of fact, work–life balance policies featured prominently in the 1997 election manifesto that brought Labour back to power after 17 years of Conservative rule. A chapter on 'work and family' included promises to 'help parents, especially women, to balance family and working life' and to introduce a 'limited unpaid parental leave' (British Labour Party 1997). These were rather vague commitments, especially insofar as extra spending was concerned, but they must be understood against the background of an election campaign in which, for the Labour Party, it was essential not to be seen as a high tax, high spend party.

The promises were followed by policies. The first high profile initiatives in this area were, in 1998, the launching of a 'national childcare strategy', which had the objective through the coordinated effort of various actors to expand childcare coverage and the publication of a Green paper. The Green paper focused on improving the quality, the affordability, and the accessibility of childcare. The document made reference to non-working mothers and to the fact that the lack of childcare was often an obstacle to employment, especially for single parents. The issue of child poverty did not feature prominently at all in this early paper, even though many of the measures put forward, such as a childcare tax credit, were to be provided on a means-tested basis (British Government 1998).

Through the national childcare strategy, the government provided public funds for developing new childcare and early education places. The actual provision of services was left to local private voluntary and public actors competing for government subsidies. Primary schools were involved in the provision of early education for 4 year olds. Local authorities were attributed a coordination and supervisory role. For younger age groups, provision depends more on private providers (Evers et al. 2005). The policy reversal initiated by the New Labour government did produce tangible results. Spending on family services has doubled between the late 1990s and 2003 to 0.8 per cent of GDP, which makes the UK the biggest spender on this item among liberal welfare states. Over the same period of time, more than 600,000 new places for the under 5 year olds were created, representing both an expansion in childcare provision and a shift from care to early childhood education (Evers et al. 2005: 200).

The development of childcare was also part of the government's anti-poverty policy, carried out mostly through a system of tax credits. A childcare tax credit was introduced in October 1999. It consisted of a means-tested tax credit available to parents working more than 16 hours a week and using approved forms of childcare. The credit covers 70 per cent of costs up to a maximum of 100 GBP for families with one child and 150 GBP for families with two or more children (Rake 2001). Eligibility depends on income, family configuration, and other factors. At the end of 1999, there were over 800,000 families receiving Working Families Tax Credit (WFTC), a number that increased to 1.1 million in May 2002, most of them eligible for the childcare tax credit (British Government 2002). The same year saw also the adoption of provision for parental leave. This remained modest by European standards, as the scheme essentially translates the minimum requirements of the EU direct-ive. Each parent can take up to 13 weeks unpaid leave before the child's fifth birthday, in addition to maternity leave (Hall 1999).

Work–life balance policies maintained a prominent place also in the second term of the Blair government. In the 2001 election manifesto, achievements in this field were mentioned proudly and prominently, and more was promised, for example a target of 1.6 million childcare places for 2004 (British Labour Party 2001). In 2002 the whole tax credit system was 'rationalized', with now a distinction being made between an 'integrated child credit' and an 'employ-ment tax credit'. The objectives behind the reform were to simplify the system and to strengthen work incentives. In the process, however, the access thresh-olds for the benefits have also been increased so that since 2003 households with children and annual income up to 50,000 GBP remain eligible for the benefit, though at a lower rate than poorer families (Daguerre 2006).

During New Labour's second term in office, work–life balance policies extended their reach upwards in the income distribution, but developed also a stronger anti-poverty orientation. This was the case of other schemes targeting disadvantaged families and neighbourhoods (like the Sure Start programme). These developments need to be seen also in the context of the government's emphasis on the eradication of child poverty. To facilitate parents' employment was considered to be the most effective strategy for dealing with child poverty (Evers et al. 2005). While during the first term, and especially in the 1997 election campaign, the main concern of the Labour Party was not to lose the median voter because of a tax and spend image, in the second term, a key issue was the internal divisions within the party. The new direction taken by work–life balance policies can be understood in relation to this development. The weakness of the opposition combined with the confidence that the general public appreciates good quality mass services provided an incentive to extend provision to the middle classes. At the same time, the expectation, strong among the party grassroots and influential left-wing figures, that a Labour government should care about the most disadvantaged and adopt redistributive policies provided the rationale for giving work–life balance policies an anti-poverty spin.

Childcare policy across time and space

The above accounts of the development of childcare in seven European countries suggest that in general our democracies do work as transmission belts between public demands and public policies, if somewhat slowly. Changes in people's demands and needs do, with a time lag, translate into new policies that are specifically designed to meet those new demands and needs. This general statement needs to be somewhat nuanced, especially in order to account for the Southern European exception, illustrated in this chapter by the Italian case.

The political mechanism that allows us to explain how new needs and demands are turned into policies is political competition, and more specifically, the fact that election-seeking politicians are after opportunities to claim credit for what they do. Investing in childcare provided them with such an opportunity. Whether in Sweden in the 1960s, France in the 1980s, Britain in the 1990s, or Germany in the 2000s, childcare policy is clearly perceived as popular. The accounts above abound with examples that support this interpretation. In Sweden, childcare became an object of competition between the Liberals, who were the first to pick it up in a party programme, and the Social Democrats (Naumann 2006: 156). As seen above, the actual or perceived popularity of childcare services forced a French candidate to political office to stick to a promise to create 2,000 new daycare centres, even though the figure was ten times bigger than what he had initially planned (Morgan 2003: 283). In Germany, the 2004 law providing subsidies to set up daycare centres was sponsored by the red–green coalition government and forced the CDU/CSU opposition to abstain in the upper chamber of parliament. The party leadership simply did not want to be seen as the obstacle to greater childcare provision (Zylka 2004b).

Childcare, and more in general work–family balance policies, have been used as instruments for credit claiming (see Morgan 2010 for a similar argument). From this point of view, we can expect that their appeal is strongest when the gap between demand and supply is greatest. To put it another way, the incentives for policy-makers to pick up the childcare issue are strongest when a relatively high proportion of women have entered the labour market and when existing provision is minimal. This claim may be illustrated with a Swedish–Italian comparison. Sweden in the early 1970s provided the most favourable conditions for childcare to appeal to vote-seeking politicians. Women began entering the labour force in great numbers but were having difficulties finding childcare. At the same time, the absence of a pre-school system and a relatively late age for beginning compulsory schooling (7 years of age) meant that the potential winners of an expansion of childcare were particularly numerous. Italy, since the mid-1990s, has witnessed a virtually uninterrupted growth in female employment (see Figure 6.1). While this development should in principle be associated with stronger demands for publicly subsidized childcare, it takes place in a completely different context. In Italy during the late 1990s to early 2000s, families have alternatives to state-subsidized services. These take various shapes and include the existing pre-school system for the age group 3–6 years, grandparents (Saraceno 2008), and immigrants (Da Roit and Sabatinelli 2005). The potential political payoff of investing in subsidized childcare is much smaller under these conditions.

While having developed a pre-school system before the massive entry of women into the labour market may have facilitated the development of comprehensive services for the age group 3–6 years, in some circumstances, the effect of this policy antecedent may be a reduced pressure for government intervention, hence lowering incentives for politicians to address the issue. In the case of Italy, this is coupled with a rather low effective age of retirement, on average around 60 years of age between 2000 and 2005 (OECD 2006), which allows grandparents to serve as providers of childcare.

Political competition plays an important role in understanding the development of childcare services across Europe. But can all parties play the credit-claiming game in this field? Historically, it is probably the case that Social Democratic parties have been more often associated with pro-childcare initiatives. Looking beyond Scandinavia, one finds an important role played by both the British Labour Party and the SPD in Germany, who tried first in the early 1970s to make progress in this direction, although without success. However, there are also several examples of non-Social Democratic parties championing childcare and work–life balance policies. As already mentioned, in Sweden the issue was brought up by the Liberals. In Denmark the key legislative act was supported by all the main parties. In Germany, the Christian Democrats in government again after 2006 clearly made work–life balance policies a key priority. Also, a Danish–Swedish comparison speaks against a strong effect of Social Democratic power. It was in the country where the Social Democrats were weaker, Denmark, that services developed first and to a larger extent (Borchorst 2002: 270). If there is a relationship between social democracy and support for childcare, it is a rather weak one.

The relationship between Christian democracy and childcare may be stronger, and negative. Christian Democratic parties when in government have generally been reluctant in promoting female employment. This may have been in order to adhere to the teachings of the Catholic Church and thus support the traditional family built around the breadwinner model. It may also be related to the fact that Christian Democratic parties were particularly influential in Western Europe in the 1980s (in government most of the time in Germany, Italy, and the Netherlands). As seen in Chapter 5, these parties championed the so-called 'labour reduction route' in order to deal with the labour market problems of the time. It entailed the reluctance to favour female employment.

Things have changed in the 2000s, though as the U-turn in family policy of the German and Dutch Christian Democrats demonstrates. In some circumstances, labour market and demographic imperatives may weigh more than traditional values. Perhaps more importantly, Christian Democrats have had troubles appealing to female and younger voters. This has resulted in a decline in their influence since the 'trente glorieurses'. Reappraising the role of government in supporting families may be seen as a strategy to reinforce the support for the Christian Democrats among these groups of voters.

7

Quantitative Evidence: The Determinants of Public Spending on Active Labour Market Policy and Childcare

The objective of this chapter is to complement the qualitative evidence presented in Chapters 5 and 6 with an account of developments in public expenditure on active labour market policy (ALMP) and childcare based on statistical analysis. Using public expenditure data to track cross-national and cross-time variation in social policies is common practice among comparativists (see, e.g., Huber and Stephens 2001; Castles 2004, 2005). Yet, this approach is not without problems. It has been pointed out that this type of data suffers from a number of weaknesses. First, it is affected by the denominator problem; in other words, GDP shifts in this parameter may give the false impression that social spending increases or decreases, whereas in fact the 'welfare effort' made in a country remains stable. Second, there is a problem related to changes in the number of beneficiaries of a programme. For example, increasing spending on pensions in the context of population ageing may be the result of an increase in the level of pensions or in the number of pensioners (Siegel 2000). These problems, however, can generally be dealt with by using control variables. Third, a more fundamental problem refers to the fact that spending tells us little about what really matters in social policies, such as how they modify the distribution of resources in society (Esping-Andersen 1990).

Despite these problems, spending data continue to be used to study cross-national variation in social policy, not only because it is readily available and of an increasingly reliable quality. The currently available level of disaggregation allows a more precise use of these indicators (Castles 2004: 10–11). In addition spending data conveniently sums up important features of policy that are difficult to measure through other channels, such as the extent of access or the level of a benefit. Of course, the appropriate controls are needed in order to avoid the problems mentioned above. In addition, one must be aware of the limitation of this kind of exercise. Analyses of trends in spending data are bound to tell only part of the story of how active social policy has developed.

Macro-level statistical analyses such as that presented in this chapter must also confront the well-known 'small N—many variables' problem. As seen in Chapter 4, on purely theoretical grounds many factors are good candidates to explain the emergence of active social policy in the OECD world. Yet the scope across which hypotheses can be tested is limited to twenty-two to twenty-three countries, and such a small number of observations is incompatible with the type of multivariate analysis that is needed when testing competing hypotheses (Shalev 2007). To deal with this problem, it has become common among comparativists to test hypotheses simultaneously across time and space, by pooling in a single database time series of the relevant indicators for different countries (pooled time series). This technique, which is described more in detail below, allows researchers to rely on much larger samples but has problems of its own. In general, pooled time series are a useful tool for identifying simple and strong effects. They are a blunt instrument. Smaller and more complex effects are more difficult to identify with certainty, given the various statistical problems involved with this kind of analysis. It is on the basis of this understanding that pooled time series are used in this chapter.

Testable hypotheses

As it is often the case with statistical analysis, the hypotheses that can actually be tested are heavily dependent on data availability. This study is no exception, which means that it will be possible to test only some of the hypotheses presented in Chapter 4. These are briefly discussed next.

Changing needs in competitive democracies

According to this hypothesis, active social policy developed in response to the emergence of new needs and demands. For both areas of active social policy, the OECD provides reasonably good indicators measuring the extent of need. In the case of ALMPs, the unemployment rate is the most obvious variable affecting need/demand for this type of policy. In relation to childcare, women's employment will be used as a proxy for the extent of demand for services.

Political parties and women's influence

As seen in Chapter 4, it has been hypothesized that a strong Social Democratic party is associated with more spending on both subsidized childcare and ALMP. It has also been hypothesized that Christian democracy, instead, is associated with a mostly passive welfare state. Hence, countries where Christian Democrats have played an important role can be expected to lag behind in the development of ALMP. Both these hypotheses can easily be tested, since data on the strength of different political parties are available.

In the field of childcare, some have hypothesized a political effect based on the influence that women have on policy-making. Of course, theoretically, subsidized childcare benefits parents regardless of their gender. However, given the reality of the division of labour within households, better provision of childcare is considerably more likely to improve the life situation of women than it is of men. For this reason, I expect indicators of women's influence in politics to be associated with higher expenditure. With regard to partisan effects we can expect a negative impact of Christian democracy because of the incompatibility between childcare and the sort of traditional family values promoted by these parties. However, as seen in Chapter 6, in recent years Christian Democratic parties' position on family issues has changed quite dramatically, particularly in Germany and in the Netherlands where reforms clearly aim at facilitating maternal employment. Therefore, I expect a weakening negative effect of Christian democracy on childcare spending.

Centripetal forces

The hypothesis on the role played by centripetal or consensual pressures is problematic for quantitative testing. Centripetal pressures are mostly the result of political institutions and how these interact with the type of power configurations that emerge from elections (Immergut 1992; Bonoli 2000). Two difficulties are involved in trying to model this effect. First, the impact of the interaction between institutions and power configuration is country specific so that it is virtually impossible to reproduce it through a quantitative indicator. For example, in France, power concentration is arguably stronger when president and prime minister belong to the same party; in Germany, when the two chambers of parliament have the same majority or in Denmark, when the country is ruled by a majority rather than a minority government. For this reason, simply including an indicator of institutionally based power concentration, such as the number of veto points, is unlikely to model adequately the impact of institutions on policy. Second, political institutions tend to be stable across time, making their inclusion in a pooled time series unreasonable. For these reasons, I do not attempt to model the impact of political institutions on the two policy areas of interest.

Less problematic is the other source of centripetal pressure discussed in Chapter 4: economic internationalization. The extent to which a country is exposed to the international economic pressures can be measured with a simple indicator of economic openness, such as the sum of imports and export as a proportion of GDP.

Timing and the crowding out effect

In Chapter 4, I hypothesized that countries in which demands for active social policies emerged earlier had an advantage because spending on these new policy areas faced less competition from spending on age-related programmes. This hypothesis can be tested by examining whether spending on old age pension impacts negatively on spending on active social policies. This effect should be discernible both across countries and over time; hence, it can be seen as suitable for analysis with a pooled time series design.

Hypotheses excluded from the statistical analysis

The other hypotheses considered in Chapter 4 will not be tested in the model. Policy learning and policy diffusion processes cannot be modelled with a simple pooled time series design. They need to be studied by careful reconstruction of countries' trajectories in a given policy field, and it is difficult to see how one could model this type of developments with measurable indicators.[1] The role of antecedents and more generally of institutional effects are also very problematic in statistical analysis because of measurement problems and also because they do not vary over time. As a result, it does not make much sense to include them in pooled time series.

The impact of public opinion is more suitable to quantitative analysis because we do have access to several databases containing information on people's policy preferences on social policies. However, as seen in Chapter 4, the problem here is one of establishing the direction of causality. Studies of public opinion and the welfare state have shown a relatively strong correspondence between what people say they want and what they do get in terms of social policies. However, it is not clear whether public opinion impacts on policy, policy shapes public opinion, or whether both effects are present. Public opinion data are unfortunately not available at a sufficiently large

---

[1] In relation to the policy diffusion hypothesis, some researchers have tried to develop a methodology were dyads of countries are compared so as to uncover similar policy development adopted at short time lags (Gilardi and Füglister 2008).

number of points in time to settle this question through empirical analysis. As argued in Chapter 4, studies relying on two or three data points per country do not produce convincing evidence. Finally, hypotheses on the impact of political competition and the use of active social policy as a credit-claiming device are also excluded from the statistical analysis.

Data

This chapter uses data on social expenditure obtained from the OECD. Even though the quality and the reliability of this data source has increased substantially over the years, there are still some problems which have resulted in two slightly different data sets—in terms of country sample and period covered—for the two policy areas.

Active labour market policies

The analysis on spending on ALMPs relies on data on twenty-two OECD countries that have been democratic since the 1980s, between 1980 and 2009.[2] Former communist and other new members of the OECD are excluded because the political and labour market dynamics are different in these contexts. Also excluded from the analysis is Luxembourg because it is a rather particular case in relation to both its labour market and its position in the international economy. Luxembourg does not have an unemployment problem (the unemployment rate is always below 3 per cent throughout the period covered, except in 1 year). In addition, the measurement of economic openness for Luxembourg is vastly overestimated because many import/export companies are based in that country. The trade openness indicator is artificially pushed up by imports that are immediately re-exported.[3]

Childcare

For the analysis of childcare, I use the OECD expenditure spending category 'family services'. This includes spending on pre-primary education, daycare centres, home-help services, and other smaller programmes (OECD 2007c: 12). Unfortunately, prior to 1998 some countries included spending on pre-

---

[2] Australia, Austria, Belgium, Canada, Denmark, Finland, France, Germany, Greece, Iceland, Ireland, Italy, Japan, Netherlands, New Zealand, Norway, Portugal, Spain, Sweden, Switzerland, United Kingdom, and the United States.

[3] The sum of import and export amounted to 256 per cent of GDP in 2003.

school programmes while others did not, making this portion of the database de facto unusable for comparative statistical analysis. Given these limitations, the analyses in this chapter concentrate on expenditure on family services as a percentage of GDP for the period covering the years 1998 to 2007 for 23 OECD countries (those covered in the ALMP analysis and Luxembourg).

Dependent variables

The dependent variables used here are OECD indicators of spending on ALMPs and childcare. Of course, spending on ALMPs is heavily dependent on the rate of unemployment, which fluctuates in every country during the period under consideration. This constitutes a problem for statistical analysis. An increase in the number of jobless may cause expenditure to rise simply because there are more beneficiaries to these programmes. Such an increase should not be mistaken for an expansion of the policy.

There are a number of different ways to suppress this unwanted effect. The simplest way is to include the rate of unemployment on the right side of the equation as a control variable. The other coefficients can then be interpreted as effects at constant unemployment rate. This is the approach used for example by Rueda (2007). Alternatively, one can standardize the dependent variable simply by dividing it by the rate of unemployment. In this case, the new dependent variable will be a measure of spending on ALMPs per percentage point of unemployment. This is the approach followed by Huo et al. (2008).

The problem of whether to use ratios or controls when dealing with the question of how to suppress an unwanted effect has been encountered in the natural sciences as well. The consensus emerging from the literature is that if the objective of the researcher is to explain the absolute size of something, then the control should be used. Ratios should be used only when the objective is to explain the proportion of something relative to something else (Bollen and Ward 1979; Smith 2005). In the case of ALMPs, a ratio would make sense if the dependent variable were spending on ALMPs as a proportion of total spending for unemployment. This ratio would have a meaningful interpretation, showing the active or passive bias of policy. If the objective is instead to control for unemployment, then the inclusion of the unemployment rate on the righthand side of the regression equation seems to be a more appropriate strategy. This is the approach followed in this chapter.

Independent variables

Since the aim of this analysis is to point out potential casual relationships, all independent variables (see Table 7.1) are lagged by 1 year.

Partisan effects—Following the above theoretical discussion, I operationalize partisan effects with two variables: the share of leftist and of religious parties in parliaments. Most studies (Esping-Andersen 1990; Huber et al. 1993; Huber and Stephens 2001) have operationalized political variables by looking at cabinet shares, in other words, the presence of the relevant political forces in government. Here I prefer parliamentary representation for three reasons. First, cabinet shares underestimate the indirect influence that a strong opposition party may have on policy, for example by putting forward a popular policy proposal that may force the government to take action in a given policy field. Second, especially in countries with majoritarian political institutions, cabinet shares overestimate the extent of variation in the political influence of the relevant actors. In these countries, for most parties this indicator resembles a dummy variable, taking only 0 and 100 per cent as values. This measure clearly does not reflect the more gradual character of the evolution of political influence. Third, in countries with multiparty systems, a strong opposition may be effectively able to veto policies that are half-heartedly supported by a coalition government. Parliamentary and government composition are obviously related. For leftist parties between 1980 and 2003, $r = 0.62$.

Economic openness—Economic openness is measured with a simple indicator of exposure to international trade: the sum of imports and exports as a proportion of GDP (trade openness).

Crowding out effect—The crowding-out hypothesis assumes a negative effect of spending on traditional social policies on new ones, such as ALMPs and childcare. Since the effect travels through spending figures, it is possible to observe it by focusing on precisely this aspect. The crowding out hypothesis is tested with the variable 'spending on old age as a percentage of GDP', lagged by 1 year. The more a country is spending on old age, the less it will be able to assign extra resources to ALMPs and childcare. While discussing this hypothesis, one should also take into account the fact that, for a variety of reasons, different countries tend to consider different levels of social expenditure as the highest acceptable level. Put another way, one can expect the crowding-out effect to kick in at a different levels in different countries. For example, in a liberal welfare state, where public spending is generally lower, the crowding-out effect may be visible at lower levels of public spending, than in a country like Sweden, where a level of state

Table 7.1. Variable description and sources (*N* = 23 OECD countries)

Variable	Mean	Standard deviation	Source
Spending on active labour market policies (ALMP) as a percentage of GDP 1981–2009	0.74	0.49	OECD, SOCX Database, 2012
Spending on family services as a percentage of GDP 1998–2007	0.64	0.43	OECD, SOCX Database, 2012
Public social expenditures as a percentage of GDP 1980–2009	21.2	5.4	OECD, SOCX Database, 2012
Spending on old age pensions as a percentage of GDP, 1980–2009	6.9	2.5	OECD, SOCX Database, 2012
Openness of the economy (sum of import and export) as percentage of GDP, 1980–2009	67.1	31.1	Armingeon et al. 2011
Standardized unemployment rate, 1980–2009	7.0	3.4	Armingeon et al. 2011
Female employment. Percentage of women aged 15–64 in employment, 1980–2009	57.1	12.6	OECD.Stat
Percentage of seats in legislature held by leftist parties, 1980–2009	34.5	16.5	Adapted from Armingeon et al. 2011
Percentage of seats in legislature held by religious-conservative parties, 1980–2004	11.0	14.5	Adapted from Armingeon et al. 2011
Percentage of seats in legislature held by women, 1997–2004	18.9	11.7	Armingeon et al. 2011

spending around 50 per cent of GDP is much more acceptable. For this reason, when testing this hypothesis, one needs to control for overall social expenditure. The inclusion of the variable 'social expenditure as a percentage of GDP' allows us to control for this and to make the putative crowding-out effect visible. The two variables (spending on old age and total social expenditure) are correlated ($r = 0.71$ over the entire data set) but according to the usual tests not strongly enough to create a multicollinearity problem.

Per capita GDP—Finally, as argued above, shifts in the denominator of social expenditure indicators, in other words, GDP, may lead to wrong conclusions concerning variations in the effort made in the various policy areas. For this reason I control for GDP, measured in purchasing power parities, in every model.

Pooled time series

The statistical technique used in this study is pooled time series, also known as times series cross-sectional (TSCS) analysis. Variables are measured at different points in time in a sample of countries. This procedure has a number of advantages. First, it allows researchers to simultaneously exploit variation across space and time to test their hypothesis. Second, it increases dramatically the number of observations (N), allowing researchers to build complex multivariate models (for example, 21 countries × 25 years = 525 potential observations). Of course the use of pooled time series makes sense only if the effects being tested can be expected to exist both across space and across time. This is the case only with variables that do change across time. Institutional variables that tend not to move (or never change) are not suitable for this kind of analysis. The variables selected for this analysis all display a reasonable degree of variation, across both space and time.

Together with these advantages, pooling time series across countries creates other problems. Generally, a pooled time series data set does not fulfil the assumptions required for OLS regression analysis to be applicable, such as the absence of correlation among residuals (autocorrelation). Over the years, a number of methods have been put forward as to how to address this issue (see, e.g., Beck and Katz 1995; Kittel 1999). For many years, the standard, was the one suggested by Beck and Katz (1995) and consisted in the inclusion of the lagged dependent variable on the right-hand side of the equation, as well as country and time dummy variables and the use of panel-corrected standard errors. More recently, an alternative approach has been put forward by Thomas Plümper and colleagues (Plümper et al. 2005). They recommend the use of a Prais–Winsten transformation for dealing with the autocorrelation problem and panel-corrected standard errors. The traditional strategy, known also as the 'Beck-Katz standard', has been criticized because the 'technical' corrections they suggest explain almost 100 per cent of the variance in most models, leaving very little to be accounted for by the variables which are of theoretical interest.

In this chapter, I follow the Plümper et al. (2005) approach as applied by Huber and Stephens (2001), but I also provide estimates for models with country and time dummies. In fact, the view that including time and country dummy variables on the right-hand side leaves little variance to be explained is convincing. At the same time, however, we can assume that numerous non-measurable country features are likely to explain large parts of the variation in public spending. In addition, external shocks and coincident (but unrelated) trends are also likely to affect our dependent variable. To limit the impact of these unwanted effects, country and time dummies are used in some of the models. The various models present different risks. For both policy areas, Model 1 and 2 present a strong risk of making a type 1 error or believing that there is a relationship when in fact there is none. Models 7 and 8, in contrast, present a high risk of making a type 2 error, in other words, concluding that there are no relationships when instead there are some. This combination of models that present different types of error risks provides an indication of the likely effects and of their robustness. In other words, the least demanding models will provide an overview of the likely effects, while the most demanding ones allow us to identify the most robust ones.

Two variants of each model are presented. This is because the control, 'public social expenditure' needed to test the crowding-out hypothesis, impacts on the significance of some theoretically interesting variables, such as the unemployment rate and the role of leftist parties. The relevance of these variables should be assessed on the basis of the models that do not contain the control 'public social expenditure'.

Results

Active labour market policies

Table 7.2 reports the coefficients obtained in the pooled time series regression of spending on ALMPs. The first hypothesis discussed above, the impact of needs, seems confirmed. Countries with a higher rate of unemployment tend to spend more on ALMPs. The result is significant in three out of four models without the control 'public social expenditure'. Obviously, this relationship is partly automatic: As the unemployment rate increases, the number of potential beneficiaries of ALMPs also increases. However, ALMPs budgets are generally not unlimited, and unemployed people may not be legally entitled to a programme once budget limits have been reached. As a result, the observation that an increase in ALMP spending follows an increase in the unemployment rate can be seen as an indication that a political decision has been made to make more funds available. Things would be different for passive spending on unemployment, where entitlements mean that higher unemployment automatically results in higher spending. The effect of unemployment can be considered particularly strong because it is visible both in the model that emphasizes cross-national differences (Model 5, with time dummies) and in the model that emphasizes differences in time (Model 3, with country dummies). One can thus rather safely conclude that a relationship exists between spending on ALMPs and unemployment.

With regard to party political variables, the hypothesis that AMLPs are essentially Social Democratic policies is not confirmed by the analysis. More in general, political parties seem to have a very limited direct impact on ALMPs. In fact, in none of the models do we see a significant partisan effect, except for a small positive effect of Christian democracy in the least demanding model (Model 1). This essentially confirms the result obtained by Rueda (2007).

Exposure to international economic competition seems to play a role as a determinant of ALMP spending. The impact is particularly strong in cross-sectional terms (Models 5 and 6), but virtually nonexistent once country

Table 7.2. Pooled time series regression analysis of spending on active labour market policies in 22 OECD countries between 1980 and 2009, Prais-Winsten regression with panel corrected standard errors

	1	2	3	4	5	6	7	8
Leftist parties in parliament	0.0003363	0.0011304	-0.0001888	0.0002766	0.0001754	0.0009775	-0.0006932	-0.0002114
Religious parties in parliament	0.0038672*	0.0011749	0.0015742	0.0008519	0.0027331	0.0003161	0.0009247	0.0002206
Trade openness	0.0027517**	0.0028334***	-0.0007553	0.0003926	0.0042051***	0.0030738***	-0.0005485	0.0005506
Public social expenditures		0.064168***		0.044805***		0.0653407***		0.040122***
Spending on old age		-0.0628084***		-0.037856**		-0.0636497***		-0.036055*
Unemployment rate	0.021367***	0.0002694	0.0218263***	0.0047408	0.0125185*	0.0002341	0.0110279	0.0009436
p.c. GDP in PPP (1,000)	0.00172	-0.00689**	0.00392	-0.00361	-0.00279	-0.00322	-0.00789	-0.00395
Constant	0.2606252*	-0.3278182**	0.1618306	-0.1255711	0.3867373	-0.5327412	omitted	omitted
Country dummies			X	X	X	X	X	X
Time dummies							X	X
R^2	0.10	0.30	0.43	0.56	0.22	0.37	0.53	0.62
Common rho	0.92	0.86	0.82	0.76	0.91	0.85	0.80	0.75
N	528	508	528	508	528	508	528	508

Notes: Significance levels:
* $p = 0.05$; ** $p = 0.01$; *** $p = 0.001$.

dummies are introduced. However, on the basis of the hypotheses made here, it would be unreasonable to expect changes in the exposure to the international economy to impact on ALMP spending on a year-by-year basis. Rather, the hypothesized mechanism, that a high level of exposure to the international economy prompts political actors to agree in support of productive social policies, requires time. As a result, we are more likely to see this effect in the cross-national comparison than in the year-to-year one. A similar result is reached by Burgoon, who finds that spending on training and relocation benefits, a large part of ALMPs, is indeed related to various indicators of exposure to the international economy (Burgoon 2001: 538).

Finally, the crowding-out effect is discernible across all models in the shape of a highly significant negative impact of spending on old age. This is the case particularly in Models 2 and 6. Controlling for total social expenditure, higher spending on old age pensions impacts negatively on the expansion of ALMPs. Having the control is important since we can expect the putative crowding-out effect to kick in at different levels of social spending in different countries, depending on how tolerant of social spending countries are. In fact, without this control variable, spending on old age is positively correlated to spending on childcare, reflecting, in my view, not so much a mutually reinforcing effect between these two areas of social policy (which would be very difficult to justify theoretically), but a tendency of countries to be more or less inclined to turn to the state to address social problems. With the control in place, spending on old age becomes negatively and strongly related to spending on childcare in all models. The fact that this effect is visible also in the models with country dummies suggests that it occurs also over time: countries that see an increase in spending on old age pensions are less likely to increase the amount they invest in ALMPs the next year. Evidence presented elsewhere suggests indeed that countries which engaged in the development of active social policies before the onset of demographic ageing are more likely to develop extensive systems of childcare and ALMP (Bonoli 2007).

Childcare

Spending on family services depends on several determinants, as shown in Table 7.3. A strong independent variable is, unsurprisingly, the proportion of women who are in employment, which yields statistically significant positive effects in four out of eight models. The effect is mostly cross-sectional, as it disappears when country dummies are introduced. However, like for the impact of economic internationalization on ALMP spending above, it is unlikely that an increase in female employment rates impact systematically on spending in the next year. The qualitative case studies presented in Chapter 6 suggest that the impact of rising female employment is less direct

Table 7.3. Pooled time series regression analysis of spending on childcare in 23 countries between 1998 and 2007, Prais-Winsten regression with panel-corrected standard errors

	1	2	3	4	5	6	7	8
Leftist parties in parliament	0.0007937	0.0009591	−0.0005078	−0.0002778	0.0011458	0.0010155	−0.0004404	−0.0002784
Religious parties in parliament	−0.0023003	−0.0052714*	0,0023293	0.0023487	−0.0032254	−0.0055123*	0.0021995	0.0025172
Proportion of women in parliament	0.0077251*	0.0040633	0.0018171	0.0014626	0.0086093**	0.0045927	0.0020298	0.0020061
Trade openness	0.0009919	0.0014723*	−0.0000732	0.0005096	0.0016011	0.0012158	0.0003876	0.0009824
Female employment rate	0.00714*	0.0063187*	−0.0000542	−0.0006962	0.0077621*	0.0063172 *	0.0004927	0.0006037
Public social expenditures		0.0462835***		0.0125675		0.0496469***		0.0142616
Spending on old age		−0.0332382**		−0.0093591		−0.0339227*		−0.0118883
p.c. GDP in PPP (1,000)	0.00194	0.00475	0.00893***	0.00886***	0.00471	0.0121*	0.00872	0.0115*
Constant	−0.1067912	−0.8468083***	0.1039241	−0.0512272	−0.260618	−1.051272***	0.0550267	−0.230383
Country dummies			X	X			X	X
Time dummies				X	X	X	X	X
R^2	0.35	0.47	0.93	0.93	0.39	0.49	0.93	0.94
Common rho	0.92	0.91	0.60	0.58	0.91	0.91	0.59	0.57
N	220	220	220	220	220	220	220	220

Notes: Significance levels:
* $p = 0.05$; ** $p = 0.01$; *** $p = 0.001$.

and rather irregular. Higher rates of female employment put pressure on governments to spend more and after some time more resources are made available. Unfortunately, pooled time series are not capable of capturing this type of real world development. However, on the basis of the other models (1,2, 5, and 6) we can conclude that here too, like in the case of ALMPs, needs and demands seem to be a necessary condition for the expansion of policy.

Of course in this field one cannot rule out a problem of reverse causality, in other words, the possibility that more spending on childcare encourages more women to enter the labour market. The relationship highlighted in the pooled time series models actually captures causal effects going in this direction rather than the opposite one, as assumed. This interpretation is plausible, but two factors suggest that most of the causal relationship goes from needs and demands to policies rather than in the opposite direction. First, the pooled time series analysis uses a time lag (1 year). Inverting the time lag does not produce stronger effects, even though in this case a direct relationship from one year to the next is more plausible, as the new childcare places made available as a result of additional spending can be quickly taken up by working parents. In fact, the relationship between spending on family services in a year $t - 1$ and female employment in year t is statistically significant in only two out of the eight models and always weaker (results not shown). Second, as seen Chapter 6 and in other qualitative studies of the emergence of childcare services in OECD countries (Leira et al. 2003; Naumann 2006), the emergence of needs and demands for better childcare provision generally comes before the development of policy.

With regard to partisan effects, contrary to expectations, I did not find a relationship between left-wing parties and spending on family services. Models without the variable 'proportion of women in parliament' show a stronger impact of left-wing party strength, but only slightly so. A somewhat stronger and negative effect is obtained in relation to Christian Democratic parties (as in Iversen and Stephens 2008). Stronger religious parties, as expected, are associated with lower spending on childcare. The effect, however, is not that strong and disappears once the country dummies are introduced. Again, the importance of the effect may be reduced by the strict assumption regarding the duration of the time lag imposed by a pooled times series design. It should be noted that models with data only up to 2005 find a much stronger negative impact of Christian Democratic strength. The effect seems to be disappearing as time goes by. This is consistent with the findings presented in Chapter 6, showing that countries under Christian Democratic government have, since the mid-2000s, significantly increased their spending on childcare (in particular Germany and the Netherlands).

The conclusion here is that Christian Democratic influence used to be associated with lower spending on childcare, but this isn't the case any longer.

With regard to trade openness, the impact is very moderate as the indicator is positively and significantly related to spending on childcare in only one model. The effect is thus much weaker than in the case of ALMPs. This is understandable because spending on childcare is less related to economic developments than spending on ALMPs, which can more easily and directly acquire a 'compensatory' dimension.

Consistent with previous studies on the impact of women's presence in political organizations and decision-making bodies on policy, I find a fairly strong impact of women's presence in parliament on spending on childcare (Bonoli and Reber 2010). The effect is significant in two of the models but disappears once the control 'public social expenditure' is introduced as well as in the models with country dummies.

Let us now turn to the hypothesized crowding-out effect, which assumes a negative relationship between spending on old age and spending on childcare. As mentioned above, this effect is visible only if one controls for total social expenditure. The effect is significant in the two models emphasizing cross-sectional differences (Models 2 and 6). In the other ones, it is not significant though in the expected direction (negative).

These findings suggest that the strongest determinants of spending on childcare are needs and demands, spending on competitor programmes (old age), and the strength of Christian Democratic parties, which can function as a brake on the expansion of childcare services. Women's descriptive representation in parliaments also seems to play a role in the field of childcare.

The determinants of spending on ALMPs and childcare

Despite the limitation discussed above, statistical analysis of spending on ALMPs and childcare provides additional helpful information in relation to the questions addressed in this book. First, in both policy areas, the existence of problem pressure, or factors that can be seen as an indication of strong needs and demands for the policy in question, play an important role. The robustness of the effects of unemployment and female employment suggests that the existence of a policy problem is a necessary condition for the development of a new policy. Second, I find relatively strong evidence of a crowding-out effect in both policy areas. Controlling for overall social expenditure, spending on old age seems to 'crowd out' spending on the new policies. Third, in both policy areas I find a positive effect of trade openness, as expected. Both policies are encouraged when countries are more exposed to international competition.

163

In the field of childcare, two additional variables play an important role. Christian Democratic strength is associated with lower spending on this programme, though this effect has become much weaker in the most recent years. Women's presence in parliament, instead, has had a positive impact. Both effects are in the expected direction and confirm the findings obtained in other studies.

This information is helpful, but on its own insufficient to tell a story of how active social policy develops across countries. Not all possible causal effects are explored, and spending data tell us little about the features of policy, including how 'active' they are. In addition, statistical analysis is able to capture association between variables, but tells us little about the mechanisms that link developments in different realms of social and political life. These weaknesses of statistical analysis can be at least partly compensated by combining these findings with those obtained in the qualitative case studies. This is the task of Chapter 8.

8

The Origins of Active Social Policy

This book started by pointing out three puzzles posed by the emergence of active social policy in relation to the mainstream theoretical perspectives in comparative social policy. First, why, in the current context of 'permanent austerity', do we see the expansion of some sectors of the welfare state? Theory would expect governments to focus on retrenchment and to use any spare cash they may have to limit its extent. Instead, since the mid-1990s a majority of advanced welfare states have increased spending on new areas of social policy. Second, the move towards active social policy clearly spans across welfare regimes, whereas institutional and political legacies are expected to further the persistence of national differences. Finally, if the reorientation does span across different welfare regimes, Southern Europe is clearly lagging behind in this movement.

The evidence presented in the previous chapters provides elements that help us make sense of each of the three puzzles. In order to turn these empirical elements into proper answers, however, they need to be connected to the hypothesis made earlier. These answers, however, are complex and clearly require us to focus on the interplay of several of the factors identified in Chapter 4 as the potential drivers of the emergence of active social policy. Socio-economic developments interact with political mechanisms and with institutions to produce the sort of policy outcomes that can be observed. In this final chapter, I try to bring these various elements together in a coherent account, or a story, of the origins of active social policy.

Post-industrial transformations as a necessary condition

The emergence of active social policy requires profound social transformations, of the type that generally go under the heading of post-industrialization. Active social policies would not have made much sense during the post-war years, when full employment and a strict gendered division of labour within households were the norm. In such a context there was little reason to develop extensive systems of active labour market policy (ALMP) and childcare.

Both the qualitative case studies and the quantitative analysis lend support to this claim. The statistical analyses presented in Chapter 7 show that among the stronger determinants of spending in each of the two policy areas covered are indicators of need and problem pressure: unemployment and female employment, respectively. In both cases the effect is rather strong. True, methodological problems such as reverse causality (in the case of childcare and female employment) or an automatic association (in the case of unemployment and ALMP spending) cannot be entirely ruled out. However, there is evidence in the qualitative case studies showing that the assumed effect is strongest in both cases. Countries developed systems of ALMP *in response* to labour market problems, and childcare systems *in response* to women's massive entry into labour markets.

The case studies provide additional useful information. With regard to childcare, they show that in a majority of countries, subsidized childcare systems develop sometime after the entry of large numbers of younger women in the labour force alongside the recognition of reconciling work and family life as a collective problem. This sequence takes place at different times in different countries, but concerns virtually all the countries covered. In Sweden, despite much talk of increasing childcare provision to bring more women to the labour market in the 1960s, it was only in the mid-1970s that childcare policy really took off (see Figure 6.1). By then, the crisis had reduced employers' interest in supporting female employment, and the take-off owed much more to women's pressures than to employers' needs. A similar story can be told in relation to other countries. In the UK a major watershed in work–life balance policies were the reforms adopted by the Blair government in the late 1990s, which also followed several years of public pressure coming from parents, women, interest groups, and so forth. Germany, in the early 2000s, followed a similar pattern of governments picking up demands for better work–life balance policies. A study by Leira and colleagues focusing on the first generation of working mothers in Norway, Italy, and Spain highlighted this sequence of events (Leira et al. 2003). On balance, this evidence suggests the causal chain goes mostly from more female employment to the development of childcare rather than the other way round.

The analysis of policy trajectories in the field ALMP provides a less clear picture. Initially ALMPs were not created in response to mass unemployment. Quite the contrary: The first instance in which one can talk of an ALMP is Sweden in the 1950s. As seen in Chapter 5, this development took place in the context of full employment and a tight labour market. The emergence of unemployment as a major social problem, however, prompted the reorientation of Swedish ALMPs, first towards the provision of alternatives to market employment (1980s), and then towards activation (1990s and 2000s). In fact, the early experiments made with ALMPs in the 1950s in Sweden, as well as the largely failed Italian and French attempts to develop a similar tool, do not really belong to the realm of social policy. The primary objective of these initiatives was neither to help disadvantaged people nor to deal with social problems. Above all, they aimed at solving an economic problem: lack of appropriately skilled labour in the expanding industrial sectors. In this respect, rather than being a social policy instrument, the early steps in ALMP were part of an arsenal of economic policy tools aimed at modernizing national economies.

ALMPs became *social* policies after the employment crisis of the mid-1970s and early 1980s. Then, as seen in Chapter 5, the existing ALMP systems, developed in order to help meet the skill needs of expanding economies, were turned into tools for fighting open unemployment. Often, the role played by ALMPs during this period was to provide an alternative to market employment, or occupation. In several cases, contribution-paying labour market programmes were used to give a chance to unemployed people to re-gain entitlement to unemployment insurance benefit, a practice that turned out to be detrimental to their long-term employability. As shown in many evaluation studies, ALMPs in the 1980s and early 1990s were not very effective in bringing people back into unsubsidized jobs.

ALMPs became *active social* policies with the 'activation turn' adopted across Europe between the mid-1990s and the early 2000s. Within this rather short time span, most of the countries covered in this book reoriented their ALMPs systems towards the promotion of labour market participation of jobless people. Activation consists of a mix of pressures (conditionality, sanctions) and enabling measures (job search assistance schemes, job subsidies) that clearly aim at putting unemployed people back into unsubsidized market jobs. Interestingly, the first movers in this phase were countries like Denmark, the UK, and the Netherlands, which in the previous decades did not develop extensive ALMP systems. In contrast, ALMP pioneers like Sweden and Germany were much slower to embrace the activation paradigm, an outcome that, as will be seen below, can be understood as an institutional effect.

Activation can be seen as a key feature of labour market policy in a post-industrial economy. Deindustrialization and globalization have resulted in a substantial decline in demand for low-skill employment in Western European countries, contributing to depressed wages and making employment opportunities scarcer (see, e.g., DiPrete 2005). In such a context, low-skill jobs tend to be low-wage, low-quality jobs, with little prospects for improvement (Esping-Andersen 1999). Low-quality jobs combined with relatively generous welfare benefits make employment unattractive for low-skill people. The result is that low-skill individuals are overrepresented among the beneficiaries of most welfare programmes. Incentive problems were less serious in the predominantly industrial labour market of the post-war years. Back then, rising productivity and rising wages in manufacturing made work attractive for the low skilled, hence the focus of labour market policy on this category of jobless people.

The evidence presented in this book supports the claim that the profound social transformations that generally go under the heading of post-industrialization are a necessary condition for the development of active social policies. An active social policy would have been pointless in the context of male full employment during the 1960s. If both those who want and those who are expected to work are in the labour market, there are few incentives for policy-makers to invest in policies that facilitate access to employment. It is only when these two conditions are not fulfilled that active social policy becomes attractive. However, social transformations, needs, and demands alone do not make policies. This is why we need to focus also on the policy-making arena.

The role of social learning

The reorientation towards active social policy may also be explained in terms of social learning. In response to the employment crises of the mid-1970s and early 1980s, different welfare regimes developed different responses, all of which presented some problems. Most problematic was clearly the labour reduction route followed in continental European countries, which was unsustainable in the medium term. Nordic and Liberal welfare states also ran into troubles in the 1990s. In Sweden, ALMPs were turned into a tool to hide open unemployment, at a very high cost for the public purse. In the Liberal welfare states, welfare state retrenchment and labour market deregulation had exacerbated incentive problems while poverty and inequality were on the increase. Active social policy provided a solution to each set of problems: More people in employment in continental Europe, more work incentives in Sweden, and more income from employment for poor households in the Liberal welfare states. We may thus conclude that the shift towards an active welfare state was at least partly motivated by the quest for the most efficient social policy mix. This was achieved through a mix of trial and error as well as imitation of what was being experimented in neighbouring countries.

The narrative accounts of policy developments lend some support to this view. Governments sometimes looked elsewhere for inspiration. In some cases, such as Denmark in 1994 or Germany in 2003–4, activation was adopted after the previously dominant passive approach became generally recognized as inadequate. On the other hand, some problems remain with this interpretation. First, while there is now evidence that ALMPs can be effective in facilitating access to employment for some disadvantaged groups, most countries reoriented their social security systems before such evidence became available.

One of the first comprehensive attempts to study the impact of modern ALMP is a study published in 2001 by two OECD economists, who conclude, rather disappointingly, that there are relatively few interventions capable of genuinely improving jobless people's chances to re-enter the labour market (Martin and Grubb 2001).

Second, the social learning explanation does not allow us to account for the delay in or lack of development of active social policies in France and in Southern Europe. As members of the European Union and of the OECD, Southern European countries are exposed to the same sort of peer pressure and advice as other Western European countries. Since the late 1990s, most notably through the European employment strategy (Goetschy 2001; de La Porte and Pochet 2002) the European Union has continuously indicated that more pro-employment reforms were needed in these countries. Despite this, we see France formally developing activation for social assistance beneficiaries only in the late 2000s (with the introduction of *Revenu de solidarité active* (RSA) in 2009, see Chapter 5). In Italy up to the present day, active social policy remains marginal, with most initiatives being taken only at the regional or local level and being rather limited.

If active social policy developed as a result of social learning processes, then the learning capacity of governments differs across countries. Social learning processes are certainly present but can be supported or hindered by developments occurring in other areas. Most notably, this is the case of the incentive structures policy-makers face in the political arena. These are discussed next.

Active social policy in the political arena

Social policies in general and active social policies in particular are highly political objects. This point has been made very clearly in much of the literature on the welfare state. This study is no exception, since what happened in the political arena is key to understanding the development of active social policies.

Affordable credit claiming

As seen in Chapter 4, some have focused on the electoral payoff Western European governments obtained dring the expansion phase of post-war welfare states (see, e.g., Alber and Flora 1981; Wilensky 1981; Ferrera 1993: 190–7). Analyses of current change, instead, have emphasized the role played by the broader economic context of 'permanent austerity' (Pierson 1998, 2001). Under these conditions, social policy is expected to entail mostly cost containment or retrenchment measures. Such measures are generally unpopular with large sections of the population throughout Europe. As a result, governments are expected to use so-called 'blame avoidance' strategies so as to limit the electoral damage that unavoidable cost containment measures might inflict upon them (Weaver 1986; Pierson 1994, 1996).

Of course today, the economic context of permanent austerity makes credit-claiming-driven expansion of the welfare state more difficult. However, politicians seeking re-election are expected to be on the lookout for credit-claiming opportunities, even though such opportunities have become increasingly rare. For most governments, increases in the generosity of transfer programmes are off limits for budgetary reasons. In this context, the idea of an active social policy provides an opportunity for what I call 'affordable credit claiming' (Bonoli 2012).

As shown in the case studies, key reforms that have led to expansion in either of the two policy areas covered were high profile exercises for the governments who initiated them. The popularity of policy is more visible in the field of childcare, where examples of its use as a credit-claiming device abound. They range from Sweden in the late 1960s, when the Liberals and the Social Democrats fought to be seen as the pro-childcare party, to France, when a candidate to political office was forced to stick to a promise of creating 2,000 new daycare centres, a figure given out by mistake and ten times bigger than intended (see Chapter 6 for details). Childcare and, more in general, work–life balance policies have clearly been used for credit claiming (see also Morgan 2010).

The credit-claiming potential in ALMP may be less obvious. Some of these policies, especially those that entail putting pressure on jobless people, are unlikely to be popular with their target groups. In this case, however, credit can be expected not by those who are targeted by the measures but by those who are in employment and see themselves as net contributors to the social security system. Public opinion data lend some support to this claim. In their analysis of public support for activation in labour market policy, Kananen et al. (2006) show that between a third and half of German, British, and Swedish respondents think that 'The unemployed should be forced to take a job quickly, even if it is not as good as their previous one'.[1] Support for the more 'enabling' variant of activation is even stronger. Considering the pro-altruism bias one tends to find in these surveys (Epstein 2006), these figures suggest that there is some potential for credit claiming in activation.

Active social policies provide opportunities for credit claiming at a relatively limited cost for the public purse. Moreover, the relatively low level of development of pro-employment and social investment policies guarantees high visibility even when only limited funds are assigned to new programmes.

---

[1] The authors used Eurobarometer data collected in 2001 (Eurobarometer 56.1).

Concretely, one additional Euro spent on childcare is going to be considerably more visible than the same amount spent to increase (or to avoid a reduction in) pensions. High profile reforms of labour market policy such as the New Deals introduced by the first New Labour government (1997–2001) in the UK have not resulted in a massive increase in spending on ALMPs. (ALMP spending in the UK remained stable between 1997 and 2000 at 0.4 per cent of GDP (OECD *Stat*).) The 2004 German law on childcare, meant to create 200,000 new subsidized childcare places, was priced at 1.5 billion Euros (Zylka 2004a), or 0.66 per cent of annual pension expenditure.[2] The new policies, also because they are developed in the context of absence of provision, offer credit-claiming opportunities that are more visible and more affordable than is the case in the field of the mature policies inherited from the post-war years.

There are other features of active social policy that make it suitable for credit claiming. First, most of the tools that go under the rubric of active social policy can be presented as win–win solutions to the social problems they are meant to address, and as a result, generate broad support. Pro-welfare groups and parties may welcome a bigger effort in this field: employers and right-of-centre parties may like the positive impact on labour supply of these policies, and perhaps, their promise to be cost-effective, at least in the medium term, by reducing reliance on transfer programmes. Second, employment-promoting social policies, as well as notions like activation and social investment, facilitate the sort of 'ambiguous agreement' that has proven instrumental in making difficult reforms possible (Palier 2005). Different actors support certain measures for very different reasons. This makes active social policies suitable for credit claiming. Moreover, many of these policies have acquired a connotation of 'modern social policy' in current debates and are as a result difficult to oppose for political actors. Take the example of the German CDU–CSU, a Christian Democratic party that has historically favoured policies supporting the male breadwinner model (van Kersbergen 1995; Seeleib-Kaiser et al. 2008), abstaining in the parliamentary vote on the Red–Green-sponsored 2004 bill providing federal subsidies for childcare for fear that a vote against could be exploited politically by the Social Democrats (Zylka 2004b).

In sum, active social policies have many of the features needed to perform credit claiming: a relatively broad constituency based on a common interest (taxpayers and parents respectively), a presumed win–win quality, some basic ambiguity, and a modern flavour. What makes them particularly attractive in the current context of permanent austerity is of course the fact that even

---

[2] In 2004 Germany spent 228 billion Euros on old age pensions, source: <http://forschung. deutsche-rentenversicherung.de/ForschPortalWeb/view3sp.jsp?chstatzr_Finanzen=37f037f0&open &viewName=statzr_Finanzen&viewCaption=Statistiken%20-%20Finanzen%20-%20Zeitreihen #37f037f0> (accessed 14 July 2010).

major, highly visible expansion in these fields is comparatively inexpensive for the public purse.

While there is potential for credit claiming in active social policy, there are also some dangers. These new policies may run against deeply held normative perceptions among sections of the electorate, in relation to the proper roles of the state and the family with regard to the care of children or in relation to prevailing notions of appropriate social citizenship rights. In the end, the German Hartz IV reforms turned out to be a major blow in terms of support for the Red–Green coalition government, and probably one of the main causes of its fall in 2005. However, this seems to be the exception rather than the rule. Other governments and political leaders who have championed activation have taken credit for it and won subsequent elections. Here examples abound: the British Labour Party and Tony Blair in 2001 and in 2005; Denmark's Poul Nyrup Rasmussen, who presided over the 1994 activation-oriented reform of unemployment policy and stayed on as Prime Minister until 2001; and the Netherlands's Wim Kok, who was instrumental in promoting the reorientation of the Dutch welfare state towards activation and stayed in power between 1994 and 2002. The credit-claiming opportunities provided by active social policies in the late 1990s and early 2000s did pay off.

The role of political parties

As seen in Chapter 4, it has been argued that both ALMPs and state-subsidized childcare are part of the social democratic project (Esping-Andersen 1990; Huber and Stephens 2001; Huo et al. 2008). The evidence presented in this book suggests that there is a connection between social democracy and active social policy, but that it is far from being a simply linear and positive relationship.

The quantitative analysis presented in Chapter 7 shows only weak and essentially non-significant partisan effects. The only exception is a negative association between Christian Democratic strength and spending on childcare. This effect was rather robust until the mid-2000s but has diminished dramatically once new data for 2006 and 2007 have become available. This suggests that the role played by Christian Democratic parties is changing as illustrated by the recent reorientation of Dutch and German family policy towards more investment in childcare and in policies that facilitate parents' employment. As seen in the case studies, key legislative acts were adopted in 2004–7 in Germany and in 2005–7 in the Netherlands. These political decisions, taken under the leadership of the Christian Democrats or with their acquiescence, have limited the negative impact Christian democracy has on childcare spending.

The case studies suggest that Social Democrats have played an important role in the development of childcare, but Social Democratic influence is not systematically associated with childcare expansion. Left-of-centre governments were in power in many countries when key political decisions in the field of childcare were taken. It was the case in the Nordic countries, but also in the UK and in Germany (2004 law). On the other hand, in other countries, like France, childcare seems to be an object of competition between parties. When solidly in power throughout most of the 1980s, the French Socialists, however, failed to expand childcare as their Nordic counterparts were doing (see also Jenson and Sineau 1995). Finally, intra-Nordic comparisons suggest that Social Democratic influence does not alone explain the expansion of childcare in those countries. In fact, publicly subsidized childcare developed faster and to a larger extent in Denmark, where the Left was weaker, than in Sweden (Borchorst 2002).

In the field of ALMP, we also find mixed evidence with regard to the role played by political parties. Statistical analysis of spending shows the absence of a clear partisan effect. In part, this result was expected, since ALMP spending refers to rather different types of policy, which can either have a left or a conservative connotation. The qualitative studies provide some additional information. Like in the field of childcare, it is often the Social Democrats who are behind major ALMP initiatives. This was true of Sweden in the 1950s and particularly true in the recent activation turn.

One striking result is the fact that several recent major reforms of labour market policy were indeed initiated by left-of-centre governments. Often a high visibility re-orientation exercise took place soon after a return to power of a left-of-centre government following a more-or-less prolonged period in opposition. This was the case in Denmark in 1994, in the UK in 1997, in the Netherlands in 1996, and in Germany in 1998. This result is surprising because activation and pro-employment policies are not traditional left-wing policies.

Two lines of reasoning can help us make sense of this development. The first one focuses on the fact that major reforms are adopted shortly after an election victory, which ends a longish period in opposition. In such circumstances, there are obviously strong expectations by the rank-and-file and by party supporters so that the newly elected government will pursue policies that are qualitatively different from what their right-of-centre predecessors did. However, the Social Democratic parties who gained power in the mid- to late 1990s found that traditional Social Democratic redistributive policies were off the menu. Economic internationalization, single currency constraints for Euro-area members, and domestically driven budgetary limits, in short what social policy analysts call the context of permanent austerity, made the expansion of the traditional spending programmes impossible. In such circumstances, Social Democrats turned to active social policy because this policy idea provided them with a much needed opportunity for affordable credit claiming. It allowed them to distinguish themselves from their competitors without endangering public finances.

A second line of reasoning refers to the image that political parties have among the electorate. Re-orienting social policies towards employment promotion is a highly ambiguous exercise from the point of view of the citizen-voters, in other words, the policy-takers. These exercises generally combine re-commodification with enabling measures; however, where most of the emphasis will lie can only be seen during the implementation phase. For this reason, it may be easier to exploit the credit-claiming potential of this type of measures for the Social Democrats, who are less likely than their right-wing counterparts to be suspected to hide retrenchment and re-commodification under the activation discourse. This mechanism is akin to the Nixon-goes-to-China explanation of why Social Democrats have often been more successful at retrenching welfare states than right-wing parties (Ross 2000; Green-Pedersen 2002).[3]

The British trajectory in ALMP illustrates well these two hypotheses. It is difficult to appropriately time the activation turn in the UK, as many elements of the new orientation were put in place by the Conservative governments since the early 1990s. In fact, New Labour's flagship programme, known as the New Deals, resembled the Conservative's 'Project Work' (Clegg 2005: 192). With the Labour Party's accession to power in 1997, however, ALMP became a high profile, highly publicized area of government policy. Already in the 1997 election manifesto, the Labour Party emphasized the mix of duties and responsibilities that was to become a trademark of the Third Way: 'The best way to tackle poverty is to help people into jobs—real jobs. The unemployed have a responsibility to take up the opportunity of training places or work, but these must be real opportunities' (Labour Party 1997: 15).

In a way, Britain provided the 'best case scenario' for the development of active social policies in the mid-1990s: a social democratic party that rose back to power after a prolonged period in opposition, during which retrenchment was pursued. The expectation on New Labour to repel at least some of the policies adopted by the Conservatives was huge among its supporters. However, the party leadership quickly excluded this option, for example by sticking to fiscal plans drawn up by the Conservatives for the first 2 years in government (Powell 1999). At the same time, active social policy was promoted in the context of the debate on the Third Way. This allowed the New Labour government to claim some difference with its Conservative predecessors,

---

[3] These authors use the phrase 'Nixon-goes-to-China logic' to explain the fact that in the 1980s and 1990s, sometimes Social Democratic parties were more successful in retrenching social policies than their right-of-centre competitors. Their traditional image as a pro-welfare party made the claim that retrenchment was indeed inevitable more credible in the eyes of voters.

without endangering public finances. This trajectory can be observed, with some minor variations, in other countries too. Key active social policy reforms were initiated by newly elected social democratic governments also in Denmark and in the Netherlands. The German sequence is similar, with the difference that the previous conservative governments did not engage in retrenchment to such a significant extent, leaving the Social Democrats under pressure to reduce social spending. This may help to explain why, in Germany, the activation turn did not occur immediately after the return to power of the Left but had to wait for their second term in office.

Countries that lagged behind in the reorientation on social policy did not go through this sequence of events. France was ruled by the Socialists throughout most of the 1980s, and under their leadership some unpopular retrenchment measures were adopted. When back in power in 1997, the French Left needed to distinguish itself not only from the short-lived conservative governments of 1993–7, but also from their Socialist predecessors. In this context, active social policy proved less attractive, and more radical left-wing policies of working time reduction and job creation schemes were pursued. Italy, too, lacks the sequence of retrenchment performed by the Right in the 1980s and the Social Democrats once back in power in the mid-1990s. Political developments in that country are more confused and affected by judicial issues, such as the corruption scandal of the early 1990s or the problem of centre-right leader Silvio Berlusconi's suitability for government. However, it is worth noting that when briefly in power, the centre-left coalition did focus on active social policies, although producing very meagre results.

An alternative explanation for the Social Democrats' enthusiasm for active social policy may make reference to the fact these parties have changed in terms of constituencies over the past two decades. This argument is used by Häusermann to account for the changing preferences of Social Democratic parties in pension reform, but can also be applied to active social policy (Hausermann 2010). As Social Democratic parties have become parties of women, middle-class professionals, and public sector workers, a traditional protective approach was replaced by emphasis on what these constituencies like most: ALMP and childcare. Two problems arise with this interpretation. First, the electoral dividend obtained from embracing the active social policy paradigm has been rather short lived for European Social Democrats. If it reflected a fundamental structural shift in the constituencies of these parties, one would have expected it to be more long-lasting. Second, active social policy as a guiding principle in welfare state matters has survived the demise of the left-wing governments elected around the mid-1990s. The active welfare state may have been promoted by Social Democrats, but its appeal has clearly gone beyond traditional party divisions. When back in government, liberal and conservative parties have tended to stick to the active orientation promoted by their social democratic predecessors, though often with a different emphasis. However, on the basis of the evidence presented in this book, it is difficult to identify clear differences in the policies adopted by governments with different political orientation. What is certain is that once the path to employment supporting social policy had been open, subsequent right-of-centre governments have clearly pursued policy along the same lines.

The Left has been both more interested and better able to exploit the mechanism of affordable credit claiming. The need to distinguish themselves from their conservative predecessors in the mid-1990s and the image of a pro-welfare party have encouraged and allowed Social Democrats to play a key role in the reorientation of social security towards employment promotion.

Women's political mobilization and childcare

As hypothesized in Chapter 4, we can expect women's political influence to be associated with the expansion of childcare services. Even though subsidized childcare benefits parents in general, given the predominant division of labour within households, women stand to gain the most from investments in this field of policy. Statistical analysis of the determinants of spending on childcare highlights the importance of women's political mobilization, namely measured by their presence in national parliaments. This finding confirms previous ones obtained with shorter time series (Bonoli and Reber 2010) and with a different indicator of women's political mobilization, in other words, women's participation in non-religious associations (Iversen and Stephens 2008).

As shown in Chapter 7 (Table 7.3), the effect is essentially a cross-sectional one. Countries where women are more present in parliament are likely to spend more on childcare. The effect remains observable after controlling for female employment, which suggests that the indicator 'proportion of women in parliament' captures more than just a trend towards greater gender equality, but also tells us something about women's political influence. The relationship is not only due to a division between the Nordic countries and the rest of the world, as sometimes happens with these type of analyses, but (as shown in Figure 8.1) concerns countries beyond Scandinavia. France is a clear outlier. Women's presence in parliament is particularly low, but spending on childcare is rather high. After reading the French case study, this should not come as a surprise. Spending on family services in France was not, for most of the twentieth century, related to facilitating women's entry into the labour force. In contrast, it was part of an effort to provide early education. When childcare was more motivated by the objective of favouring maternal employment, this was generally not in response to women's aspirations, but rather to the need of the national economy. The French childcare system may suit French women today, but it was not made to serve them in the first place.

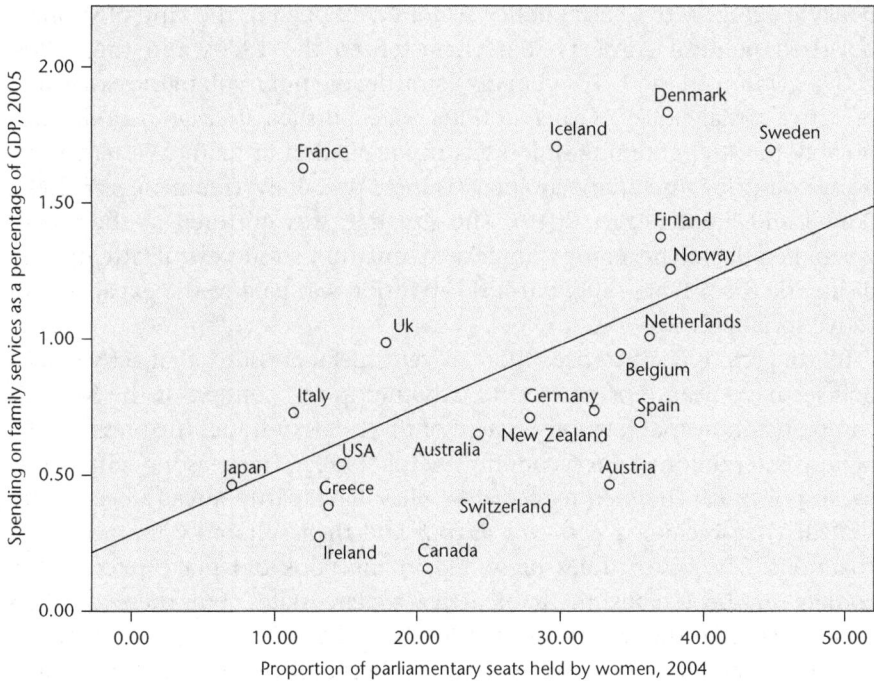

Figure 8.1. Proportion of parliamentary seats held by women and spending on family services

Sources: see Table 7.1.

The case studies provide additional evidence of the role played by women's political mobilization in the development of childcare. Feminist groups, whether within or without traditional representative structures, are often mentioned as important actors in Sweden, Denmark, and Italy. Of course, when policy is the result of the mobilization of a multitude of actors, it is difficult to estimate the influence of each one of them. The studies I have relied upon for these three countries, however, do conclude that women's political involvement in the policy debate did play a role in developing current childcare systems. On balance, the evidence provided speaks in favour of a women's political mobilization effect on childcare spending. This result is consistent also with studies carried out in other countries, including Norway (Bratton and Ray 2002), Switzerland (Ballestri and Bonoli 2003), and Spain's region of Catalunya (Gonzalez and Vidal 2004).

Active social policy as a centrist option

Many of the findings presented in this book suggest that active social policies are the result of political compromise and are particularly suitable for centrist policy-making. Active social policy seldom developed in the kind of strongly polarized political contexts that characterized the 1970s and the 1980s. Left hegemony in the 1970s in many countries did not result in the expansion of active social policy. Other options were pursued in that period, most notably the strengthening of job security regulation in many Western European countries, including Sweden, France, and Italy (Emmenegger 2009; Bonoli and Emmenegger 2010). The situation was mirrored in the 1980s, when neo-liberal hegemony translated into not-so-successful attempts to dismantle the welfare state, but little attention was paid to the expansion of active social policies.

It is in periods characterized more by centripetal pressures that active social policies have been most successful, whether in the context of the Swedish corporatist industrial relations system of the 1950s or under the pressure of a rapidly internationalizing economy in the 1990s. The reasons why active social policy can be seen as centrist policy have partly already been mentioned. They include a win–win flavour and their suitability for cross-class coalitions. The case studies presented in the book did make reference to conflict in the establishment of active welfare states, but these conflicts seldom reflected the traditional division between Left and Right or between capital and labour. In fact, many of the conflicts took place within each camp. They were often value conflicts (i.e., within the bourgeois camp) in relation to the provision of childcare. ALMPs have proved problematic for the Left, and one can clearly see a tension between Social Democrats' attachment to unconditional social rights on the one hand and the attractiveness of the idea of promoting access to employment in order to help disadvantaged people on the other.

Institutional factors

Recent studies of social policy-making have tended to emphasize the importance of institutions inherited from the past in shaping current change. Institutional explanations, however, seem of limited use in accounting for the activation turn experienced in Europe between the mid-1990s and the 2000s. This took place in countries belonging to different welfare regimes, with very different traditions in the fields of industrial relations, state involvement in economic management, coordination between economic actors, and so forth. Institutional explanations are certainly better at explaining the persistence of diversity than they are at accounting for convergence.

Yet, an institutional focus helps to account for the timing of the emergence of active social policy. The effect is clearest in the field of ALMPs, where one can see a clear role played by decisions taken in the earlier phases of development of this policy on subsequent ones. Countries like Sweden and Germany, which developed ALMP systems in the 1950s and late 1960s respectively, used this tool to provide alternatives to open unemployment during the crisis years of the 1970s and early 1980s, in a clear example of institutional conversion (Streeck and Thelen 2005). The tool was not meant to do that; it was meant to re-train jobless industrial workers so that they would be available to work in expanding industries. However, the late 1970s and early 1980s were a period of downsizing across industries. Labour market re-entry on a large scale was simply not an option. In such circumstances, existing ALMP systems took up a new role: to provide alternatives to market employment for otherwise jobless people. Other countries developed similar tools as well, but more slowly. France, the UK, the Netherlands, and even Italy adopted programmes geared towards providing an occupation to those excluded from the labour market.

Decisions taken during the 1980s proved instrumental in determining the course of ALMP in the 1990s and 2000s. Countries that developed ALMPs to a limited extent only, such as Denmark and the UK, were among the first to embark in the activation turn around the mid-1990s. The absence of a tradition in this field gave them more freedom to develop the sort of policies that made sense in the post-industrial context of the time: high levels of jobless-ness among low-skill people who face incentive problems and other practical obstacles to employment. The other countries followed suit, but later. Sweden adopted an important, activation oriented reform in 2001. In Germany, the Hartz reforms of 2003–4 signalled a watershed in labour market policy.

In contrast, in the field of childcare antecedents do not seem to matter that much. Many countries developed rudimentary childcare systems in the early twentieth century. Some of them went beyond that by institutionalizing a comprehensive pre-school system before the massive entry of women into the labour market. In the seven country samples covered in this study, this was the case in France and in Italy. A pre-school system for 3 to 6 year olds proved to be an advantage for the development of childcare policy only for France. In Italy, a high rate of coverage for the older group (100 per cent in 2004, see Table 3.5) did not impact favourably on provision for smaller children. Antecedents in childcare policy may play a role, but they do not explain the take-off in childcare provision that took place in most of the countries covered.

To understand why this is the case, one must move beyond institutions and consider political dynamics. If the expansion of subsidized childcare services is driven by credit claiming, then the potential for politicians to exploit this effect is highest when provision is low, or more precisely, when the gap between demand (high) and supply (low) is maximum. The fact that a pre-school system already exists may turn out to be a disadvantage for the development of encompassing childcare provision because it reduces the possible gains in terms of credit claiming that can be obtained from such a move.

At the end of Chapter 6, I illustrated this claim through a Swedish–Italian comparison. Sweden in the early 1970s provided the most favourable conditions for childcare to appeal to vote-seeking politicians. Women had started entering the labour force in great numbers and were having immense difficulties finding childcare. At the same time, the absence of a pre-school system and a relatively late age for beginning compulsory schooling at 7 meant that the potential winners of an expansion of childcare were particularly numerous. These were the ideal conditions for exploiting the credit-claiming potential of childcare expansion. Contrast this to Italy in the 2000s. Women are also entering the labour market in great numbers, but families have alternatives to state-subsidized services. These take various shapes and include the existing pre-school system for the age group 3–6 years, grandparents, and immigrants. As a result, the electoral payoff of investing in childcare is bound to be lower in the latter case. This helps to account for the lack of enthusiasm shown by Italian political leaders for the childcare issue.

As argued by many, institutions do impact on policies, but they do so in interaction with political factors. As a result, their impact is rather unpredictable. The case of childcare is particularly striking in this respect. Having developed an institutional antecedent in the shape of a pre-school system seems to be an obstacle, rather than an advantage, to the development of a comprehensive childcare system. This is an outcome that is both counter-intuitive and difficult to hypothesize ex ante. Yet this is what the empirical evidence presented in this book suggests. This speaks in favour of an inductive approach when developing a hypothesis on institutional effects.

Public opinion and societal values

Did active social policy develop faster and more easily in countries where predominant societal values are compatible with the new policy paradigm? The evidence presented in this book lends little support to this hypothesis. True, as mentioned in Chapter 4, measurement problems make it objectively difficult to test such a proposition. However, the narrative accounts show substantial similarities among countries in the post-war years, in relation to issues such as a strong attachment to the male breadwinner model and to a welfare state that guarantees an income stream to family fathers. In a way, prevailing societal values at the beginning of the period investigated in this book were equally inimical to the idea of an active social policy. Of course as suggested by the public opinion data on activation reported above, many things have changed since then. Still, there is no indication that the pioneers of the activation turn in the 1990s could count on some sort of 'activation friendlier' societal values.

Things may be somewhat different in relation to childcare, as the take-off in women's employment seem to be related to religion, with Catholicism having acted as a brake on female employment and, consequently, on the development of childcare services. However, there are examples of Catholic countries being relatively ahead in the provision of childcare at various stages of the development of family policy. This is the case of France, Belgium, and, at least insofar as legislation is concerned, Italy. The channel through which religion has impacted on childcare policy has been politics and in particular the strength of Christian Democratic parties and religious organizations, rather than the views held by society at large (Morgan 2006).

Does timing matter?

In Chapter 4, I hypothesized a mixed socio-economic/institutional effect, which depends on the interaction between welfare state structures and the relative timing of key socio-economic developments. Countries that have entered relatively early in the post-industrial age (i.e., 1970s and early 1980s) had an advantage when it came to reorienting their social policies, as the new policies faced limited competition from other welfare state programmes. In contrast, in countries that have developed into post-industrial societies more recently, demands for developing these new policies are in strong competition with demands for the preservation, despite population ageing, of the current level of protection, particularly in old age pensions. It should be noted that time is crucial in this argument. Whether countries manage or fail to reorient their welfare states in a way that reflects changed socio-economic circumstances depends on the relative timing of key socio-economic trends in interaction with existing welfare state structures. The key developments are post-industrialization and the increase in the cost of the industrial welfare state resulting from the combination of demographic ageing and generous pension promises. These two developments must not happen simultaneously if a welfare state is to be successfully reoriented towards active social policy.

The quantitative analyses identified a 'crowding-out' effect of pension expenditure on childcare and ALMS spending that is compatible with the hypotheses presented above. Controlling for total social expenditure (i.e., for countries' inclination to turn to the state for dealing with social problems), spending on old age is inversely related to spending on either ALMPs or childcare. A different approach to test this hypothesis yields similar results. Looking at the speed at which countries have undergone the social transformation that fall under the heading of post-industrialization, it shows that early post-industrializers have gone much further in developing active social policies. This is not only a matter of post-industrial latecomers needing time to catch up, as there is little evidence of convergence since the 1990s in spending on the two fields of policy (Bonoli 2007).

The narrative accounts provide a more nuanced view of the role of timing. Being an early adopter of active social policy is clearly an advantage for the subsequent expansion of this type of policy. However, latecomers seem to be able to catch up. Germany is probably the best example of a latecomer to active social policy and is clearly becoming one of the leaders in this field. Whether a late conversion to active social policy has a long-term impact remains largely an open question for the time being. More hindsight is arguably needed to be able to test this hypothesis in a definitive fashion.

The implications for welfare state theory

The objective of this book was above all to provide answers to the three puzzles presented in the Introduction. This has been achieved by relying mostly on existing theory. On occasions, however, theoretical approaches borrowed from the literature have had to be adapted in order to be successful in accounting for the observed developments. This suggests that some amendments to our view of what drives social policy-making are needed.

First, studies of the politics of social policy have generally focused on the interests and preferences of groups that are more or less directly targeted by policy. Typically, hypotheses are made with regard to who is likely to win and lose in the short term, and assumptions concerning policy preferences are formulated on this basis. Examples of this approach are found in relation to both the phase of expansion and of retrenchment of Western welfare states. Even more recent and sophisticated studies emphasizing the link between the composition of party constituencies and their position assume that the political impact of a social policy decision is basically limited to those who are affected by it (Häusermann 2010).

The analysis of the emergence of active social policy suggests that we need a broader understanding of the political impact of a reform, going beyond those who are directly affected by it. Large active social policy initiatives were often launched by social democratic parties competing for the middle-class vote, and the middle classes are not strongly represented among the direct beneficiaries of active social policy. This is particularly the case for ALMPs since the mid-1990s. These have targeted mostly low-skill, long-term unemployed people. In addition, activation is far from being perceived as an advantage by those who are receiving it. It is much more plausible to see the political target of the high profile activation turns adopted in countries like the UK,

Denmark, the Netherlands, and even Germany in the middle classes rather than in the receivers of the policy.

Things may be somewhat different for childcare, since subsidized childcare benefits mostly the middle classes, but much depends on how subsidies are structured. In the UK, for example, childcare tax credits are targeted on lower income families. In addition, the direct beneficiaries of childcare policy are unlikely to be numerous enough to constitute a constituency worth spending much political capital. In the field of childcare, the political target certainly includes the direct beneficiaries, but other groups are likely to be considered as well. These include broader communities of middle-class voters who see the benefit of increasing employment in the country.

If they do not have a direct stake in the policy, what drives the political response to policy change of these broader groups then? Answering this question is beyond the scope of this book. However, one can mention two areas where future research could focus in order to answer it. First, these political responses may be driven by values. Some sort of work ethic, or the belief that work is better than inactivity for everyone may be behind the support that many have given to parties promoting activation. The public opinion data referred to above lends support to this hypothesis. Second, it may be the case that the diffuse interests of tax payers, up to now considered as unlikely to lead to a change in political behaviour, may in fact play a more important role (see Pierson 1994 for a discussion of the difference between diffused and concentrated interests). Middle-class voters may support active social policy because it promises to reduce dependency on the benefits they are financing through taxation. It may be the case that in the absence of a direct interest at stake, diffused interests acquire more importance as determinants of political behaviour.

One important consequence of the above is that the visibility of a policy measure matters. If the political target of a reform is not those who are directly affected by it, then it is important that those whose support is sought are at least aware of its adoption. High visibility was a key feature of many of the reforms discussed in this book, and active social policy provides ideal conditions for obtaining maximum visibility with minimum spending.

Active social policy in the crisis

The argument and the analyses presented in this book are essentially based on observations made in the pre-2008 world. Since then, the economic and social context in which Western European welfare states operate has changed rather dramatically. Global demand shrunk starkly in 2009, resulting in unemployment hikes in many countries. After a brief revival of reflation policies of

Keynesian inspiration, most countries discovered that their ability to borrow was not unlimited and found themselves trapped in a budgetary crisis. Against this background, the objective of this section is to discuss the likely implications of the current crisis for the further development of active social policy. Of course, this exercise is difficult given that at the time of writing (March 2012), many uncertainties remain with regard to the how and when Europe will emerge from the crisis. These difficulties are compounded by the fact that not all countries have suffered equally after 2008. Germany and some surrounding countries (Austria, the Netherlands, and Switzerland) have managed to keep their unemployment rate at pre-recession levels (or even below). On the other hand, countries like Spain, Ireland, and the UK are taking the full brunt of the crisis.

There are several reasons for believing that the current crisis may impact the orientation of social policies. First, major crises in the past, like the one that started in 2008, have generally resulted in a rewriting of much social legislation. The Keynesian welfare state that emerged in the post-war years can be seen as a response to the Great Depression. More recently, the neo-liberal turn in social and economic policy in the 1980s found its origins and its justification in the oil crisis of the 1970s and the stagflation years afterwards (Hemerijck 2011). Second, the activation turn took place in good economic times, between the mid-1990s and early 2000s in most countries. The success of activation as a policy idea may of course be related to this, as the promise of a win–win solution to labour market problems sounds much more credible at times of strong job creation than during a crisis. Many voters may see it as pointless to pressure jobless people into job search when everyone has the impression that there are no jobs around. Times of crisis may be more favourable to passive social policies, such as those developed in continental Europe in the 1980s (e.g., early retirement). Third, the financial and economic crisis has provoked in most countries a public finance crisis, which severely limits the ability of governments to develop new policy initiatives and puts pressure on them to retrench across the board.

Theoretically, we can expect the crisis to impact active social policies in at least two ways. Countries may move back to more passive solutions that are likely to be politically more attractive in difficult times. However, this result implies that countries have some spare cash or at least some spare capacity to borrow or raise money. This, in most European countries, does not seem to be the case at the present time. Alternatively, active social policy may fall under the axe of budget cuts and follow a retrenchment trend.

The early indications, however, suggest that neither of these two options is likely to materialize. The reduction of labour supply through permanent income replacement benefits is definitely not on the agenda. In contrast, countries that had strengthened activation efforts in the mid-1990s to early

2000s have continued in the same direction, despite the changed economic context. In addition, early analyses of recent policy trends suggest that active social policies are generally excluded or less affected by cost-saving exercises. Retrenchment has concerned mostly old age pensions and cuts in public sector employment and wages (Hemerijck 2012b; Laulom et al. 2012).

Analysis of expenditure trends during the first 2 years of the crisis also suggests that ALMPs have not suffered. As shown in Table 8.1, spending on ALMPs either remained constant or increased in most countries during this period. Of course, this is to an extent due to the rise in the unemployment rate. However, even when dividing ALMP spending by the unemployment rate, one essentially sees stability across the board (right-hand columns). The early crisis years have not reduced the effort that OECD countries have made in ALMP.

As seen in Chapter 5, however, ALMPs can, in particular circumstances, acquire a rather passive orientation. This was the case in countries like Sweden and Germany in the years after the oil shocks of the 1970s. A 'passive' ALMP relies essentially on job creation programmes that are used to provide an alternative to market employment. In fact, the available data suggest that the initial stages of the current crisis have not seen a resurgence of job creation schemes. Spending on job creation programmes, very low by historical standards at the beginning of the recession, did not increase between 2007 and 2009. In a few countries, it even decreased. In Germany, spending went from 0.08 to 0.07 of GDP between 2007 and 2009 (though in a context of falling unemployment). In France and in the UK, the decline took place against the background of rising unemployment (from 0.2 to 0.15 per cent of GDP for France and from 0.1 to 0 per cent in the UK). True, slight increases took place in badly recession-hit countries like Spain and Ireland. These increases are nonetheless minor. Overall, one does not have the impression that ALMP is turning towards the provision of alternatives to market employment.

Instead, during the early crisis years, many countries have relied extensively on temporary unemployment benefit. This option, found mostly in continental European countries, consists in a temporary unemployment payment that allows companies facing a drop in demand to retain their workers for a limited period of time. Germany was one of the main users of this tool, known as 'Kurzarbeit', but spending on temporary unemployment benefit increased substantially also in Switzerland, Belgium, and Italy. Temporary unemployment benefit is difficult to classify according to the passive–active dichotomy. Technically, as an income replacement benefit, it should be considered as passive. However, in so far as it prevents unemployment, it can also be considered as akin to other pro-employment active policies. This view is valid only as long as the duration of the temporary unemployment benefit but allows companies to bridge surplus labour until the next recovery. If, as

Table 8.1. Spending on active labour market policies between 2007 and 2009 according to two measures

	Spending on ALMPs as a percentage of GDP			Spending on ALMPs as a percentage of GDP per percentage point of unemployment		
	2007	2008	2009	2007	2008	2009
Denmark	1.30	1.34	1.62	0.34	0.39	0.27
Finland	0.87	0.82	0.92	0.13	0.13	0.11
Norway	0.56	na	na	0.22		
Sweden	1.10	0.97	1.13	0.18	0.16	0.14
Unweighted average of Nordic countries	*0.96*	*1.04*	*1.22*	*0.22*	*0.23*	*0.17*
Austria	0.67	0.67	0.85	0.15	0.18	0.18
Belgium	1.18	1.28	1.41	0.16	0.18	0.18
France	0.93	0.84	0.98	0.11	0.11	0.10
Germany	0.73	0.80	1.00	0.08	0.11	0.13
Netherlands	1.10	1.06	1.21	0.31	0.34	0.33
Switzerland	0.57	na	na	0.17	na	na
Unweighted average of continental countries	*0.86*	*0.93*	*1.09*	*0.16*	*0.18*	*0.18*
Australia	0.30	0.31	0.32	0.07	0.07	0.06
Canada	0.29	0.29	0.35	0.05	0.05	0.04
Ireland	0.64	0.72	0.87	0.14	0.11	0.07
New Zealand	0.35			0.09		
United Kingdom	0.32	0.27	0.33	0.06	0.05	0.04
United States	0.13	0.18	0.16	0.03	0.03	0.02
Unweighted average of English-speaking countries	*0.34*	*0.35*	*0.41*	*0.07*	*0.06*	*0.05*
Greece	na	na	na	na	na	na
Italy	0.45	0.46	0.44	0.07	0.07	0.06
Portugal	0.51	0.55	0.77	0.06	0.06	0.07
Spain	0.79	0.81	0.86	0.10	0.07	0.05
Unweighted average of Southern countries	*0.52*	*0.54*	*0.62*	*0.07*	*0.07*	*0.06*
Unweighted average of above countries	*0.67*	*0.71*	*0.83*	*0.13*	*0.13*	*0.12*

Source: OECD Stat.

was the case in Italy since the 1970s, the benefit is used as an alternative to unemployment benefit for companies undergoing restructuring, then its active dimension disappears.

During the crisis years we have also seen some new initiatives in the field of ALMP. For instance, in the context of a major austerity exercise, the first budget law adopted by the Monti government in December 2011, Italy introduced a new 'Fund for financing active labour market policies'. At the time, Italy was under immense pressure from international markets to reduce its public deficit. The budget law contained essentially cuts, especially in the field of pension. However, it also decided to increase funding for ALMPs by 200 million EUR in 2012 and 300 million EUR in 2013. Of course, relative to the size of the cuts and of the deficits, this is a rather small, symbolic, effort. It nonetheless confirms that even at times of retrenchment and extreme austerity, it is important for governments to put forward some policies where they can claim credit.

In the field of childcare, and more generally in relation to work–life balance policies, there is little evidence of a U-turn since the outset of the crisis. OECD data on spending on family services are available only until 2007. As a result, it is impossible to use this source to examine trends in childcare during the crisis years. An overview of developments in selected European countries, however, suggests that little has changed in the field after 2008. In Sweden, innovations introduced by the conservative governments in the late 2000s (albeit before the crisis) have not impacted on the pro-employment orientation of childcare policy, but rather they have reduced its equality-promoting dimension (Tunbergen and Sigle-Rushton 2011). In Denmark, the childcare system remains one of the most generous worldwide, with parents still paying at most 25 per cent of the full cost of care up to the age of 6. In general, debates in the Nordic countries have focused more on issues of gender equality and choice between externally provided childcare and parental care. The four main Nordic countries now run cash-for-care schemes (a payment made to parents who care for their children, de facto an extension of parental leave). But this does not necessarily mean an abandonment of the pro-employment orientation of family policy, since childcare remains easily available. However, it has been argued that these recent initiatives have somewhat diluted the previously clear expectation of working mothers returning to work within 1 year after giving birth. Whether this will amount to a real change of direction will depend on the actual take-up of the new cash-for-care schemes over the next few years (Eydal and Rostgaard 2011).

In the Netherlands, the recent past has been characterized by retrenchment in various social policy areas, including elderly care; however, childcare has not suffered to any significant extent (van Hooern and Becker 2012). In Germany, public attention has focused on how to improve access to childcare for migrant children and how to deal with a general shortage of properly qualified childcare workers. In France, recent debates were more on the extent to which religion was to be allowed in daycare centres (*Le Monde*, 5 April 2011). In Italy, childcare expansion has occurred in some municipalities, but without significant involvement of the national government.

Recent developments in the UK are particularly instructive in relation to the argument put forward in this book. Faced by a gigantic budget problem, the Conservative–Liberal coalition government have sought to cut public expenditure across the board. Cuts have hit childcare care too, with a reduction in the rate of reimbursement of childcare expenses for low income families (childcare tax credit) from 80 to 70 per cent adopted in April 2011. Opinion polls showed that this decision proved particularly unpopular with low–middle income women voters. A few months later, however, the coalition unveiled plans to extend access to childcare tax credit to parents working less than 16 hours a week, and who were previously excluded from the scheme, at the cost of 300 million GBP (Wintour 2011). In a rather patent credit claiming exercise, the change was presented by Iain Duncan Smith, the minister responsible for work and pensions, in the left-leaning newspaper *The Guardian* (Duncan Smith 2011). Even during the tough times of budgetary consolidation, governments must pay attention to public opinion. With little spare cash, however, it is difficult to achieve much visibility. Once again, active social policy, in this case childcare, seems to have provided such an opportunity.

The years after 2008 have been characterized by unprecedented financial turmoil and economic developments. These have, above all, created much uncertainty in relation to where Western economies are heading and with regard to what the impact of the current crisis will be. The size of the shock is such that the hypothesis of a major reconsideration of the overall orientation of social policy is by all means plausible. However, after having examined the preliminary evidence we can rely upon in the early post-crisis years, it seems that the strong pro-employment policies developed in the period 1995–2007 are here to stay. In addition, even the crisis does not seem to have stopped their expansion, as shown by the few examples mentioned above. These very recent developments are consistent with the main argument put forward in this book. Even in a crisis context, active social policies provide affordable opportunities for claiming credit.

The success of a policy idea

This book has shown that the success of active social policy as a policy idea can be understood as the result of a number of interacting factors. These are found

among the independent variables known to have impacted on social policies since the post-war years.

First, socio-economic changes, going under the label of post-industrialization, have created the conditions for the expansion of active social policies. A crucial condition is the mismatch in the labour market between high supply of and low demand for low-skill labour, a key characteristic of post-industrial labour markets. Under such conditions, wages for low-skill workers are pushed downwards. Incentives to take up employment are low, especially if generous welfare arrangements are in place. As a result, activation becomes an attractive policy option. A second crucial condition is women's massive entry into the labour market, a move that has resulted in demand for childcare services and for policies that help parents reconcile work and family life more generally.

However, needs and demands alone, as political scientists know, do not create policies, and developments in the political arena have played a key role in explaining the success of the idea of an active social policy. A crucial political mechanism that helps us explain the success of active social policy is what I have termed 'affordable credit claiming'. Active social policy provided an opportunity for popular policies, and the slightly improved economic situation in the late 1990s to mid-2000s made the promises of active social policy more credible. This opportunity proved particularly attractive to Social Democrats, because, back in government after a more or less prolonged period in opposition, they needed to show that they were different from their conservative predecessors and that they could provide another answer to the at-the-time prevailing social problems.

In this account, welfare regime-based differences have lost some of their relevance. As pointed out in several places, this does not mean that differences among regimes are disappearing. On the contrary, they remain substantial. What has changed since the 1980s and the 1990s is the fact that the direction of reform is remarkably similar across welfare regimes. Countries as diverse as Sweden, Germany, and the UK have all, since the early 2000s, clearly emphasized the active approach to dealing with social problem, at least more than in the past. The notion of affordable credit claiming is compatible with this observation since it relates to the political game and can occur independently of the existing welfare state structures.

This observation leads me to the third puzzle addressed in this book: Southern Europe's apparent failure to embrace the now social policy paradigm. A number of explanations have been put forward above. First, the socio-economic developments associated with increased demands for active social policies occurred later. When the new demands emerged in the 2000s, they were in competition with spending in other areas, especially old age pensions. Second, new needs and demands emerged in the context of highly problematic public finances. Southern European countries had budgetary problems

even before the adoption of the single currency. The constraints associated with a monetary union further reduced the scope for additional spending. As the 2011–12 crisis of public finances in the weaker members of the Euro zone has shown, budgetary problems had been around for some time in countries like Italy, Spain, Portugal, and Greece. Under such budgetary pressures, even affordable credit claiming is problematic. The limited funds needed to modernize labour market policy or to develop extensive childcare are unavailable unless savings are made in other big spending areas, such as old age pensions. Third, Southern European countries have developed no-cost alternatives to active social policy, in the shape of selective labour market deregulation. This strategy has brought more people to the labour market, but has resulted in a strong new division between insiders and outsiders (Emmenegger et al. 2012). Finally, in recent years Southern European countries did not follow the sequence that I have found to be most likely to lead to the development of active social policies (i.e., a social democratic-led government back in power in the mid-1990s after a decade of retrenchment achieved by their conservative predecessors). In the 1980s, Southern European countries were still expanding their welfare states, and especially in Italy, the 1990s were characterized by a quick succession of governments of different political persuasion, providing little time for the Left, when in power, to implement this type of reform.

With regard to childcare, two additional factors seem to play a role in delaying developments in Southern Europe. First, as seen above, increases in women's political influence have often preceded the expansion of childcare services. As shown in Figure 8.1, with the exception of Spain, women's representation in parliaments tends to be very low in Southern Europe. Second, as many have pointed out, families (i.e., grandparents) play an important role in providing childcare in this part of Europe. This may reduce the electoral payoff of investing public money in childcare services.

The origins of active social policy are complex. This should not come as a surprise, considering the large variety of interventions that can be subsumed under this label. Yet, the common philosophy that underpins them justifies a comprehensive account of their development. In this book, I have shown that the policy-making logics in the two areas studied are quite similar most of the time. Both the provision of childcare and activation have required a major reassessment of the role of post-war welfare states. Countries have not turned to them easily. Instead, longish processes of social learning and policy diffusion have been observed. At the same time, these policies have proved politically attractive to policy-makers, and once this quality was recognized, the speed of their development increased dramatically. This suggests that despite crisis of public finances in several European countries, the notion of an active social policy will continue to play a role as a guiding principle of European welfare states. Active social policies are here to stay.

Bibliography

ADDISON, J. & SIEBERT, W. (1993) 'The UK Labour Market Institutions, Law and Perform-ance'. In: *Labour Market Contracts and Institutions*, J. Hartog & J. Theeuwes (eds). Amsterdam: Elsevier.

ALBER, J. (1987) 'Germany'. In: *Growth to Limits: The Western European Welfare States since World War II*, P. Flora (ed.). Florence: European University Institute.

—— & FLORA, P. (1981) 'Modernization, Democratisation and the Development of Welfare States in Europe'. In: *The Development of Welfare States in Europe and America*, P. Flora & A. J. Heidenheimer (eds). New Brunswick, NJ: Transaction Books.

ANXO, D. & NIKLASSON, H. (2006) 'The Swedish Model in Turbulent Times: Decline or Renaissance?' *International Labour Review*, 145, 339–75.

ARMINGEON, K. (2002) 'Negotiation Democracy versus Consensus Democracy: Parallel Conclusions and Recommendations'. *European Journal of Political Research*, 41, 81–105.

ARMINGEON, K. BEYELER, M. & MENEGALE, S. (2007) *Comparative Political Data Set 1960–2005*. Berne: Institute of Political Science, University of Berne.

—— & BONOLI, G. (eds) (2006) *The Politics of Post-industrial Welfare States*. London: Routledge.

ARTER, D. (1999) *Scandinavian Politics Today*. Manchester, Manchester University Press.

ATKINSON, A. B. & MICKLEWRIGHT, J. (1989) 'Turning the Screw: Benefits for the Unemployed 1979–88'. In: *The Economics of Social Security*, A. Dilnot & I. Walker (eds). Oxford: Oxford University Press.

AUST, A. & BÖNKER, F. (2004) 'Country report on Germany'. EU FP5 Project WRAMSOC, Canterbury.

BALLESTRI, Y. & BONOLI, G. (2003) 'L'Etat social suisse face aux nouveaux risques sociaux'. *Swiss Political Science Review*, 9, 35–58.

BARBIER, J.-C. (2001) *Welfare to Work Policies in Europe: The Current Challenges of Activation Policies*. Paris: Centre d'études de l'emploi.

—— (2004) 'Systems of Social Protection in Europe: Two Contrasted Paths to Acti-vation, and Maybe a Third'. In: *Labour and Employment Regulation in Europe*, J. Lind, H. Knudsen & H. Jørgensen (eds). Brussels: Peter Lang.

—— (2009) 'Réformes du marché du travail: raison garder'. *Esprit*, 95–109.

—— & FARGION, V. (2004) 'Continental Inconsistencies on the Path to Activation—Consequences for Social Citizenship in Italy and France'. *European Societies*, 6, 437–60.

—— & KAUFMANN, O. (2008) 'The French Strategy against Unemployment: Innovative but Inconsistent'. In: *Bringing the Jobless into Work? Experiences with Activation Schemes in Europe and the US*, W. Eichhorst, O. Kaufmann & R. Konle-Seidl (eds). Berlin, Springer.

—— & Ludwig-Mayerhofer, W. (2004) 'Introduction: The Many Worlds of Activation'. *European Societies*, 6, 424–36.

Barnett, W. S. & Masse, L. N. (2007) 'Comparative Benefit-Cost Analysis of the Abecedarian Program and Its Policy Implications'. *Economics of Education Review*, 26, 113–25.

Beck, N. & Katz, J. N. (1995) 'What to Do (and Not to Do) with Time-Series Cross-section Data'. *American Political Science Review*, 89, 634–47.

Benner, M. & Vad, T. (2000) 'Sweden and Denmark: Defending the Welfare State'. In: *Welfare and Work in the Open Economy*, F. W. Scharpf & V. Schmid (eds). Oxford: Oxford University Press.

Bergounioux, A. (2001) 'French Socialism and European Social Democracy'. In: *European Social Democracy Facing the Twin Revolution of Globalisation and the Knowledge Society*, R. Cuperus, K. Duffek & J. Kandel (eds). Amsterdam: Forum Scholars for European Social Democracy.

Bertone, C. (2003) 'Claims for Child Care as Struggles over Needs: Comparing Italian and Danish Women's Organizations'. *Social Politics*, 10, 229–55.

Blair, T. & Schröder, G. (1999) *The Third Way/Die neue Mitte*, London/Berlin: Labour Party/SPD.

Bleses, P. & Seeleib-Kaiser, M. (2004) *The Dual Transformation of the German Welfare State*. Houndmills, Basingstoke, Hampshire; New York: Palgrave Macmillan.

Bollen, K. A. & Ward, S. (1979) 'Ratio Variables in Aggregate Data-Analysis: Their Uses Problems and Alternatives'. *Sociological Methods & Research*, 7, 431–50.

Bonoli, G. (2000) *The Politics of Pension Reform: Institutions and Policy Change in Western Europe*. Cambridge: Cambridge University Press.

——(2001) 'Political Institutions, Veto Points, and the Process of Welfare State Adaptation'. In: *The New Politics of the Welfare State*, P. Pierson (ed.). Oxford: Oxford University Press.

——(2003) 'Social Policy through Labour Markets: Understanding National Differences in the Provision of Economic Security to Wage Earners'. *Comparative Political Studies*, 36, 983–1006.

——(2005) 'The Politics of the New Social Policies: Providing Coverage against New Social Risks in Mature Welfare States'. *Policy and Politics*, 33.

——(2007) 'Time Matters: Postindustrialisation, New Social Risks and Welfare State Adaptation in Advanced Industrial Democracies'. *Comparative Political Studies*, 40, 495–520.

——(2010) 'The Political Economy of Active Labour Market Policies'. *Politics & Society*, 38, 435–57.

——(2012) 'Credit Claiming and Blame Avoidance Revisited'. In: *The Politics of the New Welfare State*, G. Bonoli & D. Natali (eds). Oxford: Oxford University Press.

—— & Emmenegger, P. (2010) 'State-Society Relationships, Social Trust and the Development of Labour Market Policies in Italy and Sweden'. *West European Politics*, 33, 830–50.

—— & Natali, D. (2012) 'The Politics of the "New" Welfare States: Analysing Reforms in Western Europe'. In: *The Politics of the New Welfare State*, G. Bonoli & D. Natali (eds). Oxford: Oxford University Press.

—— & PALIER, B. (1997) 'Reclaiming Welfare: The Politics of French Social Protection Reform'. In: *Southern European Welfare States: Between Crisis and Reform*, M. Rhodes (ed.). London/Portland, OR: Frank Cass.

—— & —— (2008) 'When Past Reforms Open New Opportunities: Comparing Old-Age Insurance Reforms in Bismarckian Welfare Systems'. *Social Policy and Administration*, 41, 21–39.

—— & REBER, F. (2010) 'The Political Economy of Childcare in OECD Countries: Explaining Cross-national Variation in Spending and Coverage Rates'. *European Journal of Political Research*, 49, 97–118.

BORCHORST, A. (2002) 'Danish Child Care Policy: Continuity Rather than Radical Change'. In: *Child Care Policy at the Crossroads: Gender and Welfare State Restructuring*, R. Mahon & S. Michel (eds). New York/London: Routledge.

BRATTON, K. A. & RAY, L. P. (2002) 'Descriptive Representation, Policy Outcomes, and Municipal Day-Care Coverage in Norway'. *American Journal of Political Science*, 46, 428–37.

BREWER, M. (2008) 'Welfare Reform in the UK: 1997–2007'. Working Paper 2008:12. Stockholm, IFAU.

BRITISH GOVERNMENT (1998) *Meeting the Childcare Challenge: A Framework and Consultation Document*. London: HMSO Cm 3959.

—— (2002) *Working Families' Tax Credit: Estimates of Take up Rates*. London: British Government.

BRITISH LABOUR PARTY (1997) *New Labour Because Britain Deserves Better*. London: Labour Party.

—— (2001) *Ambitions for Britain: 2001 Election Manifesto*. London: Labour Party.

BROOKS, C. & MANZA, J. (2007) *Why Welfare States Persist: The Importance of Public Opinion in Democracies*. Chicago: University of Chicago Press.

BÜCHS, M. & FRIEDRICH, D. (2005) 'Surface Integration—The National Action Plan for Employment and Social-Policy Co-ordination'. In: *The Open Method of Co-ordination in Action*, J. Zeitlin, P. Pochet & E. E. Magnusson (eds). Brussels: Peter Lang.

BURGOON, B. (2001) 'Globalization and Welfare Compensation: Disentangling the Ties That Bind'. *International Organization*, 55, 509–51.

CALMFORS, L., FORSLUND, A. & HEMSTRÖM, M. (2001) 'Does Active Labour Market Policy Work? Lessons from the Swedish Experiences'. *Swedish Economic Policy Review*, 85, 61–124.

CANTILLON, B. (2010) *Disambiguating Lisbon. Growth, Employment and Social Inclusion in the Investment State*. Antwerp: University of Antwerp, Centre for Social Policy, Working Paper 10/07.

CASTLES, F. G. (2004) *The Future of the Welfare State: Crisis Myths and Crisis Realities*. Oxford: Oxford University Press.

—— (2005) 'Social Expenditures in the 1990s: Data and Determinants'. *Policy and Politics*, 33, 411–30.

CLASEN, J. (ed.) (1997) *Social Insurance in Europe*. Bristol, Policy Press.

—— (2000) 'Motives, Means and Opportunities: Reforming Unemployment Compensation in the 1990s'. In: *Recasting European Welfare States*, M. Ferrera & M. Rhodes (eds). London: Frank Cass.

CASTLES, F. G. (2005) *Reforming European Welfare States: Germany and the United Kingdom Compared*. Oxford: Oxford University Press.

——KVIST, J. & VAN OORSCHOT, W. (2001) 'On Condition of Work: Increasing Work Requirement in Unemployment Compensation Schemes'. In: *Nordic Welfare States in the European Context*, M. Kautto, J. Fritzell, B. Hvinden, J. Kvist & H. Uusitalo (eds). London: Routledge.

CLEGG, D. (2005) 'Activating the Multi-tiered Welfare State: Social Governance, Welfare Politics and Unemployment Policies in France and the United Kingdom'. PhD thesis. European University Institute, Florence.

CRESSEY, P. (2002) 'Women and Atypical Working in the United Kingdom: The Prospects for Positive Flexibility'. In: *Labour Market and Social Protection Reforms in International Perspective*, H. Sarfati & G. Bonoli (eds). Aldershot: Ashgate.

CROUCH, C. (1993) *Industrial Relations and European State Traditions*. Oxford: Clarendon Press.

DA ROIT, B. & SABATINELLI, S. (2005) 'Il modello di welfare mediterraneo tra famiglia e mercato. Come cambia la cura di anziani e bambini in Italia'. *Stato e Mercato*, 267–90.

DAGUERRE, A. (2006) 'Childcare Policies in Four Countries'. In: *The Politics of Postindustrial Welfare States*, K. Armingeon & G. Bonoli (eds). London, Routledge.

DALY, M. (2000) 'A Fine Balance: Women's Labor Market Participation in International Comparison'. In: *Welfare and Work in the Open Economy*, F. W. S. a. V. Schmidt (ed.). Oxford: Oxford University Press.

DANISH GOVERNMENT (2007) Denmark's National Reform Programme Second Progress Report. Contribution to EU's Growth and Employment Strategy (The Lisbon Strategy). Copenhagen: Ministry of Finance.

DAUNE-RICHARD, A.-M. & MAHON, R. (2001) 'Sweden: Models in Crisis'. In: *Who Cares? Women's Work, Childcare and Welfare State Redesign*, J. Jenson & M. Sineau (eds). Toronto, University of Toronto Press.

DE LA PORTE, C. & POCHET, P. (eds) (2002) *Building Social Europe through the Open Method of Co-ordination*. Brussels: P.I.E.-Peter Lang.

DIPRETE, T. A. (2005) 'Labor Markets, Inequality, and Change: A European Perspective'. *Work and Occupations*, 32, 119–39.

DOLOWITZ, D. P. & MARSH, D. (2000) 'Learning from Abroad: The Role of Policy Transfer in Contemporary Policy-Making'. *Governance: An International Journal of Policy and Administration*, 13, 5–24.

DUFOUR, P., BOISMÉNU, G. & NOËL, A. (2003) *L'aide au conditionnel. La contreparties dans les mesures envers les personnes sans emploi en Europe et en Amérique du Nord*. Montreal: Presses de l'Université de Montreal.

DUNCAN SMITH, I. (2011) 'We'll Make Work Worth It: By Supporting Childcare We'll Ensure That 80,000 Families Will Be Better off Than on Benefits'. *The Guardian*, 6 October.

EBBINGHAUS, B. (2006) *Reforming Early Retirement in Europe, Japan and the USA*. Oxford: Oxford University Press.

EICHHORST, W., GRIENBERGER-ZINGERLE, M. & KONLE-SEIDL, R. (2008) 'Activation Policies in Germany: From Status Protection to Basic Income Support'. In: *Bringing the Jobless into Work? Experiences with Activation in Europe and the US*, W. Eichhorst, O. Kaufmann & R. Konle-Seidl (eds). Berlin: Springer.

EINHORN, E. & LOGUE, J. (2003) *Modern Welfare States: Scandinavian Politics and Policy in the Global Age*, second edition. Westport CT: Greenwood Publishing Group.

EMMENEGGER, P. (2009) *Regulatory Social Policy: The Politics of Job Security Regulations*. Bern: Haupt Verlag.

——, HÄUSERMANN, S., PALIER, B. & SEELEIN-KEISER, M. (2012) *The Age of Dualisation: The Changing Face of Inequality in Deindustrializing Societies*. New York: Oxford University Press.

ENJOLRAS, B., LAVILLE, J.-L., FRAISSE, L. & TRICKEY, H. (2001) 'Between Subsidiarity and Social Assistance: The French Republican Route to Activation'. In: *An Offer You Can't Refuse: Workfare in International Perspective*, I. Lødemel & H. Trickey (eds). Bristol: Policy Press.

EPSTEIN, W. M. (2006) 'Response Bias in Opinion Polls and American Social Welfare'. *Social Science Journal*, 43, 99–110.

ERSKINE, A. (1997) 'The Withering of Social Insurance in Britain'. In: *Social Insurance in Europe*, J. Clasen (ed.). Bristol: Policy Press.

ESPING-ANDERSEN, G. (1990) *The Three Worlds of Welfare Capitalism*. Cambridge: Polity Press.

—— (ed.) (1996) *Welfare States in Transition. National Adaptations in Global Economies*. London: Sage.

—— (1999) *Social Foundations of Postindustrial Economies*. Oxford: Oxford University Press.

ESPING-ANDERSEN, G. (2000) 'Who is Harmed by Labour Market Regulations? Quantitative Evidence'. In: *Why Deregulate Labour Markets?*, G. Esping-Andersen & M. Regini (eds). Oxford: Oxford University Press.

—— (ed.) (2002) *Why We Need a New Welfare State*. Oxford: Oxford University Press.

—— (2009) *The Incomplete Revolution: Adapting to Women's New Roles*. Cambridge: Polity Press.

—— & KORPI, W. (1987) 'From Poor Relief to Institutional Welfare States, the Developement of Scandinavian Social Policy'. In: *The Scandinavian Model: Welfare States and Welfare State Research*, R. Erikson, E. J. Hansen, S. Ringen & H. E. Uusitalo (eds). London: M. E. Sharpe Publishing.

EUROPEAN COMMISSION (2007) *Towards Common Principles of Flexicurity: More and Better Jobs through Flexibility and Security*. Brussels: European Commission, Directorate-General for Employment, Social Affairs and Equal Opportunities.

EVERS, A., LEWIS, J. & RIEDEL, B. (2005) 'Developing Child-Care Provision in England and Germany: Problems of Governance'. *Journal of European Social Policy*, 15, 195–209.

EYDAL, G. B. & ROSTGAARD, T. (2011) 'Toward a Nordic Childcare Policy—The Political Processes and Agendas'. In: *Parental Leave, Childcare and Gender Equality in the Nordic Countries*, I. V. Gíslason & G. B. Eydal (eds). Copenhagen: Nordic Council of Ministers.

Fagnani, J. (2000) *Un travail et des enfants. Petits arbitrages et grands dilemmes*. Paris: Bayard.

Ferrera, M. (1993) *Modelli di solidarietà. Politica e riforme sociali nelle democrazie*. Bologna: Il Mulino.

—— (1998) 'The Four "Social Europes": Between Universalism and Selectivity'. In: *The Future of European Welfare, a New Social Contract?*, M. Rhodes & Y. Mény (eds). London: Macmillan.

—— & Gualmini, E. (2000) Italy: Rescue From Without? In *Welfare and Work in the Open Economy*, F. W. Scharpf & V. A. Schmidt (eds). Oxford, Oxford University Press.

——, Hemerijck, A. & Rhodes, M. (2000) *The Future of Social Europe: Recasting Work and Welfare in the New Economy*. Oeiras: Portuguese Ministry of Labour and Solidarity/ Celta Editora.

—— & Rhodes, M. (2000) 'Recasting European Welfare States: An Introduction'. *West European Politics*, 23, 1–10.

Fleckenstein, T. (2008) 'Restructuring Welfare for the Unemployed: The Case of Hartz Legislation in Germany'. *Journal of European Social Policy*, 18, 177–88.

Frerich, J. & Frey, M. (1993) *Handbuch der Geschichte der Sozialpolitik in Deutschland. Sozialpolitik in der Bundesrepublik Deutschland bis zur Herstellung der Deutschen Einheit (Band 3)*. Munich: Oldenburg Verlag.

Garrett, G. (1998) *Partisan Politics in the Global Economy*. Cambridge: Cambridge University Press.

Giddens, A. (1994) *Beyond Left and Right: The Future of Radical Politics*. Cambridge: Polity Press.

—— (1998) *The Third Way: The Renewal of Social Democracy*. Cambridge: Polity Press.

Gilardi, F. & Füglister, K. (2008) 'Empirical Modeling of Policy Diffusion in Federal States: The Dyadic Approach'. *Swiss Political Science Review*, 14, 413–50.

Glennerster, H. (1995) *British Social Policy since 1945*. Oxford: Blackwell.

Goetschy, J. (2001) 'The European Employment Strategy from Amsterdam to Stockholm: Has it Reached Its Cruising Speed?' *Industrial Relations Journal*, 32, 401–18.

Gonzalez, M. J. & Vidal, S. (2004) 'Where Do I Leave My Baby? Demand and Supply Factors in the Development of Early Childcare in Spain'. Paper presented at the Anual RC 19 Meeting, International sociological association, Paris, 20–22 September.

Green-Pedersen, C. (2002) *The Politics of Justification: Party Competition and Welfare-State Retrenchment in Denmark and the Netherlands from 1982 to 1998*. Amsterdam: Amsterdam University Press.

Gualmini, E. (1998) *La politica del lavoro*. Bologna: Il Mulino.

Hall, M. (1999) *UK Introduces New Rights to Time off for Family and Domestic Reasons*. Dublin: EIRO.

Hall, P. (ed.) (1989) *The Political Power of Economic Ideas: Keynesianism across Nations*. Princeton: Princeton University Press.

—— (1993) 'Policy Paradigms, Social Learning and the State'. *Comparative Politics*, 25, 275–96.

HALL, P. A. & TAYLOR, R. C. R. (1996) 'Political Science and the Three New Institutionalisms'. *Political Studies*, 44, 936–57.

HAMILTON, G., FREEDMAN, S., GENNETIAN, L., MICHALOPOULOS, C., WALTER, J., ADAMS-CIARDULLO, D. & GASSMAN-PINES, A. (2001) *National Evaluation of Welfare-to-Work Strategies*. Washington, DC: Manpower Demonstration Research Corporation.

HASSEL, A. & SCHILLER, C. (2010) *Der Fall Hartz IV. Wie es zur Agenda 2010 kam und wie es weitergeht*. Frankfurt: Campus Verlag.

HASSELPFLUG, S. (2005) *Availability Criteria in 25 Countries*. Copenhagen: Ministry of Finance, working paper No 12.

HÄUSERMANN, S. (2010) *The Politics of Welfare State Reform in Continental Europe*. Cambridge: Cambridge University Press.

HECLO, H. (1974) *Modern Social Politics in Britain and Sweden: From Relief to Income Maintenance*. New Haven, CT: Yale University Press.

HEMERIJCK, A. (2002) 'The Self-transformation of the European Social Model(s)'. In: *Why We Need a New Welfare State*, G. Esping-Andersen (ed.). Oxford: Oxford University Press.

—— (2011) 'Two or Three Waves of Welfare State Transformation?' In: *Towards a Social Investment Welfare State?*, Nathalie Morel, B. Palier & J. Palme (eds). Bristol: Policy Press.

—— (2012a) *Changing Welfare States*. Oxford: Oxford University Press.

—— (2012b) 'Stress-Testing the New Welfare State'. In: *The Politics of the New Welfare State*, G. Bonoli & D. Natali (eds). Oxford: Oxford University Press.

—— & SCHLUDI, M. (2000) 'Sequences of Policy Failures and Effective Policy Responses'. In: *Welfare and Work in the Open Economy*, vol. I: *From Vulnerability to Competitiveness*, F. W. Scharpf & V. A. Schmidt (eds). Oxford: Oxford University Press.

——, UNGER, B. & VISSER, J. (2000) 'How Small Countries Negotiate Change. Twenty-Five Years of Policy Adjustment in Austria, the Netherland, and Belgium'. In: *Welfare and Work in the Open Economy*, vol. II: *Diverse Responses to Common Challenges*, F. W. Scharpf & V. A. Schmidt (eds). Oxford: Oxford University Press.

HERING, M. (2004) 'Turning Ideas into Policies: Implementing Modern Social Democratic Thinking in Germany's Pension Policy'. In: *Social Democratic Party Policies in Contemporary Europe*, G. Bonoli & M. Powell (eds). London: Routledge.

HINRICHS, K. (2000) 'Elephants on the Move: Patterns of Public Pension Reform in OECD Countries'. *European Review*, 8, 353–78.

HØGELUND, J. (2003) *In Search of the Effective Disability Policy*. Amsterdam: Amsterdam University Press.

HOHNEN, P. (2000) 'When Work Is Like a Gift: An Analysis of New Forms of Exclusion On the Danish Labour Market'. Copenhagen: Danish Institute of Social Research, Working paper 2000/11.

HOOP, R. (2004) 'Social Policy in Belgium and the Netherlands: Third Way or Not?' In: *Social Democratic Party Policies in Contemporary Europe*, G. Bonoli & M. Powell (eds). London: Routledge.

HUBER, E., RAGIN, C. & STEPHENS, J. D. (1993) 'Social Democracy, Christian Democracy, Constitutional Structure, and the Welfare State'. *American Journal of Sociology*, 99, 711–49.

—— & Stephens, J. D. (2001) *Development and Crisis of the Welfare State: Parties and Policies in the Global Markets*. Chicago: University of Chicago Press.

—— & Stephens, J. D. (2000) 'Partisan Governance, Women's Employment, and the Social Democratic Service State'. *American Sociological Review*, 65, 323–42.

Huo, J. (2009) *Third Way Reforms: Social Democracy after the Golden Age*. Cambridge: Cambridge University Press.

——, Nelson, M. & Stephens, J. D. (2008) 'Decommodification and Activation in Social Democratic Policy: Resolving the Paradox'. *Journal of European Social Policy*, 18, 5–20.

ILO (1999) *Denmark: Flexibility, Security and Labour Market Success*. Geneva: ILO.

Immergut, E. M. (1992) *Health Politics: Interests and Institutions in Western Europe*. Cambridge: Cambridge University Press.

Iversen, T. (1999) *Contested Economic Institutions: The Politics of Macroeconomics and Wage Bargaining in Advanced Democracies*. Cambridge: Cambridge University Press.

—— & Stephens, J. (2008) 'Partisan Politics, the Welfare State, and Three Worlds of Human Capital Formation'. *Comparative Political Studies*, 41, 600–37.

—— & Wren, A. (1998) 'Equality, Employment, and Budgetary Restraint: The Trilemma of the Service Economy'. *Wold Politics*, 50, 507–46.

Jenson, J. (1989) 'Paradigms and Political Discourse: Protective Legislation in France and the United States before 1914'. *Canadian Journal of Political Science*, 22, 235–58.

—— (2002) *From Ford to Lego: Redesigning Welfare Regimes*. Boston: Annual Meeting of the American Political Science Association.

—— (2009) 'Redesigning Citizenship Regimes after Neoliberalism: Moving towards Social Investment'. In: *What Future for Social Investment?*, N. Morel, B. Palier & J. Palme (eds). Stockholm: Institute for Future Studies.

—— (2011) 'Redisigning Citizeship Regimes after Neoliberalism: Moving towards Social Investment'. In: *Towards a Social Investment Welfare State?*, Nathalie Morel, B. Palier & J. Palme (eds). Bristol: Policy Press.

—— & Saint-Martin, D. (2006) 'Building Blocks for a New Social Architecture: The LEGO (tm) Paradigm of an Active Society'. *Policy and Politics*, 34, 429–51.

—— & Sineau, M. (1995) 'Family Policy and Women's Citizenship in Mitterrand's France'. *Social Politics*, 2, 244–69.

Jessoula, M., Graziano, P. & Madama, I. (2010) ' "Selective Flexicurity" in Segmented Labour Markets: The Case of Italian "Mid-Siders" '. *Journal of Social Policy*, 39, 561–83.

Joint-Lambert, M.-T. (1994) *Les politiques sociales*. Paris: Presses de Sciences Po.

Kamerman, S., Neuman, M., Waldfogel, J. & Brooks-Gunn, J. (2003) *Social Policies, Family Types and Child Outcomes in Selected OECD Countries*. Paris: OECD Social, Employment and Migration. Working Paper No. 6.

Kananen, J., Taylor-Gooby, P. & Larsen, T. (2006) 'Public Attitudes and New Social Risk Reform'. In: *The Politics of Postindustrial Welfare States*, K. Armingeon & G. Bonoli (eds). London: Routledge.

Katzenstein, P. J. (1985) *Small States in World Markets: Industrial Policy in Europe*, Ithaca, NY: Cornell University Press.

Kautto, M. (2001) 'Moving Closer? Diversity and Convergence in Financing of Welfare States'. In: *Nordic Welfare States in the European Context*, M. Kautto, J. Fritzell, B. Hvinden, J. Kvist & H. Uusitalo (eds). London: Routledge.

King, D. (1995) *Actively Seeking Work? The Politics of Unemployment and Welfare Policy in the United States and Great Britain*. Chicago: University of Chicago Press.

KITTEL, B. (1999) 'Sense and Sensitivity in Pooled Analysis of Political Data'. *European Journal of Political Research*, 35, 225–53.

KLUVE, J., CARD, D., FERTIG, M., GÓRA, M., JACOBI, L., JENSEN, P., LEETMAA, R., NIMA, L., PATACCHINI, E., SCHAFFNER, S., SCHMIDT, C. M., KLAAUW, B. V. d. & WEBER, A. (2007) *Active Labor Market Policies in Europe: Performance et Perspectives*. Berlin/Heidelberg: Springer.

KNIJN, T. & OSTNER, I. (2002) 'Commodification and De-commodification'. In: *Contested Concepts in Gender and Social Politics*, B. Hobson, J. Lewis & B. Siim (eds). Chelthenam: Edward Elgar.

KORPI, W. (1983) *The Democratic Class Struggle*. London: Routledge and Kegan Paul.

KREMER, M. (2005) 'How Welfare States Care: Culture, Gender and Citizenship in Europe'. PhD thesis, University of Utrecht.

KUHN, T. (1962) *The Structure of Scientific Revolutions*. Chicago: University of Chicago Press.

KVIST, J., PEDERSEN, L. & KÖHLER, P. A. (2008) 'Making All Persons Work: Modern Danish Labour Market Policies'. In: *Bringing the Jobless into Work? Experiences with Activation in Europe and the US*, W. Eichhorst, O. Kaufmann & R. Konle-Seidl (eds). Berlin: Springer.

LAULOM, S., MAZUYER, E., TEISSIER, C., TRIOMPHE, C. E. & VIELLE, P. (2012) *European Economic, Employment and Social Policy: How Has the Crisis Affected Social Legislation in Europe?* Brussels: ETUI Policy Brief 2.

LEIRA, A., TOBIO, C. & TRIFILETTI, R. (2003) 'Kinship and Informal Support as Resources for the First Generation of Working Mothers in Norway, Italy and Spain'. In: *Working Mothers in Europe: A Comparison of Policies and Practices*, U. Gerhard, T. Knijn & A. Weckwert (eds). Cheltenham: Edward Elgar.

LEITNER, S. (2008) 'Varianten von Familialismus. Eine historisch vergleichende Analyse der Kinderbetreuungs- und Altenpflegepolitik in kontinentaleuropäischen Wohlfahrtsstaaten'. Habilitation Thesis. University of Göttingen.

LEPRINCE, F. (2003) L'accueil des jeunes enfants en France. Etat des lieux et pistes d'amélioration. Paris: Haut Conseil de la population et de la famille.

LEVY, J. (1999) 'Vice into Virtue? Progressive Politics and Welfare Reform in Continental Europe'. *Politics and Society*, 27, 239–73.

LEWIS, J. (1980) *The Politics of Motherhood*. Lomdon: Croom-Helm.

—— (1992) 'Gender and the Development of Welfare Regimes'. *Journal of European Social Policy*, 2, 159–73.

—— (2006) 'Gender and Welfare in Modern Europe'. *Past and Present*, 39–54.

LIJPHART, A. (1968) *The Politics of Accommodation: Pluralism and Democracy in the Netherlands*. Berkeley/Los Angeles: University of California Press.

—— (1984) *Democracies: Patterns of Majoritarian and Consensus Government in Twenty-One Countries*. New Haven, CT/London: Yale University Press.

LOVENDUSKI, J. & NORRIS, P. (2003) 'Westminster Women: The Politics of Presence'. *Political Studies*, 51, 84–102.

MABBET, D. (1995) *Trade, Employment and Welfare: A Comparative Study of Trade and Labour Market Policies in Sweden and New Zealand, 1880–1980*. Oxford: Clarendon Press.

MADSEN, P. (2002) 'The Danish Model of Flexicurity: A Paradise with Some Snakes'. In: *Labour Market and Social Protection Reforms in International Perspective*, H. Sarfati & G. Bonoli (eds). Aldershot: Ashgate.

MANOW, P. (1997) *Social Insurance and the German Political Economy*. Cologne: Max-Planck-Institut für Gesellschaftsforschung.

—— & SEILS, E. (2000) 'Germany: Adjusting Badly'. In: *Welfare and Work in the Open Economy*, F. W. Scharpf & V. A. Schmid (eds). Oxford: Oxford University Press.

MARTIN, J. & GRUBB, D. (2001) 'What Works and for Whom: A Review of OECD Countries' Experiences with Active Labour Market Policies'. *Swedish Economic Policy Review*, 8, 9–56.

MJOSET, L. (1987) 'Nordic Economic Policies in the 1970s and 1980s'. *International Organization*, 41, 403–56.

MOREL, N. (2007) 'L'Etat face au social. La (re)définition des frontières de l'Etat-providence en Suède'. PhD Thesis. Univérsité Paris I, Sorbonne.

MORENO, L. (2000) 'The Spanish Development of Southern European Welfare'. In: *The Survival of the European Welfare State*, S. Kuhnle (ed.). Chicago: University of Chicago Press.

MORGAN, K. J. (2002) 'Forging the Frontiers between State, Church, and Family: Religious Cleavages and the Origins of Early Childhood Education and Care Policies in France, Sweden, and Germany'. *Politics and Society*, 30, 113–48.

—— (2003) 'The Politics of Mothers' Employment—France in Comparative Perspective'. *World Politics*, 55, 259–89.

—— (2005) 'The "Production" of Child Care: How Labor Markets Shape Social Policy and Vice Versa'. *Social Politics*, 12, 243–63.

—— (2006) *Working Mothers and the Welfare State: Religion and the Politics of Work-Family Policies in Western Europe and the United States*. Stanford, CA: Stanford University Press.

—— (2010) *The End of the Frozen Welfare State? Innovation in Work-Family Policies in Western Europe*. Montreal. Paper prepared for the 17th Annual Conference of Europeanists, 15–17 April.

—— & ZIPPEL, K. (2003) 'Paid to Care: The Origins and Effects of Care Leave Policies in Western Europe'. *Social Politics*, 10, 49–85.

MÜLLER, W. & STRØM, K. (eds) (1999) *Policy, Office or Votes? How Political Parties in Western Europe Make Hard Decisions*. Cambridge: Cambridge University Press.

MYLES, J. (2006) 'Comment on Brooks and Manza, ASR, June 2006—Welfare States and Public Opinion'. *American Sociological Review*, 71, 495–8.

—— & Pierson, P. (1997) *Friedman's Revenge: The Reform of 'Liberal' Welfare States in Canada and the United States*. Florence: European University Institute.

—— & Pierson, P. (2001) 'The Comparative Political Economy of Pension Reform'. In: *The New Politics of the Welfare State*, P. Pierson (ed.). Oxford: Oxford University Press.

—— & Quadagno, J. (1997) 'Recent Trends in Public Pension Reform: A Comparative View'. In: *Reform of Retirement Income Policy*, K. G. Banting & R. Boadway (eds). Kingston: Queen's University.

NATALI, D. (2002) 'La ridefinizione del welfare state contemporaneo. La riforma delle pensioni in Francia e in Italia'. PhD Thesis. Florence, European University Institute.

NAUMANN, I. (2005) 'Child Care and Feminism in West Germany and Sweden in the 1960s and 1970s'. *Journal of European Social Policy*, 15, 47–63.

—— (2006) 'Childcare in the West German and Swedish Welfare States from the 1950s to the 1970s'. PhD Thesis. Florence, European University Institute.

NEAL, A. C. (1984) 'Employment Protection Laws: The Swedish Model'. *International and Comparative Law Quarterly*, 33, 634–62.

NICKELL, S. (2003) 'Labour Market Institutions and Unemployment in OECD Countries'. CESifo DICE Report, 13–26.

NORRIS, P. (2002) *Democratic Phoenix: Reinventing Political Activism*. Cambridge: Cambridge University Press.

OECD (2000a) *Early Childhood Education and Care Policy in Denmark*. Paris: OECD.

—— (2000b) *Employment Outlook*. Paris: OECD.

—— (2002) *Babies and Bosses—Reconciling Work and Family Life: Australia, Denmark, The Netherlands* (vol. 1). Paris: OECD.

—— (2003) *Employment Outlook*. Paris: OECD.

—— (2005) *Extending Opportunities: How Active Social Policy Can Benefit Us All*. Paris: OECD.

—— (2006) *Live Longer, Work Longer: A Synthesis Report*. Paris: OECD.

—— (2007a) 'Activating the Unemployed: What Countries Do'. *OECD Employment Outlook*, 207–41.

—— (2007b) *Babies and Bosses—Reconciling Work and Family Life: A Synthesis of Findings for OECD Countries*. Paris: OECD.

—— (2007c) *SOCX Interpretative Guide*. Paris: OECD.

OECD (2008a) *Growing Unequal: Income Distribution and Poverty in OECD Countries*. Paris: OECD.

—— (2008b) *OECD Economic Surveys: The Netherlands 2008*. Paris: OECD.

ORENSTEIN, M. A. (2003) 'Mapping the Diffusion of Pension Innovation'. In: *Pension Reform in Europe: Process and Progress*, R. Holzmann, M. Orenstein & M. Rutkowski (eds). Washington, DC: World Bank.

ORLOFF, A. (2006) 'From Maternalism to "Employment for All": State Policies to Promote Women's Employment across the Affluent Democracies'. In: *The State after Statism*, J. Levy (ed.). Cambridge, MA: Harvard University Press.

PALIER, B. (2002) *Gouverner la sécurité sociale. Les réformes du système français de protection sociale depuis 1945*. Paris: Presses Universitaires de France.

—— (2005) 'Ambiguous Agreement, Cumulative Change: French Social Policy in the 1990s'. In: *Beyond Continuity: Institutional Change in Advanced Political Economies*, W. Streeck & K. Thelen (eds). Oxford: Oxford University Press.

—— (2010) 'The Long Conservative Corporatist Road to Welfare Reforms'. In: *A Long Good Bye to Bismarck? The Politics of Welfare Reform in Continental Europe*, B. Palier (ed.). Amsterdam: Amsterdam University Press.

—— & Thelen, K. (2010) 'Institutionalizing Dualism: Complementarities and Change in France and Germany'. *Politics and Society*, 38, 119–48.

PECK, J. (2001) *Workfare States*. New York: Guildford Press.

PIERSON, P. (1993) 'When Effect Becomes Cause. Policy Feedback and Political Change'. *World Politics*, 45, 595–628.

—— (1994) *Dismantling the Welfare State? Reagan, Thatcher, and the Politics of Retrenchment.* Cambridge: Cambridge University Press.

—— (1996) 'The New Politics of the Welfare State'. *World Politics*, 48, 143-179.

—— (1998) 'Irresistible Forces, Immovable Objects: Post-industrial Welfare States Confront Permanent Austerity'. *Journal of European Public Policy*, 5, 539–60.

—— (2000) 'Increasing Returns, Path Dependence, and the Study of Politics'. *American Political Science Review*, 94, 251–67.

—— (2001) 'Coping with Permanent Austerity: Welfare State Restructuring in Affluent Democracies'. In: *The New Politics of the Welfare State*, P. Pierson (ed.). Oxford: Oxford University Press.

—— (2004) *Politics in Time.* Princeton, NJ: Princeton University Press.

PLANTENGA, J. (1996) 'For Women Only? The Rise of Part-Time Work in the Netherlands'. *Social Politics*, 3, 57–71.

PLÜMPER, T., TROEGER, V. E. & MANOW, P. (2005) 'Panel Data Analysis in Comparative Politics: Linking Method to Theory'. *European Journal of Political Research*, 44, 327–54.

POGGIONE, S. (2004) 'Exploring Gender Differences in State Legislators' Policy Preferences'. *Political Research Quarterly*, 57, 305–14.

POLANYI, K. (1957 [1944]) *The Great Transformation.* Boston: Beacon Press.

POWELL, M. (1999) *New Labour, New Welfare State? The 'Third Way' in British Social Policy.* Bristol: Policy Press.

RAKE, K. (2001) 'Gender and New Labour's Social Policies'. *Journal of Social Policy*, 30, 209–31.

RANDALL, V. (1995) 'The Irresponsible State? The Politics of Child Daycare Provision in Britain'. *British Journal of Political Science*, 25, 327–48.

—— (2000) 'Childcare Policy in the European States: Limits to Convergence'. *Journal of European Public Policy*, 7, 346–68.

REDAELLI, M. (2006) *Part-time Emplyoment in Italy.* Presentation made at the EIPA seminar 'Part-time Employment in Europe', Milan, 8–10 February.

RHODES, M. (2000) 'Restructuring the British Welfare State'. In: *Welfare and Work in the Open Economy*, F. W. Scharpf & V. A. Schmidt (eds). Oxford: Oxford University Press.

RILEY, D. (1983) *War in the Nursery.* London: Virago.

RIMLINGER, G. V. (1971) *Welfare Policy and Industrialisation in Europe, America, and Russia.* New York: John Wiley & Sons.

ROSS, F. (2000) '"Beyond Left and Right": The New Partisan Politics of Welfare'. *Governance: An International Journal of Policy and Administration*, 13, 155–83.

ROSTGAARD, T. & FRIDBERG, T. (1998) 'Denmark'. In *Caring for Children and Older People: A Comparison of European Policies and Practices*, (SFI) S. r. i. (ed.). Copenhagen: SFI, Social Security in Europe, no. 6.

ROTHSTEIN, B. (1985) 'The Success of the Swedish Labour Market Policy: The Organizational Connection to Policy'. *European Journal of Political Research*, 13, 153–65.

RUEDA, D. (2007) *Social Democracy Inside Out: Partisanship and Labor Market Policy in Industralised Democracies.* Oxford: Oxford University Press.

SAINSBURY, D. (ed.) (1994) *Gendering Welfare States.* London: Sage Publications.

—— (1999) Le genre et la construction des Etats-providence. In: *Comparer les systèmes de protection sociale en Europe du Nord et en France*, MIRE (ed.). Paris: MIRE-DREES.

SAMEK LODOVICI, M. & Semenza, R. (2008) 'The Italian Case: From Employment Regulation to Welfare Reforms?' *Social Policy and Administration*, 42, 160–76.

SARACENO, C. (1990) 'Women, Family and the Law, 1750–1942'. *Journal of Family History*, 15, 427–42.

—— (2003) *Mutamenti delle famiglie e politiche sociali in Italia*. Bologna: Il Mulino.

—— (ed.) (2008) *Families, Ageing and Social Policy: Intergenerational Solidarity in European Welfare States*. Cheltenham: Edward Elgar.

SCARBROUGH, E. (2000) 'West European Welfare States: The Old Politics of Retrenchment'. *European Journal of Political Research*, 38, 225–59.

SCHARPF, F. W. (1991) *Crisis and Choice in European Social Democracy*. Ithaca, NY: Cornell University Press.

—— (1997) *Games Real Actors Play: Actor-Centered Institutionalism in Policy Research*. Boulder: Westview Press.

—— (2000) 'Economic Changes, Vulnerabilities, and Institutional Capabilities'. In: *Welfare and Work in the Open Economy*, vol. I: *From Vulnerability to Competitiveness*, F. W. Scharpf & V. A. Schmidt (eds). Oxford: Oxford University Press.

SCHLANSER, R. (2011) *Qui utilise les crèches en Suisse? Logiques sociales du recours aux structures d'accueil collectif pour la petite enfance*. Lausanne, IDHEAP, Cahier No. 264.

SCHMIDT, V. A. (2002) 'Does Discourse Matter in the Politics of Welfare State Adjustment?' *CPS Comparative Political Studies*, 35/2, 168–93.

SCHULTHEIS, F. (1996) 'La famille, un catégorie du droit social? Une comparaison franco-allemande'. In: *Comparer les systèmes de protection sociale en Europe*, MIRE (ed.). Paris: Ministère du Travail et des affaires sociales.

SCHWINDT-BAYER, L. A. (2006) 'Still Supermadres? Gender and the Policy Priorities of Latin American Legislators'. *American Journal of Political Science*, 50, 570–85.

SEELEIB-KAISER, M. & FLECKENSTEIN, T. (2007) 'Discourse, Learning and Welfare State Change: The Case of German Labour Market Reforms'. *Social Policy and Administration*, 41, 427–48.

——, VAN DYK, S. & ROGGENKAMP, M. (2008) *Party Politics and Social Welfare: Comparing Christian and Social Democracy in Austria, Germany and the Netherlands*. Cheltenham: Edward Elgar.

SHALEV, M. (2007) 'Limits and Alternatives to Multiple Regression in Comparative Research'. *Comparative Social Research*, 24, 261–308.

SHONFIELD, A. (1964) *Modern Capitalism*. Oxford: Oxford University Press.

SIAROFF, ALAN (1994), 'Work, Welfare and Gender Equality: A New Typology'. In: *Gendering Welfare States*, Diane Sainsbury (ed.). London: Sage, 83–100.

—— (2000) 'Women's Representation in Legislatures and Cabinets in Industrial Democracies'. *International Political Science Review*, 21, 361–80.

SIEGEL, N. A. (2000) 'Jenseits der Expansion? Sozialpolitik in westlichen Demokratien 1975–95'. In: *Wohlfahrtsstaatliche Politik. Institutionen, politischer Prozesse und Leistungsprofil*, M. G. Schmidt (ed.). Opladen: Leske und Budrich.

SIMONIN, B., BUREAU, M.-C., LEHL, C., GOMEL, B., DANTEC, E. L., LEMAÎTRE, V., LEYMARIE, C. & SCHMIDT, N. (2002) *Les institutions locales et le programme 'emplois-jeunes' dans les activités culturelles et socioculturelles*. Paris: Centre d'Etudes sur l'Emploi.

SMITH, R. J. (2005) 'Relative Size versus Controlling for Size—Interpretation of Ratios in Research on Sexual Dimorphism in the Human Corpus Callosum'. *Current Anthropology*, 46, 249–73.

SOL, E., SICHERT, M., VAN LIESHOUT, H. & KONING, T. (2008) 'Activation as a Socio-economic and Legal Concept: Laboratorium, the Netherlands'. In: *Bringing the Jobless into Work? Experiences with Activation Schemes in Europe and the US*, W. Eichhorst, O. Kaufmann & R. Konle-Seidl (eds). Berlin/Heidelberg: Springer.

SPIES, H. & VAN BERKEL, R. (2001) 'Workfare in The Netherlands: Young Unemployed People and the Jobseekers Employment Act'. In: *An Offer You Can't Refuse: Workfare in International Perspective*, I. Lødemel & H. Trickey (eds). Bristol: Policy Press.

STREECK, W. & THELEN, K. (2005) 'Introduction: Institutional Change in Advanced Political Economies'. In: *Beyond Continuity: Institutional Change in Advanced Political Economies*, W. Streeck & K. Thelen (eds). Oxford: Oxford University Press.

SVENSSON, C. (2001) 'Swedish Social Democracy and the Third Way—A Delicate Affair'. In: *European Social Democracy Facing the Twin Revolution of Globalisation and the Knowledge Society*. R. Cuperus, K. Duffek & J. Kandel (eds). Amsterdam: Forum Scholars for European Social democracy, 217–26.

SWEDISH GOVERNMENT (2002) *Sweden's Action Plan for Employment*. Stockholm: Swedish Government.

SWENSON, P. A. (2002) *Capitalists against Markets: The Making of Labor Markets and Welfare States in the United States and Sweden*. Oxford: Oxford University Press.

SWERS, M. (2001) 'Understanding the Policy Impact of Electing Women: Evidence from Research on Congress and State Legislatures'. *Ps-Political Science and Politics*, 34, 217–20.

——(2005) 'Connecting Descriptive and Substantive Representation: An Analysis of Sex Differences in Cosponsorship Activity'. *Legislative Studies Quarterly*, 30, 407–33.

TAYLOR-GOOBY, P. (2004) 'New Risks and Social Change'. In: *New Risks, New Welfare?* P. Taylor-Gooby (ed.). Oxford: Oxford University Press.

——(2008) 'The New Welfare Settlement in Europe'. *European Societies*, 10, 3–24.

THELEN, K. (2004) *How Institutions Evolve: The Political Economy of Skills in Germany, Britain, the United States and Japan*. Cambridge: Cambridge University Press.

——& STEINMO, S. (1992) 'Historical Institutionalism in Comparative Politics'. In: *Structuring Politics: Historical Institutionalism in Comparative Analysis*, S. Steinmo, K. Thelen & F. Longstreth (eds). Cambridge: Cambridge University Press.

THORGAARD, C. & VINTHER, H. (2007) 'Rescaling Social Welfare Policies in Denmark: National Report', Working Paper 2007/10. Copenhagen: Danish National Institute of Social Research.

TIMONEN, V. (2004) 'New Risks—Are They Still New for the Nordic Welfare States?' In: *New Risks, New Welfare*, P. Taylor-Gooby (ed.). Oxford: Oxford University Press.

TORFING, J. (1999) 'Workfare with Welfare: Recent Reforms of the Danish Welfare State'. *Journal of European social Policy*, 9, 5–28.

TREIB, O. & FALKNER, G. (2004) 'The EU and New Social Risks: The Need for a Differentiated Evaluation'. 14th Biennial Conference of Europeanists 'Europe and the World: Integration, Interdependece, Exceptionalism', Chicago.

——— & ——— (2006) 'The EU and New Social Risks: The Need for a Differentiated Evaluation'. In: *The Politics of Postindustrial Welfare States: Adapting Post-war Social Policies to New Social Risks'*, K. Armingeon & G. Bonoli (eds). London, Routledge.

TSEBELIS, G. (2002) *Veto Players; How Political Institutions Work*. Princeton, NJ: Princeton University Press.

TUNBERGER, P. & SIGLE-RUSHTON, W. (2011) 'Continuity and Change in Swedish Family Policy Reforms'. *Journal of European Social Policy*, 21, 225–37.

VAN HOOREN, F. & BECKER, U. (2012) 'One Welfare State, Two Care Regimes: Understanding Developments in Child and Elderly Care Policies in the Netherlands'. *Social Policy and Administration*, 46, 83–107.

VAN KERSBERGEN, K. (1995) *Social Capitalism: A Study of Christian Democracy and the Welfare State*. London/New York: Routledge.

VAN OORSCHOT, W. & BOOS, C. (2001) 'The Battle against Numbers: Disability Policies in the Netherlands'. In: *Disability Policies in European Countries*, W. van Oorschot & B. Hvinden (eds). The Hague: Kluwer Law International.

VANDENBROUCKE, F., HEMERIJCK, A. & PALIER, B. (2011) *The EU Needs a Social Investment Pact*. Brussles: OSE, Opinion paper 5.

VEDDER, P., BOUWER, E. & PELS, T. (1996) *Multicultural Child Care*. Clevedon: Cromwell Press.

VIEBROCK, E. & CLASEN, J. (2009) 'Flexicurity and Welfare Reform: A Review'. *Socio-economic Review*, 7, 305–31.

VISSER, J. (2002) 'The First Part-time Economy in the World: A Model to be Followed?' *Journal of European Social Policy*, 12, 23–42.

——— & HEMERIJCK, A. (1997) *'A Dutch Miracle' Job Growth, Welfare Reform and Corporatism in the Netherlands*. Amsterdam: Amsterdam University Press.

VOLKENS, A. (2004) 'Policy Change of European Social Democrats, 1945–98'. In: *Social Democratic Party Policies in Contemporary Europe'*, G. Bonoli & M. Powell (eds). London: Routledge.

WEAVER, K. (1986) 'The Politics of Blame Avoidance'. *Journal of Public Policy*, 6, 371–98.

WHITE, S. (2001) *New Labour: The Progressive Future?* Basingstoke: Palgrave.

WILENSKY, H. (1981) 'Leftism, Catholicism and Democratic Corposartism: The Role of Political Parties in the Recent Development of the Welfare State'. In: *The Development of Welfare States in Europe and America*, P. Flora & A. J. Heidenheimer (eds). New Brunswick, NJ: Transaction Books.

WILENSKY, H. L. (1975) *The Welfare State and Equality: Structural and Ideological Roots of Public Expenditures*. Berkeley/Los Angeles: University of California Press.

WILTHAGEN, T. & TROS, F. (2004) 'The Concept of "Flexicurity": A New Approach to Regulating Employment and Labour Markets'. *Transfer* 10, 166–86.

WINTOUR, P. (2011) 'Coalition to Boost Childcare Pot by £300m to Target Low-Earning Women'. *The Guardian*, 6 October.

WOOD, S. (2001) 'Labour Market Regimes under Threat? Sources of Continuity in Germany, Britain, and Sweden'. In: *The New Politics of the Welfare State*, P. Pierson (ed.). Oxford: Oxford University Press.

WORLD BANK (2001) *Social Protection Sector Strategy: From Safety Net to Springboards.* Washington, DC: World Bank.

ZYLKA, R. (2004a) 'Germany Struggles to Close Daycare Gap'. *Deutsche Welle Online* (<http://www.DW-World.de>), 21 July.

——(2004b) 'Unionsfraktion lehnt Kita-Gesetz nicht mehr ab'. *Berliner Zeitung,* 28 October.

Index

Index